Religion and Science

About the Author

Dr. Hamid Rezania is professor of Philosophy of Religion, Religious Studies and Islamic Theology at Islamic Seminary and Universities, Head & authorized representative of Almustafa International University (MIU), South of India, member of Iran Metaphysic Association, member of Hekmate Islami Sadra Association, Director of Educational and Cultural Institute, (Hekmat Rooyesh), Qom, Iran.

Dr. Hamid Rezania has also served as Faculty and Director at the department of Religious Studies of Religions University (URD). He hold B.A. in Education "Instructional Management" from Shiraz University, Master of Islamic Philosophy (Imam Baqer University at Qom), Master of Islamic Theology (Imam Khomeini Institute at Qom) and Ph.D. in Philosophy (Pune University, India). Rezania has published several books and articles in Arabic, Persian and English and participated in about 20 international and inter-disciplinary seminars, conferences and academic workshops. In addition to his teaching and writing Dr. Rezania serves as consultant in the fields of education, morality, and especially relationship between religion and science.

RELIGION AND SCIENCE

A Philosophical Approach

Hamid Rezania

CONCEPT PUBLISHING COMPANY PVT. LTD.
NEW DELHI-110059

ISBN-13: 978-81-8069-915-3

First Published 2012.

Published and Printed by

Concept Publishing Company Pvt. Ltd.
A/15-16, Commercial Block, Mohan Garden
New Delhi-110059 (India)
T: 25351460, 25351794, *F*: 091-11-25357109
E: publishing@conceptpub.com, W: www.conceptpub.com
Editorial Office: H-13, Bali Nagar, New Delhi-110 015, India.

Cataloging in Publication Data--Courtesy: D.K. Agencies (P) Ltd. <docinfo@dkagencies.com>

Rezania, Hamid.
Religion and science : a philosophical approach / Hamid Rezania.
p. cm.
Includes bibliographical references (p.) and index.
ISBN 9788180699153

1. Religion and science—Philosophy. I. Title.

DDC 215 23

Albert Einstein

"Religion without science is blind and science without religion is lame."

Alfred Whitehead

"Religion will not regain its old power until it can face change in the same spirit as does science."

Preface

Man's completeness is certainly dependant on many human sources; mostly scientists or scholars of religion. But whereas Science and Religion are specifically supposed as the main sources of such purpose, there is a question on their efficient collaboration. They both insist on their point of views while today many natural mysteries are already discovered or getting soon found. When the religion is defined as a way of life and man's purification, we cannot believe or imagine the science, the rationality in opposite to the religion. In the age of constant clash between the faith and rationality, it seems there is a serious doubt on the fulfilment of their ideological integrity. It is possible that religion and science converge in the future world and their convergence would bring lasting peace and happiness to humanity.

This book attempts to invite all theologians, scientists and scholars have a helpful dialogue to reach an effective convergence on these both main sources of human studies. I am very grateful to Mr. Ashok Kumar Mittal and his colleagues in Concept Publishing Company Pvt. Ltd. for their valuable cooperation, and all people who helped me to work out this book. I request the distinguished readers to send me their helpful comments.

Pune 2012
rezania110@gmail.com

Hamid Rezania

Acknowledgements

My most sincere expressions of gratitude must go to every single member of my family (my dear wife and my lovely children), my lovely teachers especially Dr. Kalicharan Rauta who supported me with his critical mind, and tolerated my polemics with his always original, thoughtful conceptions and relatives, friends for their patience during the preparation of this work and without whose constant encouragement and moral support throughout the course of the study and without whose blessings this work would have never seen the light of the day or its present shape.

Hamid Rezania

Contents

1

Introduction

Religion and Science: Terms Briefly Explained

In this book, I am concerned with the natural sciences as well as Hinduism and Islam as religions. Religion and science are two major sources that have guided mankind in historical times. Both of them have greatly influenced all aspects of human life. In certain cases both religion and science have looked into those problems and clashes that needed urgent attention. There is a popular belief that religion and science are two basically opposite poles. There are several definitions of religion, which imply a relationship not merely between man and man, but also between man and some moral power that attempts to find out the ways to reach human perfection.

Some definitions have pointed out that whenever and wherever man has a sense of dependence on external moral powers, which are conceived as mysterious as, and higher than, man's own, there is religion. The feeling of awe and self-abasement with which man is filled in the presence of such mysterious powers is essentially a religious emotion, the root of worship and prayer. The internal aspect of religion is the body of ideas, convictions and emotions concerning man's relations with God, while its external aspect is the system of prayers, ceremonies and rites through which the religious feeling is manifested.

On the other hand, science has a different method and different definition. Many scientists believe that science is applied to solving modern problems of a technological and humanistic nature. The question of whether religion is compatible with science has occupied a prominent place in the discussions of the nineteenth century and some thinkers have held the view that science and religion are incompatible. In the midst of this controversy it may be said that both schools of thought have firmly held their views. The course of history shows that historically religion has frequently opposed science and free enquiry. It has not encouraged scientific knowledge.

Some of the causes of conflicts between science and religion are listed below:

1. The first cause of conflict between science and religion is that the boundary between the two is continuously shifting. What was unknown till yesterday is known today and thus the boundaries of the known go on expanding for ever.
2. The second cause of conflict is that science possesses a faith of its own. The scientific pursuit of empirical truth is opposed to religion's pursuit of the non-empirical.
3. The third cause of conflict is that religion is subjected to scientific analysis.

There are also those who believe that religion and science are not opposed to each other. These thinkers argue that religion and science are two aspects of the facts of life. One aspect touches the soul while the other indicates material advancement. Religion gives peace to a scientifically advanced and worried society. Religion and science both try to pierce into the realm of unknown. These thinkers argue that in every society there are eminent scientists who believe in God. They, therefore, feel that it is not correct to say that both are absolutely opposed to each other. It cannot be denied that there is conflict between the two. Religion fears that the free enquiry of science may damage or shatter its image, if not wholly, at least partially.

It can be asserted that Ethics and Religion could solve many problems of mankind; for example, faith and purification to complete goodness will open new horizons for human perfection. What is the place of ethics in this relationship? The present study will attend to deal with these issues of significance as far as the relationship between religion and science is concerned.

One of the fundamental ideas of Islam is that empirical Science does not have any conflict with Religion. Science is God's sign and His reminder in nature. One who believes that religion is a personal belief (idea), emphasizes on the relationship between Religion and Science, while religion is a relationship of man with God. Religion and Science both have a social, political and psychological dimension. Attention to science is in Islamic views, a religious duty. Religion and Science both are concerned with the real and the timeless issues of life in general in the universe.

With the advent of Marx and Darwin's views in the nineteenth century, some had thought that the growth of new science (i.e., empirical science) could remove the age of religion. Yet what we find is a much greater religious optimism and credence in the twentieth century. Many religious activities are being broadly performed even more than earlier. Right from the Russian Revolution of 1917, even after seventy years of fighting against religion in the USSR, religion could not be removed and eradicated from man's nature and his world.

The following two questions need urgent attention:

(a) Why has Religion remained constant and stable and may perhaps even expand further?
(b) What is the root of this reality, such that in spite of all problems, shocks and plagues, the tree of religion has remained stable and persistent?

The relationship between man and religion is internal and intuitive, without any mediator. Man's perception of himself is so different from his understanding of things. This difference is based on an ancient understanding that has been with man perennially. There are some features of human nature that we cannot find in the external world. Man feels the world of freedom internally. He can make decisions freely. There is no form of life behaving in this fashion in nature. Man knows that he has a perspective faculty and that he can discover or understand others too. Man and nature have differences in ethics, values, willingness, and in love, too. The requirement for religion is a necessity for man. Although, some thinkers have denied this claim, the real and the best witness of this phenomenon is the history of the human race.

Man has some basic questions which science is able to answer. The main responsibility of science is that of answering man's questions. Science could not satisfy man in some of the deepest questions. Science could not give responses to some of these questions. Therefore, the agitation and commotions have continued.

Ethics, justice and values, etc., are holy concepts for men. Man has arrived at this point through Science and without the co-operation of religion, but the sciences are not concerned with the state of values, though religions are. Science alone cannot make man happy, hopeful and serious about looking for the goal of life. Science itself is not enough for his happiness. The experience of the Second World War has made it clear that science by itself and without religion could not bring happiness and goodness. Science during that period was used only for making war more destructive and killing more and more persons. The world is not free from war even for one day. Science without religion cannot lead man towards happiness. Science is a powerful instrument that man can use effectively when he wants to remove or decrease his suffering.

In the theistic religions the source of science goes back to the notions of God. The limits of conflict between religion and science should be known in order to understand what has happened, in the Middle Ages and in the world of Christianity and the world of Islam. This is a fundamental idea of Islam that the empirical Science does not conflict with Religion. According to Islam, science is God's sign and His reminder in the nature.

Man in his search for truth, has used in the span of history different methods and different ways. Some people are attached to the metaphysical and religious ways. Others like to make this search through empirical and positive experiences. These two methods or two ways are known as the methods of religion and science. We know that science without religion will be useless or even will be dangerous for humanity. Similarly, religion without science cannot guide men alone.

The present study consists of six chapters. In the beginning of the present research work, in the first chapter, the concepts of religion and science are briefly explained and the view that there is a conflict between religion and science is discussed in various aspects, especially with reference to Islam and Hinduism. From the seventeenth century to the twentieth century this view was being challenged and its course through the centuries has been discussed briefly.

The next chapter—the second chapter—presents the discussion on following points:

- Definitions of religion and science and their place in the discipline of philosophy.

- The relationship between religion and science—in conflict or in a cooperative bond.
- Types of relationships between religion and science and the latest views about the same.
- The nature of scientific method and religious method, and the differences between them.
- The three illustrative examples of clashes between religion and science; Galileo, Marx and Darwin, and their contributions to science and their challenges to the domain of religion. The main topic of the present research study is presented briefly in the second chapter.

In the third chapter, the Islamic view and its reaction against the position of religion and science is discussed. Islam is not opposed to scientific and technological progress. On the contrary, Islam encourages science. The only two points that are stressed are:

1. Scientific, technological and social progress shall not result in man waxing proud and thereby disregarding his Creator.
2. This endeavour and progress shall be utilized to improve the condition of men and shall never be used in propagating sin or to buttress the foundations of cruelty and oppression.

Islamic sciences are *sciences* in the context of traditional religious ideas of *Islam,* including its *ethics* and *philosophy.* The modern advancement of science in the Islamic world can be seen as part of the broader movement of getting a deeper knowledge of science as well as its relation with religion.

The fourth chapter discusses the relationship between science and religion from the viewpoint of Hinduism, which has a special philosophy, in several schools, as is the case in other religions. Hinduism has two main branches; *Astika* and *Nastika* (Orthodox and Heterodox). The views of three interpreters of its scriptures (Vivekanand, Mahatma Gandhi and Dr. Sarvepalli Radhakrishnan) regarding the subject, are further discussed.

Ethics, a major branch of philosophy, is the study of *values* and *customs* of a person or group. It covers the *analysis* of *concepts* such as "*right*" and "*wrong*", "*good*" and "*evil*", and "*responsibility*". Ethics is divided into three primary areas: meta-ethics (the study of the concept of ethics), normative ethics (the study of how to determine ethical values), and applied ethics (the study of the use of ethical values). The relationship between ethics and religion and the role of ethics in relation to modern science with special reference to Hinduism and Islam is discussed in the fifth chapter. The views on Marxist Theory and the Darwinian Theory of Evolution are further discussed in the light of the views of Professor S.H. Nasr and Gandhi. It appears that all approaches have some strengths and weaknesses and the choice of a solution on the basis of their positive points is a logical and necessary selection. The relationship between ethics and religion and modern science is very strong, taking into consideration the main purpose of religion. In other words: religions have to improve the moral activities in human life, and lead men to goodness and happiness.

The last chapter is an attempt to present a viable and plausible solution to the issue of the nature of relationship between religion and science.

2

History of Religion and Science

Understanding the Concept of Religion

At times the word "religion" appears to be so simple that any man could understand the meaning. At other times it appears to be very difficult to understand. A number of modern scholars of religions have commented on the difficulty of defining what religion is.

There are many different religions in the world. Religions try to answer important but mysterious questions like "Where did the world come from?" and "What happens to us after we die?" When people believe that they have answers to these questions, they often start new religions, or add their new ideas to old religions.[1]

Many religions believe in supernatural beings such as spirits, angels, devils, polytheistic gods, or a monotheistic god (such as the Christian, Islamic, or Judaic God), who can influence people and the world. People who teach or write about religion often say that they got their ideas from a supernatural being.

Many religions are very old, but new religions are always being created when some people are not satisfied with the answers from the old religions. Things which are considered important and good by religions are called sacred or holy. Many religions have sacred books that give the most important ideas and stories of their religions.

Religions usually say how people should behave in order to be happy together or to please God. Many religions believe that people who live in a right way will go to Heaven for ever after they die, or that people who live in a wrong way will go to Hell. Some religions believe in the Resurrection—by which God will bring some, most, or all dead people to life again one day; other religions believe in Rebirth—that people will be born again as new persons or as an animal after they die. Usually this is believed to be according to how a person acts in the present life. Some religions believe in a mixture of all of these ideas.

All religions teach people to be good and to help each other; unfortunately religions also sometimes create problems. This is partly because the questions of religion are so important to people, and because it is difficult to be sure which answers are correct. Many people are unhappy when other people do not agree with their ideas about religion, or when they think that people will cause problems for their religion.

Etymology of the word "Religion"

There are many definitions of religion, and most have struggled to avoid an overly sharp definition on the one hand, and meaningless generalities on the other. Some have tried to use formalistic, doctrinal definitions and others have tried to use experiential, emotive, intuitive, valuation and ethical factors.

We have some philosophical and some theological definitions. There are other kinds of definitions as well: social, political and psychological definitions.

- In Latin "religio" means: to connect.
- The word "religion" generally indicates all forms of ceremonial community worship.

The Cambridge Encyclopaedia points out that various dictionaries have made many attempts to define the word religion.[2] However, no single definition will suffice to encompass the varied sets of traditions, practices, and ideas which constitute the different religions.

The Webster Dictionary[3] states that religion means any specific system of belief and worship, often involving a code of ethics and philosophy.

The two important components of religions are:

1. One's belief and worship in a deity or deities.
2. One's ethical behaviour towards other persons.

One definition makes the point by stating that "a community striving to come to the pure essence of the worship of YHWH" and cites definitions from an unknown dictionary: "religion (ri-lij'[uh] n) n.

A. The beliefs, attitudes, emotions, behaviour, etc., constituting man's relationship with the powers and principles of the universe, especially with a deity or deities; also, any particular system of such beliefs, attitudes, etc.
B. An essential part or a practical test of the spiritual life.
C. An object of conscientious devotion or scrupulous care: e.g. His work is a religion to him.
D. Religious practice or belief.
E. An organized system of belief that generally seeks to understand purpose, meaning, goals, and methods of spiritual things. These spiritual things can be God, people in relation to God, salvation, after life, purpose of life, order of the cosmos, etc.

Religion is defined as the beliefs, attitudes, emotions, behaviour, etc., constituting man's relationship with the powers and principles of the universe especially with a deity or deities, as well as any particular system of such beliefs, attitudes, etc.

Religion also means the relation of 'uman beings' to that which they regard as holy and sacred, spiritual or divine[4].

Religion is defined in terms such as any specific system of belief and worship, often involving a code of ethics and a philosophy. This definition would exclude religions that do not engage in worship[5].

The English word "*religion*" is derived from the Middle English "*religioun*" which came from the Old French "*religion*". It may have been originally derived from the Latin word "*religo*" which means "*good faith*," "*ritual*," and other similar meanings. It may have come from the Latin "*religre*" which means "to tie fast."

The *Encyclopaedia of Religion* describes religion in the following way:

> "In summary, it may be said that almost every known culture involves the religious in the above sense of a depth dimension in cultural experiences at all levels—a push, whether ill-defined or conscious, towards some sort of ultimacy and transcendence that will provide norms and power for the rest of one's life. When more or less distinct patterns of behaviour

> are built around this depth dimension in a culture, this structure constitutes religion in its historically recognizable form. Religion is the organization of life around the depth dimensions of experience—varied in form, completeness, and clarity in accordance with the environing culture."[6]

Therefore, "Religion", sometimes used interchangeably with *faith,* is commonly defined as *belief* concerning the *supernatural, sacred,* or *divine,* and the practices and institutions associated with such belief. In its broadest sense some have defined it as the sum total of answers given to explain mankind's relationship with the universe. Occasionally, the word "religion" is used to designate what should be more properly described as a "religious organization"—that is, an organization of people that support some religion, often taking the form of a *legal entity.*

The Problems with Definitions

Defining the word "*religion*" is fraught with difficulty. All of the definitions mentioned contain at least one or the other deficiency. Some exclude beliefs and practices that many people passionately defend as religious. For example, one definition might include belief in a personal deity or some supernatural entities. This excludes such non-theistic religions as Buddhism and religious Satanism which have no such belief.

Some definitions equate "*religion*" with "*Christianity*," and thus consider two out of every three human beings in the world as non-religious. Some definitions are so broadly written that they include beliefs and areas of study that most people do not regard as religious. For example, David Edward's definition would seem to include cosmology and ecology, fields of investigation that most people regard as scientific studies and non-religious in nature. Some define "*religion*" in terms of "the sacred" and/or "the spiritual", and thus necessitate the creation of two more definitions. Sometimes, definitions of "religion" contain more than one deficiency.

There is also some problem for the definition of religion: various methodologies in definition make different interpretations, such as social, political, psychological, etc.

On the other hand, some of the definitions have social aspects that need to be discussed separately and also some are based on a secular approach. Most of these definitions mention only one aspect of religion and do not describe the essence of religion.

Some further Definitions

Herbert Spencer: Religion is the recognition that all things are manifestations of a power which transcends our knowledge or religion is a tool for explaining the secret of the world[7].

Napoleon Bonaparte: Religion is excellent stuff for keeping common people quiet[8].

Thomas Edison: Religion is all bunk[9].

These are functional definitions for religion[10].

Bradley said: Religion is rather the attempt to express the complete reality of goodness through every aspect of our being[11].

Mathew Arnold: Religion is ethics heightened, enkindled lit up by feeling[12].

The following are normative definitions:

Karl Heinrich Marx (1818-1883): Religion is the sight of the oppressed creature, the heart of heartless world, just as is the spirit of a spiritless situation; it is the opiate of the people[13].

Bertrand Russell: Religion is something left over from the infancy of our intelligence[14].

Friedrich Daniel Ernest Schleiermacher (1768-1834): The essence of religion consists in the feeling of an absolute dependence[15].

Emil Durkheim (1858-1917): "Society has to be present within the individual. Religion is as a mechanism that shored up or protected a threatened social order." According to Durkheim, religion has been the cement of society in the past, but he held that the collapse of religion would not lead to a moral implosion. Durkheim was specifically interested in religion as a communal experience rather than an individual one. His view is that religious phenomena occur when a separation is made between the profane (the realm of everyday activities) and the sacred (the realm of the extraordinary and the transcendent). These are different depending on what man chooses them to be. An example of this is wine at communion, as it is not only wine but represents the blood of Christ. Durkheim believed that religion is 'society divinized', as he argues that religion occurs in a social context. He also, in line with our forefathers, who tried to find a replacement for dying religions, urged people to unite in a civic morality, on the basis that we are what we are as a result of society.

Durkheim condensed religion into four major functions:

1. Disciplinary, forcing or administrating discipline.
2. Cohesive, bringing people together, a strong bond.
3. Vitalizing, to make more lively or vigorous, vitalise and boost the spirit.
4. Euphoric, a good feeling, happiness, confidence, well-being.[16]

Our Compromise Definition

Religion defined in comprehensive terms: A very broad definition of religion can be attempted: "Religion is any specific system of belief about the deity, often involving rituals, a code of ethics, a philosophy of life, and a worldview." (A worldview is a set of basic, foundational beliefs concerning deity, humanity and the rest of the universe.) Thus we would consider Christianity, Islam, Judaism, Native American Spirituality, and Neo-Paganism to be religions. Thus, any collection of doctrines or any specific system of beliefs that springs from the revelation of prophets for human guidance and illustrated by descriptive or normative statements constitutes a religion.

The Need for Religion

It is not possible to separate man's way of thinking from his way of living and his dealing with life. Man is a wise and understanding being who thinks for himself, wants to comprehend his surroundings and tries to know the beginning and the end of everything, in order to be able to understand the mysteries of the world and the beings around him. He tries to discover: How did this world begin? Where is it going to? Why is he here in this life? What is the goal of his existence? Where will he end?

What does life itself mean? How should he conduct his life? Man has always been looking for convincing answers to these questions.

The answer to these questions either leads him to happiness and welfare, or to wretchedness and misfortune. The answers, though short in their form and brief in their expression, are yet great in their meanings, important in their reality and deep in their effects.

It is these answers which define how man should live, behave, and understand life and estimate the importance of his own existence. By providing correct answers one may resolve an important crisis of thought—the crisis from which man has long been suffering. Unable to find correct answers, he has been tormented by anxiety and uncertainty and forced to wander through an abyss of suffering in life, and soundly evaluate life and man's existence. The correct answers to these questions have always been confined to two contradictory theories, both in their truth and in the resulting constructions that are based upon them. The answer, given through religion, lights the path of righteousness and faith with rational proof; the second given by error and denial, aims at invoking a mist to obliterate clear visibility, to envelope man's conscience and prevent it from directing itself towards Truth or God, the Beginning and the End of existence.

The answer of religion offers, through its call and message, an interpretation of the universe and life, and an explanation of man's existence, and of his links with them; while the other answer bases its explanation as a retort to the idea of faith, denying its reasoning and explanation. Religion bases its interpretation and viewpoint on believing that this universe, life and man have a Creator, a Lord, a God-head; and that man's existence on this earth is neither a meaningless and aimless one, nor a random happening. Life and man have their goals and values exceeding the time span of man's existence on the earth's surface. He has a supreme objective to pursue, embodying it through his attitudes, his deeds and his general activities in a world that goes beyond perception and the time spent in this world.

Etymology of the word "Science"

The word *science* comes from the Latin word *scientia* for 'knowledge', which in turn comes from *scio*—'I know'. The Indo-European root means 'to discern' or 'to separate'. akin to the Sanskrit *chyati*, 'he cuts off; Greek *schizein*, 'to split'; Latin *scindere*, 'to split'. From the Middle Ages to the Age of Enlightenment, science or *scientia* meant any systematic or exact recorded knowledge. Science, therefore, had the same sort of very broad meaning that philosophy had at that time. In some languages, including French, Spanish, Portuguese, and Italian, the word corresponding to science still carries this meaning.

From classical times to the advent of the modern era, philosophy was divided into natural philosophy and moral philosophy. In the 1800s, the term natural philosophy gradually gave way to the term Natural Science. Natural science was gradually specialized to its current domain, which typically includes the physical sciences and biological sciences. The social sciences, inheriting portions of the realm of moral philosophy, are currently also included under the auspices of science to the extent that these disciplines use empirical methods. As currently understood, moral philosophy still retains the study of ethics, regarded as a branch of philosophy and one of the three classical normative sciences[17].

Understanding the Concept of Science

According to *Webster's New Collegiate Dictionary*, the definition of science is "knowledge attained through study or practice," or "knowledge covering general truths of the operation of general laws, especially as obtained and tested through scientific method [and] concerned with the physical world".

Science refers to a system of acquiring knowledge. This system uses observation and experimentation to describe and explain natural phenomena. The term science also refers to the organized body of knowledge people have gained using that system. Less formally, the word science often describes any systematic field of study or the knowledge gained from it.

Most scientific investigations use some form of the scientific method. Science as defined above is sometimes called pure science to differentiate it from applied science, which is the application of research to human needs. Fields of science are commonly classified along two major lines:

- Natural sciences, the study of the natural world; and
- Social sciences, the systematic study of human behaviour and society.

The *Oxford English Dictionary* defines science as:

1. The state or fact of knowing; knowledge or cognizance of something specified or implied; also, with wider reference, knowledge (more or less extensive) as a personal attribute. (Now only theological and philosophical.)
2. (a) Knowledge acquired by study; acquaintance with or mastery of any department of learning. Also (plural) (a person's) various kinds of knowledge. (b) Trained skill.
3. (a) A particular branch of knowledge or study; a recognized department of learning. (b) Contradistinguished from *art*. (d) a craft, trade or occupation requiring trained skill.
4. In a more restricted sense: A branch of study which is concerned either with a connected body of demonstrated truths or with observed facts systematically classified and more or less colligated by being brought under general laws, and which includes trustworthy methods for the discovery of new truth within its own domain.
5. The kind of knowledge or of intellectual activity of which the various *sciences* are examples. In modern use, chiefly: The sciences (in sense 4) as distinguished from other departments of learning; scientific doctrine or investigation. (b) In modern use, often treated synonymous with 'Natural and Physical Science', and thus restricted to those branches of study that relate to the phenomena of the material universe and their laws, sometimes with implied exclusion of pure mathematics.

Another dictionary[18] states that science means:

1. (a) The observation, identification, description, experimental investigation, and theoretical explanation of phenomena.
   (b) Such activities restricted to a class of natural phenomena.
   (c) Such activities applied to an object of inquiry or study.
2. Methodological activity, discipline, or study: I have got packing a suitcase down to a science.
3. An activity that appears to require study and method: The science of purchasing.
4. Knowledge, especially that gained through experience.
5. The state or fact of knowing; knowledge or cognizance of something specified or implied; also with wider reference, knowledge (more or less extensive) as a personal attribute.

6. (a) Knowledge acquired by study; acquaintance with or mastery of any department of learning. (b) Trained skill.

In the modern use, science is often treated as synonymous with "natural and physical science" and thus restricted to those branches of study that are related to the phenomena of the material universe and their laws, sometimes with implied exclusion of pure mathematics. This is now the dominant sense in ordinary use[19].

In another definition, "Science is devoted to formulating and testing naturalistic explanations for natural phenomena. It is a process for systematically collecting and recording data about the physical world, then categorizing and studying the collected data in an effort to infer the principles of nature that best explain the observed phenomena. Science is not equipped to evaluate supernatural explanations for our observations; without passing judgment on the truth or falsity of supernatural explanations, science leaves their consideration to the domain of religious faith. Because the scope of scientific inquiry is consciously limited to the search for naturalistic principles, science remains free of religious dogma and is thus an appropriate subject for public school instruction."[20]

It seems that the word *science* as used, is equivocal, and has several meanings.

Sometimes it is used as certainty, to denote positive and certitude knowledge of science in this meaning *versus* the illusional propositions.

Science is used also as an organization of acquired statements and proposition such as philosophical or natural or historical sciences.

Experimental sciences can also be divided according to subject. belonging to humanities and natural, therefore, includes sciences, like psychology or sociology and economics or chemistry and physics, etc.

The meaning of science in relationship between religion and science is experimental science that includes natural and humanities. In the Islamic and religious views, science has another interpretation that will be discussed in the next chapter.

Experimental science is known to arrive at and find natural laws or canons and to explain the facts or their quality a position that is used with objectivity and experimentation, prediction and selection and hypothetic-deductive method.

The philosophical discussion of the relationship between modern science and religion has tended to focus on Christianity, because of its dominance in the west.

Sciences, Classification

Science (*scientia*) is an analogy, legitimately but diversely applicable to many differing senses and to many disciplines in a set in which demonstrated knowledge ranks as the prime analogue. To illustrate, the various ways in which the sciences can be classified are first considered. Then the different ways in which the sciences have been classified—according to some interpretations—by certain key figures in the history of thought, are sketched, with an emphasis upon the classification proposed by St. Thomas Aquinas.

Scientific Method

Science can be defined as a systematic study of the nature and the behaviour of the material and physical universe based on observation, experiment and measurement. It is a method of approach to the entire empirical world. It is furthermore an approach, which does not aim at "persuasion", at the finding of "ultimate reality" or at "conversion"[21]. Procedures for attaining scientific knowledge are known as scientific methods. These methods include formulating theories and testing them against observation or experiment. Ancient and medieval thinkers called any systematic body of knowledge a 'science', and their methods were aimed at knowledge in general.

According to the most common model for scientific knowledge, formulated by Aristotle, induction yields universal propositions from which all knowledge in a field can be deduced. This model was refined by medieval and early modern thinkers, and further developed in the nineteenth century by Whewell and Mill[22]. As Kuhn observed, idealized accounts of scientific method must be distinguished from descriptions of what scientists actually do. The methods of careful observation and experiment have been in use from antiquity, but became more widespread after the seventeenth century. Developments in instrument making, in mathematics and statistics, in terminology, and in communication technology have altered the methods and the results of science.

'Method' comes from the Greek *meta* (after) plus *hodos* (path or way). A method is a way to achieve an end; a scientific method is a way to achieve the ends of science. What those ends are depends on what science is or is taken to be. The word 'science' now means primarily natural science, examples of which are physics, astronomy, biology, chemistry, geology and psychology, and it applies secondarily to social sciences such as economics and sociology. Discussions of method focus on the cognitive aims of science, which may include knowledge, understanding, explanation, or predictive success, with respect to all or part of nature or to some domain of natural or social phenomena. Abstractly described, the scientific method is the means for attaining these aims, especially by forming models, theories, or other cognitive structures and testing them through observation and experiment. Investigations of the scientific method may describe the methods actually employed by scientists, or they may formulate proposals about the procedures that should be followed to achieve scientific knowledge.

Goals of Science

It has been said that it is virtually impossible to make inferences from the human senses which actually describe what "is". On the other hand, people can form hypotheses based on observations that they make in the world. By analyzing a number of related hypotheses, scientists can form general theories. These theories benefit society or human individuals who make use of them. For example, Newton's theories of physics allow us to predict various physical interactions, from the collision of one moving billiard ball with another, to trajectories of space shuttles and satellites. Relativity can be used to calculate the effects of our sun's gravity on mass light years away. The social sciences allow us to predict (with limited accuracy for now) things like economic turbulence and also to better understand human behaviour and to produce useful models of society and to work more empirically with government policies. Chemistry and biology together have transformed our ability to use and predict chemical and biological reactions and scenarios. In modern times though, these segregated scientific disciplines (notably the latter two) are more often being used together in conjunction to produce more complete models and tools. One goal of science is to explain and utilize multiple known phenomena with one theory or set of theories.

Despite popular impressions of science, it is not the goal of science to answer all questions. The goal of the sciences is to have publicly testable thoughts about the world. Science cannot possibly address nonsensical, or non-testable questions, so the choice of which questions to answer becomes important. Science does not and cannot produce absolute and unquestionable truth. Rather, science tests some aspects of the world and provides a reasonable theory to explain them.

Science is not a source of subjective value judgments, though it can certainly speak to matters of ethics and public policy by pointing to the likely consequences of actions. What one projects from the currently most reasonable scientific hypothesis onto other realms of interest is not a scientific issue, and the scientific method offers no assistance for those who wish to do so. Scientific justification (or refutation) for many things is, nevertheless, often claimed.

Science is a useful tool and it is a growing body of understanding that allows us to contend more effectively with our surroundings and to better adapt and evolve as a social whole, as well as independently.

Individualism is a tacit assumption underlying most empiricist accounts of science, which treat science as if it were purely a matter of a single individual confronting nature, testing and predicting by using hypotheses. In fact, science is always a collective activity conducted by a scientific community. This can be demonstrated in many ways, perhaps the most fundamental and trivial of which is that scientific results must be communicated with language. Thus, the values of scientific communities permeate the science they produce.

For a large part of recorded history, science had little bearing on the everyday lives of people. Scientific knowledge was gathered for its own sake, and it had few practical applications. However, with the dawn of the Industrial Revolution in the eighteenth century, this rapidly changed. Today, science has a profound effect on the way we live, largely through technology—the use of scientific knowledge for practical purposes.

Some forms of technology have become so well established that it is easy to forget the great scientific achievements that they represent. The refrigerator, for example, owes its existence to a discovery that liquids take in energy when they evaporate, a phenomenon known as latent heat. The principle of latent heat was first exploited in a practical way in 1876, and the refrigerator has played a major role in maintaining public health ever since. The first automobile, dating from the 1880s, made use of many advances in physics and engineering, including reliable ways of generating high-voltage sparks, while the first computers emerged in the 1940s from simultaneous advances in electronics and mathematics.

Other fields of science also play an important role in the things we use or consume everyday. Research in food technology has created new ways of preserving and flavouring what we eat. Research in industrial chemistry has created a vast range of plastics and other synthetic materials, which have thousands of uses in the home and in industry. Synthetic materials are easily formed into complex shapes and can be used to make machine, electrical, and automotive parts, scientific and industrial instruments, decorative objects, containers, and many other items.

Alongside these achievements, science has also brought about technology that helps save human life. The kidney dialysis machine enables many people to survive kidney diseases that would once have proved fatal, and artificial valves allow sufferers of coronary heart disease to return to active living. Biochemical research is responsible for the antibiotics and vaccinations that protect us from infectious diseases, and for a wide range of other drugs used to combat specific health problems. As a result, the majority of people on the planet now live longer and healthier lives than ever before.

However, scientific discoveries can also have a negative impact in human affairs. Over the last hundred years, some of the technological advances that make life easier or more enjoyable, have proved to have unwanted and often unexpected long-term effects. Industrial and agricultural chemicals pollute the global environment, even in places as remote as Antarctica, and city air is contaminated by toxic gases from vehicle exhausts. The increasing pace of innovation means those products become rapidly obsolete, adding to a rising tide of waste. Most significantly of all, the burning of fossil fuels such as coal, oil, and natural gas releases into the atmosphere carbon dioxide and other substances known as greenhouse gases. These gases have altered the composition of the entire atmosphere, producing global warming and the prospect of major climate change in years to come.

Science has also been used to develop technology that raises complex ethical questions. This is particularly true in the fields of biology and medicine. Research involving genetic engineering, cloning, and *in vitro* fertilization gives scientists the unprecedented power to bring about new life, or to devise new forms of living things. At the other extreme, science can also generate technology that is deliberately designed to harm or to kill. The fruits of this research include chemical and biological warfare, and also nuclear weapons, by far the most destructive weapons that the world has ever known.

Differences between Science and Religion

Scientific findings and religious beliefs are normally quite separate; Science deals with the study of nature, its forces, processes and development. It is based on the analysis of empirical evidence. It assumes, as a working hypothesis, that processes and events happen due to natural causes, not through divine intervention. It rarely intrudes in matters of morality, the existence and nature of deity, spirituality, etc. Religion deals with matters of faith. Its main basis is often revelation from a deity—orally transmitted from generation to generation, recorded in a sacred text, or *revealed to individuals through prayer.* Most faith groups teach of the existence of one or more deities who created the universe, and continue to play a major role in managing it—sometimes bypassing the laws of nature to create miracles. A main function of religion is to teach moral principles, mankind's relationship to the god(s) or goddess(es), behaviour towards other humans, spiritual matters, etc. The main battles between religion and science are in areas in which they overlap. Here, both often hold conflicting positions.

Many people feel that their own religious tradition is absolutely true, whereas science and all other faiths are artificial and deeply flawed belief systems, invented by error-prone humans. This attitude often fuels religious conflict, sometimes escalating into mass crimes against humanity and genocide. The result is that different religious traditions battle each other, as well as disagree with the findings of science[23].

Science and Religion: From Conflict to Convergence

The history of human intellectual development in Western civilization reveals that human consciousness has grown through three different stages of evolution. The early Greek civilization was dominated by philosophy which was characterized by the theme of reason. Still its final objective was to reach the Ultimate Reality through the mediation of pure reason.

The Middle Ages were dominated by religion, which stood on the strong foundations of faith and belief.

The Post-Renaissance period is dominated by science, which seeks to reach at concrete facts. The history of human thoughts further reveals that there has been constant conflict between the devotees of religion, philosophy and science. It goes without saying that religion and science appear to be perfect strangers. They are totally different world views and their outlook on life and of life, is mostly antagonistic and conflicting.

Philosophical discussion of the relation between modern science and religion has tended to focus on Christianity, because of its dominance in the West. The relations between science and Christianity have been too complex to be described by the 'warfare' model popularized by A.D. White (1896) and J.W. Draper (1874). An adequate account of the past two centuries requires a distinction between conservative and Liberal positions. Conservative Christians tend to see theology and science as partially intersecting bodies of knowledge. God is revealed in 'two books': the Bible and Nature. Ideally, science and theology ought to present a single, consistent account of reality; but in fact there have been instances where the results of science have (apparently) contradicted Scripture, in particular with regard to the age of the universe and the origin of the human species.

Liberals tend to see science and religion as complementary but non-interacting, as having concerns so different as to make conflict impossible. This approach can be traced to Immanuel Kant, who distinguished sharply between pure reason (science) and practical reason (morality). More recent versions contrast science, which deals with the what and how of the natural world, and religion, which deals with meaning; or contrast science and religion as employing distinct languages. However, since the 1960s a growing number of scholars with liberal theological leanings have taken an interest in science and have denied that the two disciplines can be isolated from one another[24].

Topics within science that offer fruitful points for dialogue with theology include Big-Bang cosmology and its possible implications for the doctrine of creation, the 'fine-tuning' of the cosmological constants and the possible implications of this for design arguments, and evolution and genetics, with their implications for a new understanding of the human individual.

Perhaps of greater import are the indirect relations between science and theology. Newtonian physics fostered an understanding of the natural world as strictly determined by natural laws; this in turn had serious consequences for understanding divine action and human freedom. Twentieth century developments such as quantum physics and chaos theory call for a revised view of causation. Advances in the philosophy of science in the second half of the twentieth century provide a much more sophisticated account of knowledge than was available earlier, and this has important implications for methods of argument in theology.

1. Religion and Western Predecessors of Science

Western interest in a systematic account of the natural world is an inheritance from the ancient Greeks rather than from the Hebrew tradition, which tended to focus on the human world. The Greek concept of nature was not set over against a concept of super nature, as it has been in more recent centuries, so it is possible to say that Greek philosophy of nature was inherently theological. Early Christian scholars were divided in their approach to Greek natural philosophy, some making great use of it for apologetic purposes, others rejecting it.

After the fall of Rome, the centre of scholarship shifted eastward. Islamic scholars in the Middle Ages were largely responsible for preserving the learning of the Greeks, as well as for significant scientific developments of their own in the fields of optics, medicine, astronomy and mathematics. It was through Muslims in Spain that important scientific works by Aristotle were introduced to Western Europe in the twelfth century. The influence of these works on Christian thought culminated in Thomas Aquinas' 'Two Summas'.

2. Early Modern Science and Worldview

At the end of the nineteenth century, White (1896) and Draper (1874) promoted the view of science and religion as traditional enemies. However, revisionist history at the end of the twentieth century presents a much more complex picture. It is true that the Catholic Church silenced Galileo in 1633, while René Descartes' mechanics conception of matter was condemned, and that fear of censorship had a generally chilling effect on scientific theorizing throughout the seventeenth century. However, it must be noted that not all of the

Catholic officials were opposed to Galileo. In addition, a number of the century's greatest scientists were Catholic: Pierre Gassendi, Marin Mersenne, Blaise Pascal and Nicolas Steno, as well as Galileo and Descartes. The Jesuit order was home to a number of scientists who were not outstanding theorists but contributed significantly to experimental science.

In the early modern period, it is difficult to distinguish conflicts between science and religion on the one hand from intra-theological conflicts and conflicts between the new science and the Aristotelian scholastic synthesis on the other. The Galileo affair needs to be interpreted in the light of both these complications, since it is not possible to understand the resistance to Galileo's astronomy without recognizing the fact that it called into question an entire socio-political order founded on a picture of the cosmos and of the place of humans in it. The affair was also an internal church struggle concerning the proper interpretation of Scripture. Galileo followed Augustine's rule that an interpretation of Scripture should be revised when it is found to conflict with other knowledge. This put him in conflict with conservative church officials who adopted a more literalist interpretive strategy. A further complication is the fact that the new science was often liberally mixed with magic and astrology, which the Catholic Church condemned both because they dabbled with the demonic and because of suspicion that they confirmed Calvinist views of determinism against the Catholic view of free will.

Robert Merton (1938) argued that Puritanism promoted the scientific revolution, a thesis still debated over half a century later. While Merton's thesis was overstated, it is likely that a particular reformed doctrine of the sovereignty of God—that God's sovereignty excludes all active contributions of lesser beings to his work—made the modern scientific and philosophical conception of matter as inert or passive more acceptable to Isaac Newton, Robert Boyle and other Protestants than it would otherwise have been. Here again it is important to recognize the interplay of Aristotelians and intra-theological disputes. The mechanical conception of matter was a direct rejection both of Neo-Platonist magical conceptions and of the Aristotelian teleological and organic view, that 'forms' inherent in substances provided built-in powers and goals. At the same time, it furthered theological convictions first expressed by late medieval nominal theologians. It is one of the great ironies of history, then, that Newton's mechanical conception of the material universe so quickly evolved into Pierre Simon de Laplace's purely materialist and determinist view, the latter being absolutely incompatible with religion.

3. Indirect Relation

If direct conflicts between Christian theology and the various theories of modern science have often been overemphasized, the deleterious effects on theology of indirect conflicts between religion and science have received much too little attention. These indirect interactions can be considered under the headings of metaphysics and epistemology.

Metaphysics

'Descartes' mechanical view of matter as pure extension, accompanied by a view of mind as 'thinking substance', inaugurated a metaphysical dualism that has replaced older and more nuanced views of Christian anthropology. In so far as this dualism has been shown to be philosophically untenable, Christianity, with its view of the soul and after life, has appeared untenable as well.

The clockwork image of the universe as a closed system of particles in motion, strictly governed by the laws of physics (the image epitomized in the nineteenth century by the work of Laplace), created insuperable problems in accounting for divine action. A popular variety of deism offered the most reasonable account: God was the creator of the universe, and responsible for the laws of nature, but has no ongoing interaction with the natural world or with human history. The alternatives for theists were accounts of miraculous interventions or an account of God as an immanent sustainer of natural processes. The former seemed to make God irrational (contradicting God's own decrees) or inept (needing to readjust the system). The latter view made it difficult to maintain any more, the sense of God's personal involvement in human life than was possible for the deists. Much of the difference between liberal and conservative Christianity can be traced to theories of divine action: conservatives tend to take an interventionist view, liberals an immanent, view.

Epistemology

Medieval theologians had two sets of epistemological categories at their disposal, those relating to scientia (demonstrative or scientific knowledge) and those relating to *opinion* ('probable' beliefs, including those based on authority). So those theological conclusions that could not be deduced from first principles could, happily, be based on unimpeachable authority, the very word of God. However, in the modern period, the range of *scientia* contracted to the spheres of mathematics and formal logic; Hume and Kant both provided powerful critiques of deductive arguments for the existence of God and of natural theology generally. Furthermore, when probable knowledge took on its contemporary sense of knowledge based on the weight of empirical evidence, appeals to authority became irrelevant, and most judged it impossible to provide empirical evidence for theological claims. Thus, the central question for modern liberal theologians has been how, if at all, theology is possible.

Liberal theology diverged from more traditional accounts as a result of its strategies for meeting the problems raised directly or indirectly by science.

Following Friedrich Schleiermacher, many liberal theologians have understood religion to constitute its own sphere of experience, unrelated to that of scientific knowledge. Theological doctrines are expressions of religious awareness, not accounts of a supernatural realm. God works immanently, and not by interventions in either the natural world or human history. Thus, liberal theology has avoided direct conflict with modern science, at the cost (or with the beneficial consequence) of a radical revision of the very concepts of religion and theology. However, Ian Barbour's *Issues in Science and Religion* (1966) presented an encyclopaedic overview of the points at which scientific claims are relevant to religious thought, and in Myths, Models, and Paradigms (1974) he argued for significant epistemological similarities between science and religion. Since then, a growing number of scholars from the liberal wing of Christianity have begun to call the modern division of territory into question.

4. Geology, Evolution and the Age of the Earth

Physics and astronomy were the main scientific issues for theologians in the seventeenth and eighteenth centuries; Geology and Biology held an analogous place in the nineteenth and twentieth. For centuries, the biblical narrative from creation to Christ and the projected *Last Judgement* provided the skeletal outline for accounts of natural as well as human history. For instance, the story of Noah and the Flood served as a useful explanation for marine fossils found high above sea level. However, by the seventeenth century, the short span of history calculated from the Bible was being challenged from a number of directions. (James Ussher, a seventeenth-century Irish archbishop, has been credited with the calculation that creation took place a mere 4004 years before Christ.) Although sporadic attempts to reconcile geological history with Genesis continue up to the present, in the eighteenth century a large number of geologists already recognized that the Flood hypothesis could not explain the growing body of knowledge regarding rock stratification and the placement of fossils. A much longer history of the Earth, prior to human history, had to be presumed. At the same time, Egyptian and Chinese records were calling into question the short span of human history calculated from the Bible.

While some contemporary opposition to evolutionary theory involved 'young earth' chronology, in the nineteenth century, negative reactions to Charles Darwin's *The Origin of Species* (1859) were more often objections to Social Darwinism and to the claim that humans were kin to the 'lower animals'; other negative reactions focused on the fact that natural selection provided an alternative to divine design for explaining the fit of organisms to their environments, thus undermining an important apologetic argument. Nonetheless, many theologians and other believers readily accepted the theory and judged the changes it required in theology to be salutary rather than mere accommodation.

5. Biological Sciences

The theory of evolution was a surprisingly hot issue again at the end of the twentieth century. A Gallup poll published in the magazine *US News and World Report* (December 23, 1991) reported that a majority of North American Christians were skeptical of the macro evolutionary paradigm. The best explanation for this resistance is probably the fact that the issue had come to be framed in terms of creation *versus* chance as an account of the origin of the human species. That the issues can be formulated in these terms is due in part to a (defective) theory of divine action that contrasts God's creative acts with natural processes, rather than allowing that God may work through natural processes, including those that involve random events. The controversy was exacerbated by the use made of evolutionary biology by proselytizing atheists.

Genetics provides a new area for dialogue between religion and the biological sciences. Studies showing a genetic basis for human characteristics and behaviour raise questions about the status of the human person—for example, questions about freewill and determinism—that have been the province of philosophy and religion. Of particular interest are studies of twins suggesting a genetic factor in religious behaviour.

Genetic research in general and genetic engineering in particular have raised a number of ethical questions that relate to theological ethics. For example, while most people favour genetic treatment for illnesses, many are opposed to germ-line intervention, which would affect all succeeding generations.

Some objections are based on quasi-religious positions: scientists should not 'play God'. This line of thinking calls for theological scrutiny: are not human beings themselves created in order to participate in God's ongoing creative process? It is noteworthy that in 1991, the US National Institute of Health awarded its first grant ever to a theological institution to the Centre for Theology and the Natural Sciences (Berkeley, California) to study the theological and ethical implications of the Human Genome Initiative, the project to map human DNA.

6. Cosmologies

Physical cosmology is the branch of science that studies the universe as a whole. Beginning in the 1920s, developments in this field have sparked lively debate at the interface between theology and science. The Big-Bang theory, based on the expansion of the universe and a variety of other data, postulates that the universe originated in an extremely dense, extremely hot 'singularity' some 15 to 20 billion years ago. Many Christians, including Pope Pius XII, greeted this theory as a confirmation of the biblical doctrine of creation. It was not only religious people who saw it as such; Frederick Hoyle defended a steady-state model of the universe, in which hydrogen atoms come into being throughout an infinite time span, partly because he saw it as more compatible with his atheism.

The discussion among theologians on the relevance of Big-Bang cosmology to the doctrine of creation involves controversy over the very nature of theology. As mentioned above, it has been common among liberal theologians since Schleiermacher to claim that religious meaning is entirely independent of scientific fact. Theologians who hold this position claim that the doctrine of creation, having to do only with the relation of all that exists to God, says nothing about the temporal origin of the universe, and is, therefore, equally compatible with any cosmological model.

A more recent area of research that has occasioned theological speculation can be referred to as the issue of the anthropoid principle. A number of factors in the early universe had to be adjusted in a remarkably precise way to produce the universe we have. These factors include the mass of the universe, the strengths of the four basic forces (electromagnetism, gravitation, and the strong and weak nuclear forces), and others.

Calculations show that if any of these numbers had deviated even slightly from its actual value, the universe would have evolved in a radically different manner, making life as we know it—and probably life of any sort—impossible. An example of the fine-tuning' required is that if the ratio of the strength of electromagnetism to gravity had varied by as much as one part in 1040, there would be no stars like our sun.

Many claim that this apparent fine-tuning of the universe for life calls for explanation. To some, it appears to provide grounds for a new design argument. Others believe that it can be explained in scientific terms—for example, by suggesting that there are vastly many universes, either contemporaneous with our own or in succession, each of which instantiates a different set of fundamental constants. One or more of these universes would be expected to support life, and it is only in such a universe that observers would be present to raise the question of fine-tuning. Whether or not the fine-tuning is taken as evidence for the existence of God, it has important consequences for theology in that some philosophers believe that it argues against an interventionist account of continuing creation and divine action, since the prerequisites for human existence were built into the universe from the very beginning.

7. Physics and Metaphysics

A variety of developments in physics since the end of the nineteenth century have called into question the determinist worldview. Quantum physics has introduced indeterminacy into the worldview of physics. Quantum theory generally allows only for probabilistic predictions regarding classes of events, not for prediction of individual events. It is unclear whether this limitation represents only a limit of human knowledge, or whether it signifies genuine indeterminacy in nature. However, scholarly opinion tends towards the latter view. Thus, most physicists reject the determinism of the Newtonian worldview, at least at this level. 'Quantum non-locality' refers to the peculiar fact that electrons and other sub-atomic entities that have once interacted continue to behave in coordinated ways, even when they are too far apart for any known causal interaction in the time available. This phenomenon calls radically into question the Newtonian picture of the universe as discrete particles in motion, interacting by means of familiar physical forces. If Newtonian determinism had strong implications for theories of divine action, it is surely the case that these developments in quantum physics must have theological implications as well. What these implications are is still very much an open question.

A more recent development, which cuts across physics and the other natural sciences, is chaos theory. This is the study of systems whose behaviour is highly sensitive to changes in initial conditions. What this means can be illustrated with an example from classical dynamics: the movements of a billiard ball are governed in a straightforward way by Newton's laws, but very slight differences in the angle of impact of the cue stick have greatly magnified effects after several collisions; moreover, initial differences that make for large differences in later behaviour are too small to measure, so the system is intrinsically unpredictable. Chaotic systems are found throughout nature—in thermodynamic systems far from equilibrium, in weather patterns and even in animal populations. Chaos theory is relevant to discussions of divine action not because chaotic systems are indeterminate (that is, not causally determined) and thus open to divine action without violation of the laws of nature. Rather, the recognition of the ubiquity of chaotic systems shows the intrinsic limitations of human knowledge, and leads to the negative but important conclusion that one is rarely (or never) in a position to know that God is not acting in natural processes.

Another development throughout science with important implications for the issue of determinism and divine action is the recognition of 'top-down causation'. The sciences can be conceived as a hierarchy in which higher sciences study progressively more complex systems: physics studies the smallest, simplest components of the universe; chemistry studies complex organizations of physical particles (atoms and molecules); biochemistry studies the extremely complex chemical compounds making up living organisms, and so on. The dream of the logical positivists was to provide an account of the sciences wherein the laws of the higher-level sciences could all be reduced to the laws of physics. This concept of explanatory reductionism followed naturally from the ontological reductionism that has become an important tenet of the modern scientific worldview: if all entities and systems are ultimately made up of the entities studied by physics, their behaviour ought to be understandable in terms of the laws of physics. So, ontological and explanatory reductionism entails causal reductionism, or 'bottom-up causation'. If the laws of physics are deterministic, we have a deterministic account of the whole of nature.

However, it has become apparent that the behaviour of entities at various levels of the hierarchy of complexity cannot always be understood entirely in terms of the behaviour of their parts; attention to their interaction with non-reducible features of their environments is also required. Thus, the state or behaviour of a higher-level system exercises top-down causal influence on its components.

Arthur Peacocke (1990) has used this development in scientific thought to propose new directions for understanding divine action. In his 'panentheist' view, the universe is 'in' God, and God's influence on the cosmos can then be understood by analogy with top-down causation throughout the hierarchy of natural levels. While this proposal does not answer questions about how God affects specific events within the cosmos, it does dissolve the long-standing problem of causal determinism.

8. Epistemology and Language

The shift from medieval epistemology to modern empiricism required radical revision of religious epistemology. Various strategies were employed during the modern period to show theology to be epistemologically respectable. However, the increasing prevalence of atheism in scholarly circles suggests that these strategies have not been successful. At a point in intellectual history that some would call the end of the modern period, theories of knowledge have changed enough that the question of the epistemic status of theology needs to be examined afresh.

The concern here will be only with changes relating directly to science. Theologians' statements have sometimes been dismissed on the grounds that they describe states of affairs that are unimaginable or non-picturable.

However, quantum theory and other recent scientific developments describe a physical reality that is equally unimaginable and, some would say, calls into question traditional two-valued logic. This line of argument is intended to point out that a view of knowledge more humble than that of the modern period is called for; reality is more complex and mysterious than anything our language and concepts allow us to capture.

It has often been said (especially by theologians) that theology differs radically from science in that science is objective while all religious knowledge is self-involving, the product of an interaction between God and the human subject. Another way in which science has tempered older views of knowledge, and narrowed the difference between science and theology, is in its recognition that scientific knowledge itself is interactive.

Measurements are interactions with the phenomena being measured, especially at the subatomic level.

Most modern thinkers have judged it impossible to provide empirical support for theology. However, beginning with the work of Ian Barbour (1974), there has been an investigation of the ways in which theological reasoning resembles that of science, including accounts of suitable data for theology. This development was made possible by advances in philosophy of science that show science itself to be a more complicated, and a more human, enterprise than the positivists assumed.

9. Religion's Implications for Science

Most of this entry has focused on the implications of science for religion.

However, it is also the case that religion has implications for science. It has been argued that Christian doctrine was an important contributor to the rise of modern science: God's freedom entailed that features of the natural world could not be deduced *a priori* from rational principles, yet God's goodness and faithfulness suggested that the world would not be so chaotic as to be unintelligible. The very existence of religion is a valuable reminder that there are boundaries beyond which scientific explanation cannot go, and its doctrines help to answer questions that lie beyond those boundaries.

The Newtonian era saw the separation of natural philosophy (science) from natural theology, and since then it has been a methodological presupposition of science that it should provide purely natural explanations.

Science has thereby set boundaries on its own competence, but this does not mean that what is beyond its competence is, therefore, unimportant (or non-existent). Cosmology and physics raise questions they cannot answer.

Why is the behaviour of natural processes law-like? What caused the Big Bang? Why is there a universe at all? While theology and science may interact in minor ways within each of their proper domains, it is here that theological explanation comes into its own.

For further explanation some important viewpoints of both philosophers and scientists about the position of religion will be presented. Prior to this, the types of relationship between religion and science will be discussed.

Types of Relationships

According to some philosophers and great thinkers,[25] there are four approaches and ways in which science and religion can be related to each other:

1. *Conflict:* The conviction that science and religion are fundamentally irreconcilable.
2. *Contrast:* The claim that there can be no genuine conflict since religion and science are each responding to radically different questions.
3. *Contact*: An approach that looks for dialogue, interaction, and possible "consonance" between science and religion, and especially for ways in which science shapes religious and theological understanding.
4. *Confirmation*: A somewhat quieter, but extremely important perspective that highlights the ways in which, at a very deep level, religion supports and nourishes the entire scientific enterprise.

A grasp of these four approaches should help to pass safely through the thicket of issues that make up the subject matter of this thesis.

1. Conflict

Many scientific thinkers are quite certain that religion can never be reconciled with science. They hold that it is hard to imagine how a scientist could honestly also be religious, at least in the sense of believing in God. Their main reason for drawing this conclusion is that religion apparently cannot demonstrate the truth of its ideas in a straightforward way, whereas science can. Religion, according to them, tries to sneak by without providing any concrete evidence of God's existence. Science, on the other hand, is willing to test all of its hypotheses and theories against "experience". Religion cannot do this in a way that is satisfying to an impartial witness, skeptic's claim, so there must be a "conflict" between the scientific and religious ways of understanding.

Both historical and philosophical considerations seem to substantiate such a grim verdict. Historically, we need only recall the obvious examples—as it was noted; the church's persecution of Galileo in the seventeenth century, and the widespread religious and theological aversion to Darwin's evolutionary theory in the nineteenth and twentieth centuries. The slow pace by which religious thought comes to terms with such scientific ideas, and the fact that many theists still have distaste for them, suggest that religion will never get along with science. Since so many believers in God—especially Catholics—have resisted the findings of astronomy, physics, and biology, is it any wonder that religion comes across as inherently hostile to science?

More important than this historical point, however, are the religion and theology present to scientific skeptics. The main problem here is that religious ideas seem to be experientially non-testable. That is, they apparently exempt themselves from the rigours of public examination. If empirical scrutiny shows a scientific hypothesis to be mistaken, then science willingly discards it and tries out alternatives, subjecting these also to the same rigorous process of inspection.

It seems to skeptics that religious teachings are "unfalsifiable". Karl Popper (1902-1994), argued that[26] genuine science must strive to come up with evidence that will show its ideas to be mistaken. That is, science has to risk the "falsification" of its various claims. For example, since relativity theory predicts that light waves will always bend in the presence of gravitational fields, scientists should look for possible instances in which this prediction might not be true. Then if they cannot find any evidence to the contrary, this means that relativity is a pretty strong theory for weathering all attempts at falsification. Falsifiability is the mark of a theory's scientific status. Willingness to allow its ideas to be falsified purifies science and shows it to be a truly open and honest way of learning about the nature of things.

But can religion display a comparable openness? Scientific skeptics (i.e., those who reject religion in the name of science) declare that religion lacks the robust probity of science. The God-hypothesis, for example, seems to be completely beyond falsification, so it cannot pass muster before the courts of science. Can you imagine any situations and experiences that might lead you to deny God's existence? If you cannot, then the idea of God must be unfalsifiable and, therefore, is not to be taken seriously.

Religion is based, skeptics often claim, on *a priori* assumptions or "faith", whereas science takes nothing for granted. In addition, religion relies heavily on untamed imagination, whereas science sticks to observable facts. And religion is highly emotional, passionate and subjective, whereas science strives to remain disinterested, dispassionate and objective. These antitheses seem to add up to nothing less than an insuperable mutual hostility between science and religion.

The skeptics are not the only ones to insist that religion clashes with science. Biblical literalists (people who think the words of the Bible are literally true) also often see a conflict between their faith and some well established scientific theories. Whenever scientific ideas do not correspond with the letter of the Bible (which is quite often), biblical literalists argue that science must be wrong and religion right. This is especially the case with regard to evolution, but also with miracles, the creation of the universe, the origin of life, and other issues. Many Christians maintain that the Bible teaches the "true" science and that secular science should be rejected if it does not correspond with the letter of scripture. In addition to biblical literalists, there are still other critics who think that science is the enemy of religion. They argue that it was the coming of science that caused most of the emptiness and meaninglessness in modern life and culture. When science separated the experience of "facts" from our human need for eternal "values", they argue, it emptied the cosmos of any real meaning. And since the main business of religion is to teach us the meaning of things, it cannot be reconciled with science.

The conflict between religion and science is what naturally occurs to our minds when we think about this subject. It seems as though, during the last half-century, the results of science and the beliefs of religion had come into a position of frank disagreement, from which there can be no escape, except by abandoning either the clear teaching of science or the clear teaching of religion. This conclusion has been urged by controversialists on both sides; not by all controversialists, of course, but by those trenchant intellects which every controversy calls out into the open. In the seventeenth century the doctrine of the motion of the earth was condemned by a Catholic tribunal. A hundred years ago the extension of time demanded by geological science distressed religious people, Protestant and Catholic. And today the doctrine of evolution is an equal stumbling block. These are only a few instances illustrating a general fact. But all our ideas will be in a wrong perspective if we think that this recurring perplexity was confined to contradictions between religion and science and that in these controversies religion was always wrong and science always right. The true facts of the case are very much more complex, and refuse to be summarized in these simple terms. Science is even more changeable than theology. No man of science could subscribe without qualification to Galileo's beliefs, or to Newton's beliefs, or to all his own scientific beliefs of ten years ago.

Galileo said that the earth moves and that the sun is fixed; the Inquisition said that the earth is fixed and that the sun moves; and Newtonian astronomers, adopting an absolute theory of space, said that both the sun and the earth move[27]. But now we say that any one of these three statements is equally true, provided that you have fixed your sense of 'rest' and 'motion' in the way required by the statement adopted. At the time of Galileo's controversy with the Inquisition, Galileo's way of stating the facts was, beyond question, the most fruitful procedure for scientific research. But in itself, it was not truer than the formulation of the Inquisition. At that time the modern concepts of relative motion were in nobody's mind, so that the statements were made in ignorance of the qualifications required for their more perfect truth. Yet this question of the motions of the earth and the sun expresses a real fact in the universe, and all sides had got hold of important truths concerning it. But, with the knowledge of those times, the truths appeared to be inconsistent[28].

2. *Contrast*

Many scientists and theologians, on the other hand, find no such opposition between religion and science. Each is valid, they argue, though only in its own clearly defined sphere of inquiry. We should not judge religion by the standards of science, nor *vice versa*, because the questions each asks are so completely disparate, and the content of their answers so distinct, that it makes no sense to compare them with each other. If religion and science were both trying to do the same job, then they might be incompatible, but they have radically dissimilar tasks, and if we just keep them in their separate jurisdictions, preventing them from invading each other's territory, there can never be any real "problem" of science and religion.

According to this "contrast" approach, the impression that religion conflicts with science is almost always rooted in a previous confusion, or "conflation[29]" of science with either a religious or a secular belief system. To avoid conflict then the contrast into an undifferentiated smudge, it was, after all, the inability of medieval theology to distinguish religion clearly from science that made Galileo's ideas seem so hostile to believers in the seventeenth century. The church's failure to acknowledge the separate domains of science and religion led its officials to condemn Galileo's novel ideas as though they were an invasion of their own territory. This, of course, was a most unfortunate misunderstanding, leading as did too much of the hostility that many scientists still feel towards religion.

However, we should now know better: religion and science have no business meddling in each other's affairs in the first place. To avoid possible combat, our second approach claims, we should carefully contrast science with religion. Science and religion are such completely independent ways of understanding reality that it is meaningless to place them in opposition to each other.

Conflation, in this view, is an unsatisfactory attempt to avoid conflict by carelessly commingling science with belief. Instead of respecting the sharp differences between science and religion, conflation weaves them into a single fabric where they fade into each other, almost to the point of becoming indistinguishable. Today, for instance, many conservative Christians argue that since the *Bible* is divinely inspired and inerrant, it gives us the most reliable scientific information about beginnings of the universe and life. Some of them call their fusion of science and belief "creation science" and they renounce the Darwinian theory of the evolution, in favour of a literalist interpretation of the biblical accounts of the world's creation. They insist that since the biblical stories are "scientific" they should be taught in public schools as the best alternative to evolutionary biology.

In any case, two things can be opposed to each other only if they are playing the same game. For example, it makes no sense to compare a move in chess, either favourably or unfavourably, with a play in baseball. A completely disparate set of rules governs each game, and so it is senseless to say that one is better than the other. Likewise, since science and religion do not belong on the same playing field together, there is no point in comparing one with the other. We should not place them in competition or conflict. Advocates of this approach typically emphasize that the "game" science plays is one examining the natural world empirically, while religion's is that of expressing the ultimate meaning that transcends the empirically known world. Science is concerned with *how* things happen in nature, religion with *why* there is anything at all rather than nothing. Science is about *causes*, religion about *meaning*. Science deals with solvable *problems, religion* with unsolvable *mystery*. Science answers specific questions about the workings of nature, whereas religion expresses concern about the ultimate ground of nature. Science is concerned with particular truths; religion is interested in explaining why we should seek truth at all.

Where many theologians allow for clear logical distinctions between the tasks of science and religion, the contrast approach sees such differences as a reason for sharply *segregating* the two. Only by drawing an unbroken line between them can we avoid the conflation that leads to conflict. Contrast envisages science and religion as independent, autonomous ways of knowing. Only by putting them in separate camps, it insists, can we prevent eventual warfare between them. And so it holds that the whole ugly affair between Galileo and the church could have been avoided if theology had not intruded into an area that today we would cede to science alone.

Many theologians and scientists are understandably attracted to the concept of contrast, because it seems to keep everything so clean, allowing us to embrace both the discoveries of science and the beliefs of religion without any fear of possible antagonism.

3. Contact

The method of contrast may be an important step towards clarity, but it still fails to satisfy those who seek a more unified picture of reality.

As Ian Barbour would say, it is helpful first approximation, but contrast leaves things at a frustrating impasse. The urge to discover the coherence of all our ways of knowing is too powerful for us to suppress indefinitely, and so it could be suggested that we consider a third approach, one that we shall simply call *contact.*

This way of relating religion to science is not willing to leave the world divided into the two realms defined by the contrast position. Yet it does not wish to revert to the superficial harmony of conflation either. It agrees that science and religion are logically and linguistically distinct, but it knows that in the real world they cannot be as easily compartmentalized as the contrast position supposes. After all, religion in the West has helped shape the history of science, and scientific cosmology has in turn influenced theology. It is impossible to separate them completely even though we can try to make clear logical distinctions in our definitions of them.

In addition, it seems unlikely that just any old cosmology will be compatible with just any old theology, as the contrast position would seem to allow. The kind of world described by evolutionary biology and big bang physics for example, cannot peacefully coexist with the picture of God that Newton, Descartes, and perhaps even Thomas, Aquinas idealized. Whether they are aware of it or not, theologians always bring at least implicit cosmological assumptions to their talk about God, and it is only honest that they acknowledge this fact. It often happens; however, that their cosmological assumptions are scientifically out of date. The contact approach, therefore, is concerned that theology always remains positively "consonant" with cosmology.

Theology cannot rely too heavily on science, but it must pay attention to what is going on in the world of scientists. It must seek to express its ideas in terms that take the best of science into account lest it becomes intellectually irrelevant.

For this reason, the contact approach looks for an open-ended conversation between scientists and theologians. The term "contact" implies coming together without necessarily fusing. It allows for interaction, dialogue, and mutual impact but forbids both conflation and segregation. It insists on preserving differences, but it also cherishes relationship.

Contact proposes that scientific knowledge can broaden the horizon of religious faith and that the perspective of religious faith can deepen our understanding of the universe. It does not strive to prove God's existence from science but is content simply to interpret scientific discoveries within the framework of religious meaning. It does not seek to shore up religious doctrines by appealing to scientific concepts that may on the surface seem to point directly to a divine designer. The days in which scientific ideas could be used to seal arguments for God's existence are over. Still, it is convinced that, without in any way interfering with scientists' own proper methods, religious faith can flourish alongside of science in such a way as to co-produce with it a joint meaning that is more illuminating than either can provide on its own. The kind of religion we are discussing in this work, for example, characteristically strives to instil in its followers a special way of looking at things, and this perspective, as it turns out, is ideally suited to frame recent developments in biology and physics. Rooted in the story of Abraham, the prophetic faith traditions invite their followers to look for the promise that lies in all things. Judaism, Christianity, and Islam think of genuine "faith" as a confidence that new life and undreamed of possibilities are latent even in the most desperate of situations. The authentic religious attitude, then, is a steadfast conviction that the future is open and that an incalculable fulfilment awaits the entire cosmos.

It should, however, be mentioned here, that in recent philosophical discussions of the nature of science, the ways of science and theology do not appear nearly as divergent as either the conflict or the contrast position insinuates. Science no longer appears quite so pure and objective as we used to think, nor theology so impure and subjective. Both science and theology generate imaginative metaphors and theories to interpret certain kinds of "data" but in neither case is it always clear just where metaphor or theory leaves off and "fact" begins. Indeed the consensus of philosophers is that there are no un-interpreted facts. And so we are now more aware than ever before, that in both science and theology there is an aspect of human "construction" which we previously failed to notice. This does not mean that our ideas are, therefore, inevitably unobjective, but it does mean that we cannot enshrine as absolutely reliable any particular form of expression that we employ in our quest for truth.

Science and religion, therefore, make meaningful contact with each other only when they agree to play by the rules of what we are calling critical realism. Good science, in this covenant, hopes to approximate, more or less, the way things are in nature, but it is always willing to be critical of its ways of representing the world. And a theological method committed to the same principles of critical realism allows that our religious symbols and ideas are also always in need of constant correction, but that in a finite way they too may point towards a Transcendent Reality, one that is infinitely elusive but also always truly "there".

Scientific theories and religious metaphors, in this epistemological contract, are not just imaginative concoctions, as much of modern and post-modern thought asserts. Rather, they bear an always tentative relationship to a *real* world and its ultimate ground. This world beyond our representations is always only incompletely grasped, and its presence constantly "judges" our hypotheses, inviting us continually to deepen our understanding both in science and religion. Hence, it is their mutual sharing in this critical openness to the real that provides the basis for genuine "contact" between science and religion.

4. Confirmation

The confirmation approach may be stated as follows; religion's claim that the universe is a finite, coherent, rational, ordered totality, grounded in an ultimate love and promise, provides a general vision of things that consistently nurtures the scientific quest for knowledge and liberates science from association with imprisoning ideologies.

Science, to be more specific, cannot even get off the ground without rooting itself in a kind of *a priori* "faith" that the universe is a rationally ordered totality of things. Scientists always rely on a tacit faith (which they seldom reflect on in an explicitly conscious way) that there is a real world that hangs together intelligibly, that the human mind has the capacity to comprehend at least some of the world's intelligibility, and that no matter how far we investigate, there will still be further intelligibility to uncover. Without this kind of trust there could be no incentive to look for the order present in nature or to keep looking deeper into the specifics of this order.

Thus, it seems that "faith", in the sense of basic trust in the limitless rationality of the real, is not opposed to science but is its very well spring. Science, like all human knowing, has what some philosophers call a "fiduciary"[30] aspect (from the Latin *fideo*, to trust). Without this element of trust there would be no incentive to pursue the truth through science in the first place.

It would be more cautious not to let religion intrude into the actual work of science, but it is better to say that religion does provide confirmation of the trust that inevitably underlies science. Religion cannot add anything to the list of scientific discoveries and is much more intimately connected to the epistemological roots of scientific inquiry than the other approaches have enunciated.

Religion, taken as a confirmation of the faith assumptions out of which science springs, and not as an alternative source of scientific hypotheses, will not obstruct, but only encourage, the work of science.

Religion comes about in human culture because of our awareness of the fact that trust can fail, and its central mission is continually to revive this trust. It does not initiate our trust, since a capacity to trust in reality seems native to us, but instead functions to revive our trust when it fails.

There are numerous experiences that can lead us to doubt the intelligibility of the universe.

The point of religion, though, is to encourage us to trust anyway. It seeks to restore our hope in the face of despair, to help us adhere to the conviction that there is a final meaning and promise that can light up even those experiences that seem to make the universe absurd. The word "God" points us towards this mysterious meaning and promise, towards that which guarantees the word's ultimate coherence and trustworthiness.

Religious symbols, stories, and teachings persuade us that there is an infinitely wider perspective than our own, and that our own minds are not encompassing enough to take in the whole horizon of being at any given moment, but that nonetheless things do make sense in terms of an effort to continually press onward, beyond the narrowness of current understanding, and to go in search of this transcending breadth and depth.

Religion, invites us to assume a posture of trust in the ultimate intelligibility of things. If we abandon ourselves to such a trust, it does not lead us into conflict with science but instead prepares our consciousness for the journey of scientific discovery.

"Confirmation" goes further than the "contact" approach by attaching itself directly onto the faith that scientists have to possess as they embark on their forays into the world's endless intelligibility. The place to locate religion in relation to scientific conversation, therefore, is not as the answer to specific scientific questions (since this would be conflation), but as a response to the source question concerning the reason why we should go forth on the adventure of truth-seeking in the first place. The business of religion is not to place itself alongside of science as a competing set of answers to scientific questions, but to confirm the scientist's trust in reality's coherence.

In this section, an attempt is made to clarify the relationship of religion to science and avoid both unnecessary conflation and dualism by presenting the view that religious expression is most appropriately concerned with grounding our trust and not with solving scientific questions. The implications of religion for science are much more radical, intimate, and nourishing than the other three approaches have allowed us to see.

Three Examples of Clash: Galileo, Marx and Darwin

1. Galileo's (1564-1642)[31] *View and Christian Scriptures*

As we noted earlier, there are broadly speaking two ways of looking at the relationship between science and religion (conflict and harmony), there are also two ways to approach historical episodes. One way is to start, from the outset, with either a harmony or a conflict model in place, being convinced, for example, that there is a harmony between science and religion; and then to turn to the case in question and attempt to read everything in terms of that position. The alternative is to begin with an open mind in regard to which model is correct, being thereby free to approach the episode as a way to determine which model is correct. (There are also shades of grey between these two alternatives.)

In Galileo there is a bold commitment to the idea of unity (that there is one God behind both Scripture and nature). For Galileo, the same God who created the things that we discover through science also wrote all of the Scriptures. He did not ignore the *Bible*, but he knew very well that if his doctrine was proved right, then it could not contradict the Scriptures when they were rightly understood.

The assumption of unity led Galileo to a harmonious view of the relation between religion and science: since there is one God behind the book of nature and the book of Scripture, then there is a harmony between true science and true religion, once science is properly proved, and Scripture properly interpreted. If we begin from the presupposition of unity, then it is inevitable that we will be led to a metaphoric interpretation of anything that apparently contradicts what we are learning in the new science. His type of argument is valid: but since it begins from the presupposition of unity, it does nothing to answer the question about which is the appropriate way to approach these episodes.

The neutrality principle of Galileo and Calvin guarantees harmony by insulating religion from scientific advances *via* the blanket understanding that Scripture teaches us how to go to heaven, not how the heavens go. Neutrality is an independent view of the relation between science and religion, offering a global recipe for reading Scripture. However, this is not simply a response to new developments in science, invented to avoid the Church's censure. It is rather the natural outworking of a fundamentally religious and universally unquestioned view of the world: that one and the same mind created the world and wrote Scripture.[32]

Another example of a clash of views is taken from modern physical science. Since the time of Newton and Huygens in the seventeenth century, there have been two theories as to the physical nature of light. Newton's theory was that a beam of light consists of a stream of very minute particles, or corpuscles, and that we have the sensation of light when these corpuscles strike the retinas of our eyes. Huygens's theory was that light consists of very minute waves of trembling in all-pervading ether, and that these waves are travelling along a beam of light. The two theories are contradictory. In the eighteenth century Newton's theory was believed, in the nineteenth century Huygens's theory was believed.

2. Karl Marx (1818-1883) and Religion[33]

According to Karl Marx, religion is like other social institutions in that it is dependent upon the material and economic realities in a given society. It has no independent history; instead it is the creature of productive forces. As Marx wrote, "The religious world is but the reflex of the real world".

According to Marx, religion can only be understood in relation to other social systems and the economic structures of society. In fact, religion is only dependent upon economics, nothing else—so much so that the actual religious doctrines are almost irrelevant. This is a functionalist interpretation of religion: understanding religion is dependent upon the social purpose which religion itself serves, and not on the content of its beliefs.

Marx's opinion is that religion is an illusion that provides reasons and an excuse to keep society functioning just as it is.

Much as capitalism takes our productive labour and alienates us from its value, religion takes our highest ideals and aspirations and alienates them from us, projecting them onto an alien and unknowable being called god.

Marx has three reasons for disliking religion. First, it is irrational—religion is a delusion and a worship of appearances that avoids recognizing the underlying reality. Second, religion negates all that is dignified in human beings by rendering them servile and more amenable to accepting the *status quo*. In the preface to his doctoral dissertation, Marx adopted as his motto the words of the Greek hero Prometheus who defied the gods to bring fire to humanity: "I hate all gods", adding that they "do not recognize man's self-consciousness as the highest divinity".

Third, religion is hypocritical. Although it might profess valuable principles, it sides with the oppressors. Jesus advocated helping the poor, but the Christian church merged with the oppressive Roman state, taking part in the enslavement of people for centuries. In the Middle Ages the Catholic Church preached about heaven, but acquired as much property and power as possible[34].

Martin Luther preached about the ability of each individual to interpret the *Bible*, but sided with aristocratic rulers and against peasants who fought against economic and social oppression. According to Marx, this new form of Christianity, Protestantism, was a production of new economic forces as early capitalism developed. New economic realities required a new religious superstructure by which the system could be justified and defended.

Marx's most famous statement about religion comes from a critique of Hegel's Philosophy of Law:[35]

Religious distress is at the same time the expression of real distress and the protest against real distress. Religion is the sigh of the oppressed creature, the heart of a heartless world, just as it is the spirit of a spiritless situation. It is the opium of the people.

The abolition of religion as the illusory happiness of the people is required for their real happiness. The demand to give up the illusion about its condition is the demand to give up a condition which needs illusions.

The quote is presented dishonestly because saying "Religion is the sigh of the oppressed creature". leaves out that it is also the "heart of a heartless world." This is more a critique of society that has become heartless and is even a partial validation of religion that it tries to become its heart. In spite of his obvious dislike of and anger towards religion, Marx did not make religion the primary enemy of workers and communists. Had Marx regarded religion as a more serious enemy, he would have devoted more time to it.

Marx is saying that religion is meant to create illusory fantasies for the poor. Economic realities prevent them from finding true happiness in this life, so religion tells them this is OK because they will find true happiness in the next life. Marx is not entirely without sympathy for religion: people are in distress and religion does provide solace, just as people who are physically injured receive relief from opiate-based drugs[36].

The problem is that opiates fail to fix a physical injury—you only forget your pain and suffering. This can be acceptable, but only if you are also trying at the same time to solve the underlying causes of the pain. Similarly, religion does not fix the underlying causes of people's pain and suffering—instead, it helps them forget why they are suffering and causes them to look forward to an imaginary future when the pain will cease instead of working to change present circumstances here and now. Even worse, this "drug" is being administered by the oppressors who are responsible for the pain and suffering.

Karl Marx wrote that religion was "an opiate of the people." Although those words were not published in The German Ideology, they best describe his various views on religion. Marx wrote that there was a social relationship between the upper class or bourgeoisie and religion. The upper class that owned the means of production, used religion as a tool to keep the working class or proletariat oppressed and poor. Marx's criticism of religion was that it had so many ulterior motives that there was no actual spiritual meaning. He argued that religion existed because of the state of society and its class struggles. The existence of religion also helped to limit or avoid change in society. Marx also believed that religion stripped us of our true humanity. "It is self-evident, moreover, that "spectres", "bonds", "the higher being", "concept", "scruple", are merely the idealistic, spiritual expression, the conception apparently of the isolated individual, the image of very empirical fetters and limitations, within which the mode of production of life and the form of intercourse coupled with it move." God or any higher power was something invented to deposit fear into humans. God was something to blame for our own inefficiencies and failures. He also wrote that humans give too much credit to God for their own accomplishments.[37]

Is Religion the Opiate of the Masses?

This quote is reproduced a great deal and is probably the only Marx quote that most people are familiar with. Unfortunately, if someone is familiar with it they are likely to be familiar with only a small portion which, taken by itself, tends to give a distorted impression of what Marx had to say about religion[38].

Religious distress is at the same time the expression of real distress and the protest against real distress. Religion is the sigh of the oppressed creature, the heart of a heartless world, just as it is the spirit of a spiritless situation. It is the opium of the people. The abolition of religion as the illusory happiness of the people is required for their real happiness. The demand to give up the illusion about its condition is the demand to give up a condition which needs illusions.

It [religion] presents man to himself in terms which distort the true ideal of human liberation and conceal the misery of his actual condition[39].

Usually all one gets from the above is that "Religion is the opium of the people" (with no ellipses to indicate that something has been left out).

Sometimes "Religion is the sigh of the oppressed creature" is included. If you compare these with the full quotation, it is clear that a great deal more is being said than what most people are aware of.

In the above quotation, Marx is saying that the purpose of religion is to create illusory fantasies for the poor. Economic realities prevent them from finding true happiness in this life, so religion tells them that this is OK because they will find true happiness in the next life. Although this is a criticism of religion, Marx is not without sympathy: people are in distress and religion provides solace, just as people who are physically injured receive relief from opiate-based drugs.

The quote is not, then, as negative as most portray it to be (at least about religion). In some ways, even the slightly extended quote which people might read is a bit dishonest because saying "Religion is the sigh of the oppressed creature". deliberately leaves out the additional statement that it is also the "heart of a heartless world."

What we have is a critique of society that has become heartless rather than of religion which tries to provide a bit of solace. One can argue that Marx offers a partial validation of religion in that it tries to become the heart of a heartless world. For all its problems, religion doesn't matter so much—it is not the real problem. Religion is a set of ideas, and ideas are expressions of material realities. Religion is a symptom of a disease, not the disease itself.

Still, it would be a mistake to think that Marx is uncritical towards religion—it may try to provide heart, but it fails. For Marx, the problem lies in the obvious fact that an opiate drug fails to fix a physical injury—it merely helps you forget pain and suffering. This may be fine up to a point, but only as long as you are also trying to solve the underlying problems causing the pain. Similarly, religion does not fix the underlying causes of people's pain and suffering—instead, it helps them forget why they are suffering and gets them to look forward to an imaginary future when the pain will cease.

Even worse, this "drug" is administered by the same oppressors who are responsible for the pain and suffering in the first place. Religion is an expression of more fundamental unhappiness and symptom of more fundamental and oppressive economic realities. Hopefully, humans will create a society in which the economic conditions causing so much pain and suffering would be eradicated and, therefore, the need for soothing drugs like religion will cease. Of course, for Marx, such a turn of events is not to be "hoped for" because human history was leading inevitably towards it.

So, in spite of his obvious dislike of and anger towards religion, Marx did not make religion the primary enemy of workers and communists, regardless of what might have been done by twentieth century communists. Had Marx regarded religion as a more serious enemy, he would have devoted more time to it in his writings. Instead, he focused on economic and political structures that in his mind served to oppress people.

For this reason, some Marxists could be sympathetic to religion. Karl Kautsky, in his Foundations of Christianity, wrote that early Christianity was, in some respects, a proletarian revolution against privileged Roman oppressors. In Latin America, some Catholic theologians have used Marxist categories to frame their critique of economic injustice, resulting in "liberation theology".

Marx's relationship with and ideas about religion are more complex than most realize. Marx's analysis of religion has flaws, but despite them his perspective is worth taking seriously. Specifically, he argues that religion is not so much an independent "thing" in society but, rather, a reflection or creation of other, more fundamental "things" like economic relationships. That is not the only way of looking at religion, but it can provide some interesting illumination on the social roles that religion plays. He opposed religion because it is a counter revolutionary force, i.e. it is a conservative force within society that mitigates against social change. Religion supports the *status quo* on two grounds: it consoles the proletariat; in addition, it justifies the position of the capitalist bourgeoisie. The religion which in Marx's view is the opiate of the masses and religious suffering, is at the same time an expression of real suffering. Religion is the sigh of the oppressed creature, the sentiment of a heartless world, and the soul of soulless conditions. It is the opium of the people. The abolition of religion as the illusory happiness of men, is a demand for their real happiness. The call to abandon their illusions about their condition is a call to abandon a condition which requires illusions. The criticism of religion is, therefore, the embryonic criticism of this vale of tears of which religion is the halo. He said also that that religion for the capitalist class is a justification of their position of privilege (e.g., it is God's will/plan).

Religion undercuts the revolutionary urge of the proletariat, thus preserving the capitalist's position of privilege. Religion provides rationalizations for the existing class system (e.g., laws of *karma*).

Marx's view of God draws on the German theologian Feuerbach: God is a projection of man's own qualities and powers.

Theology is nothing other than a mystified form of anthropology, thus, when one speaks of God as knowledge, wisdom, and love, one is speaking of man's own powers.

Criticisms of Karl Marx's Analysis of Religion

Turning now to the causes of the emergence of secularism in the West, why is it that secularism came into being in the West from the sixteenth century onwards, whereas it did not develop in the world of Islam and in the East as a whole? What was the factor behind the growth of secularism in the West? First and foremost, according to Dr. Soroush (an Iranian thinker) secularism had a natural birth in the West. In other words, it was an infant that spent the appropriate length of time in the womb of the West's history and, when it had reached its full term, it came into this world; its birth was not accompanied by a Caesarean section and bleeding. We can attribute this to two causes.

The first cause was the confrontation and clash between science and religion. The quarrel between science and religion was a very fateful quarrel in the history of Europe. And it was not a product of a conspiracy, ill will, malice or religiosity. In fact, it was a very natural quarrel: there was growth in the natural sciences, in geology, biology, astronomy. And new information came to light that was in conflict with the contents of Scripture and the conflict intensified to the point where it became impossible to hide or deny. There was Copernicus, Kepler, Galileo and Newton and, later, Buffon and Darwin.

Some of these people were religious themselves. As it happens, Galileo was a religious man. Copernicus was once a priest. Kepler was someone who had gone several steps beyond the common religion of the masses to the point of being superstitious. But the product of these people's work was something that was not in any way in keeping with the contents of Scripture, especially on the subject of the motion of the earth and the sun and the planets. The Church tolerated these ideas for a while but eventually the quarrel flared up. The status that the Church and Scripture acquired thereafter never went back to what it had been before the quarrel. In all fairness, despite all its hostility towards science, the Church did not go down the path of fanaticism. The Church allowed the publication of Copernicus's book. In *The Revolutions of the Heavenly Spheres*, Copernicus explicitly stated that the earth was in motion and that the sun was still, whereas, according to Scripture, it was the sun that moved and the earth that was still. From the 400 copies of the book that were published in the sixteenth century, 200 still exist today. The tales about Galileo having been put to death are all untrue. Of course, they did put Galileo under house arrest. The Church allowed the publication of Copernicus's book but wrote an introduction to it. And the important point that was made in this introduction was "what is stated in this book is a theory and not the absolute truth". This was a laudable and sensible solution. The big and small discoveries that were being made here and there gradually robbed Scripture of the status that it had had hitherto. Religion lost its former power and status and from then on it was no longer the actor on the social and political stage that it had been before. As long as religion was strong, it was in the political arena. When faith diminished and religion's status declined, this actor ended up playing a smaller role. It was not as if anyone evicted religion from the political stage; it just grew weaker and moved to the sidelines. It was a natural birth. The political stage is for powerful players.

When religion was strong, there was no need for anyone to invite religion onto the political stage. And, when it grew weak, it inevitably left the stage; there was no need for anyone to evict it.

The second cause was the rupture that occurred in Christianity; that is, the birth of Protestantism from the ribs of Catholicism. This Protestantism reduced the Church's strength; in fact, it stood exactly opposite the Church. Martin Luther was the first person to translate the *Bible* into German. And he said that everyone was his or her own priest and he rejected the authority of the Church.

These two events together weakened the Christian Church so that it departed from the game of power, and this departure meant that there was now a separation between religion and the State. Some people imagine that, in European countries, some people drew up Constitutions stating that, henceforth, there must be a separation between religion and politics. This was not at all the case. The fact that this has been stated in European Constitutions was the effect of this development, not its cause. At any rate, the secularism that was born was a tolerant secularism. It was not militant. Since it knew that religion was weak, it felt no need to attack it. As recently as about 30 or 40 years ago, many sociologists were of the view that not just Christianity but all religions were on the decline. They believed that history was moving in the direction of political secularism. So, what do you do when faced with weaklings? You are tolerant and you tell yourself that they pose no danger, they are doing no harm, let them have their mosque or church, let them observe their rituals. Secularism proceeded on the assumption that it should be neutral towards religions and view them all in the same light. As far as secularism is concerned, it makes no difference that there are Christians, Muslims, Jews and/or Zoroastrians in society, because it assumed that they were all being left behind by history.

Secularism in this sense both led to the separation of religion and the State and adopted a neutral approach to religions. Former US Secretary of State Colin Powell said with pride: "In the US now, you can see mosques and synagogues alongside churches, and they are all coexisting peacefully." And, in fact, this is something to be proud of and it is a very laudable situation.

As interesting and insightful as Marx's analysis and critiques are, they are not without their problems—historical and economic. Because of these problems, it would not be appropriate to accept Marx's ideas uncritically. Although he certainly has some important things to say on the nature of religion, he can't be accepted as the last word on the subject.

First, Marx does not spend much time looking at religion in general; instead he focuses on the religion with which he is most familiar: Christianity. His comments do hold for other religions with similar doctrines of a powerful god and happy afterlife, they do not apply to radically different religions. In ancient Greece and Rome, for example, a happy afterlife was reserved for heroes while commoners could only look forward to a mere shadow of their earthly existence.

Perhaps he was influenced in this matter by Hegel, who thought that Christianity was the highest form of religion and that whatever was said about that also automatically applied to "lesser" religions—but that isn't true.

A second problem lies with his claim that religion is wholly determined by material and economic realities. Not only is there nothing else fundamental enough to influence religion, but the influence cannot run in the other direction, from religion to material and economic realities. This is not true. If Marx were right, then capitalism would appear in countries prior to Protestantism because Protestantism is the religious system created by capitalism—but we don't find this. The Reformation comes to sixteenth century Germany which is still feudal in nature; real capitalism doesn't appear until the nineteenth century. This caused Max Weber to theorize that religious institutions end up creating new economic realities. Even if Weber is wrong, we see that there is clear historical evidence for a position directly to that of Marx with.

Marxists have tried valiantly to refute those critiques or revise Marx's ideas to render them[40] immune to the problems described above, but they haven't entirely succeeded (although they certainly disagree—otherwise they wouldn't still be Marxists).

We do not have to restrict ourselves to the idea that religion is only dependent upon economics and nothing else, such that the actual doctrines of religions are almost irrelevant. Instead, we can recognize that there are a variety of social influences upon religion, including the economic and material realities of society. By the same token, religion can in turn have an influence upon society's economic system.

Whatever one's final conclusion about the accuracy or validity of Marx's ideas on religion, we should recognize that he provided an invaluable service by forcing people to take a hard look at the social web in which religion always occurs. Because of his work, it has become impossible to study religion without also exploring its ties to various social and economic forces. People's spiritual lives can no longer be assumed to be totally independent of their material lives, and in addition to this point it has to say that we can find many social reforms that are founded on religions such as Gandhian movement the Islamic revolution of Iran and the case of the Tobacco concession in Iran (1891)[41].

3. Darwin's[42] (1802-1882) Theory and Religion

Does evolution rule out God's existence and is it against all religious scriptures? In 1859, Charles Darwin published *On the Origin of Species*, his famous treatise on what we now call "evolution". It is one of the most important books of science ever written, and even today experts consider it to be a generally accurate account of the story of life.

Theologically speaking, however, it caused a fierce storm of controversy, and we are still wrestling with the question of what to make of it. Does Darwin's theory perhaps put the final nail in religion's coffin? Or can there perhaps be a fruitful encounter of religion with evolutionary thought?

For many scientists, evolution means that the universe is fundamentally impersonal and Godless. In fact, some of them (Steven Weinberg), asserts that evolution refutes the idea of an "interested" god much more decisively than physics does. Only a brief look at Darwin's theory will show why it disturbs the traditional religious belief in a loving and powerful Deity.

Darwin observed that all living species produce more offspring than ever reach maturity. Nevertheless, the number of individuals in any given species remains fairly constant. This means that there must be a very high rate of mortality, since more young are produced than ever reach maturity. To explain why some survive and others do not, Darwin argued that some are better "adapted" to their environment than others. It appears that the most "fit" are the ones that survive to produce offspring. The vast majority of individuals and species lose out in the struggle for existence, but during the long voyage of evolution there emerges a staggering diversity of life, millions of new species, and eventually the human race.

What, then, is so theologically disturbing about the theory? What is it about evolution that places in question even the very existence of God? It can be summarized in three propositions:

1. The variations that lead to differentiation of species are purely random, thus suggesting that the workings of nature are "accidental" and irrational. Today the source of these variations has been identified as genetic mutations, and most biologists still follow Darwin in attributing these to "chance."
2. The fact that individuals have to struggle for survival, and that most of them suffer and lose out in this contest, points to the basic cruelty of the universe, particularly towards the weak.
3. The mindless process of natural selection by which only the better adapted organisms survive points to a universe, that is, essentially blind and indifferent to life and humanity[43].

These three inseparable ingredients—randomness, struggle, and blind natural selection all seem to suggest that the universe is impersonal, utterly unrelated to any "interested" God. Darwin himself, after reflecting on the "cruelty", randomness, and impersonality in evolution, could never again return to the benign theism of his ancestral Anglicanism. Though he did not completely lose his religious faith, many of his scientific heirs have been much less hesitant to equate evolution with atheism. From the middle of the last century until today prominent thinkers have welcomed Darwinian ideas as the final victory of skepticism over religion T.H. Huxley, Darwin's "bulldog" as he was known, thought evolution was antithetical to traditional theism. Ernst Haeckel, Karl Marx, Friedrich Nietzsche, and Sigmund Freud all found Darwin's thought congenial to their atheism. And numerous others in our own time closely associate evolution with unbelief. Given this coalition of evolution and hostility to theism it is hardly surprising that the idea of evolution has encountered so much resistance from some religious groups[44]. Darwin himself, however, did not envisage so unambiguous a union between evolution and skepticism. If he moved towards unbelief at all it was not without undergoing a great deal of personal anguish and mental reservation. In 1860, a year after the publication of *The Origins*, he wrote:

"There seems to me too much misery in the world. I cannot

> persuade myself that a beneficent and omnipotent God would have designedly created the Ichneumon date with the express intention of their feeding within the living bodies of caterpillars, or that cat should play with mice."[45]

It seems that one question still remains; we must ask here whether the Darwinian or the neo-Darwinian picture of nature in evolution is after all compatible with or fits into the four categories we are following throughout this chapter:

1. Conflict: Any wonder that we skeptics find in evolution the most compelling scientific reasons for rejecting religion? The three features of chance, struggle, and blind natural selection are so antithetical to any conceivable notion of divine providence or design, that we find it hard to understand how any scientifically educated person could still believe in God. In this position evolution is incompatible with any and all religious interpretations of the cosmos, not just with Christian fundamentalism. The commonness of chance variations, which today are called genetic "mutations," definitively refutes the idea of any ordering deity.

The fact of struggle and waste in evolution positively demonstrates that the cosmos is really not cared for by a loving God. Theology after Darwin will have to look these facts squarely in the face, and we don't think it can survive the encounter.

2. *Contrast:* According to this position science and religion are such disparate ways of looking at the world that they cannot meaningfully compete with each other. This means that evolution, which may be quite accurate as a scientific theory, bears not the slightest threat towards religion. "Conflict" arises not from the science of evolution itself, but from two different kinds of conflation. On the one hand, "scientific creationists" try to combine religious scriptures or biblical accounts of creation with modern "science," and on the other hand, scientific skeptics generally collapse evolutionary theory into an ideology of their own, "scientific materialism".

There is no will to examine scientific creationism and then follow that up with a critique of materialist evolutionism. It is emphasizing, though, that there is no way attaching scientific theories of evolution.

Scientific materialists generally write about evolution as though it were inherently anti-theistic. They are uncritically espousing the assumptions of a secularist intellectual culture. Their species of conflation may be called simply "evolutionism," an often subtle bonding of Darwinian ideas with hidden premises of secularism, naturalism, and the belief system it has been calling scientific materialism.[46]

Evolution is a purely scientific theory that need not be cast in either materialist or religious terms. When stripped of any materialist overlay, evolutionary theory neither supports nor contradicts theism. The important thing is that we conscious beings are here, and this is a significant enough fact irrespective of how we arrived. The particulars of the evolutionary past are useful for scientists to study, but they are not important for defining who we really are or what our relation to God is. When our species came along, with its capacity for freedom, goodness, and love, it is clear that evolution had leapt onto a new plane altogether. No matter what our evolutionary past was like, the core of our human existence lies now beyond the realm of scientific illumination. So in response to materialist conviction that human consciousness "is but a tiny, late-arising twig" on the bush of life, we would submit that there are other plausible ways of looking at the same phenomenon, including a religious perspective that points to our inherent and eternal value. In the case of the apparent contradictions that evolutionary theory poses to theism we would reply very briefly as follows:

1. In the first place, the "chance" character of the variations which natural selection chooses for survival may easily be accounted for on the basis of our inevitable human narrowness and ignorance. Allegedly "random" genetic mutations may not really be random at all. They could very well be mere illusions resulting from the limitedness of our human perspective. According to religious faith, a purely human angle of vision is always exceedingly restricted. Hence, what appears to be absurd chance from a scientific perspective could be quite rational and coherent from that of God's infinite wisdom?
2. Second, evolutionist complaints about the struggle, suffering, waste and cruelty of natural process add absolutely nothing new to the basic problem of evil of which religion has always been quite fully aware. Faith is always faith "in spite of "all the difficulties that defy reason and science. In fact, more than a few of our number consider evolution's severity to be

quite consistent with the ancient religious theme that the earth is a "soul school" whose often stern lessons make us worthy of eternal life. If life posed no hardships, and if evolution were totally benign, how would we ever be aroused to develop our moral and spiritual character?

3. There is no more theological difficulty in the remorseless laws of inertia, gravity or any other impersonal aspects of science. Gravity, like natural selection, has no regard for our inherent personal dignity either. It pulls toward earth the weak and powerful alike—at times in a deadly way. But very few thinkers have ever insisted that gravity is a serious argument against God's existence. Perhaps natural selection should be viewed no less leniently.

At any rate, our contention is that humans cannot learn the nature of ultimate reality simply by pondering purely natural laws and occurrences.

Nature itself provides evidence neither for nor against God's existence. Something as momentous as the reality of God can hardly be decided by a superficial scientific deciphering of the natural world. Hence, we are neither troubled nor heartened by evolutionary theory.

3. *Contact*: Its sharp portrayal of the ideological biases in both creationism and evolutionism is very helpful. Contrast may be an essential step in the process of thinking clearly and effectively about the relationship of evolution to religion.

For many scientists and religious thinkers contrast does not go nearly far enough. Evolution is more than just another innocuous scientific theory that theology can innocently ignore. When we think about religion in the post-Darwinian period we cannot have exactly the same approach that Augustine, Avicenna, Maimonides, Aquinas, or for that matter our grandparents and parents had, so we may need to recast all of theology in evolutionary terms.

Without fusing science with religion, theology is making fruitful contact with the same Darwinian ideas that evolutionists consider antithetical to God's existence. In fact for many of us, evolution is an absolutely essential ingredient in our thinking about God today. As the Roman Catholic theologian Hans Kung puts it, evolutionary theory now makes possible: (1) a deeper understanding of God—not above or outside the world but in the midst of evolution; (2) a deeper understanding of creation—not as contrary to but as making evolution possible; and (3) a deeper understanding of humans as organically related to the entire cosmos.[47]

A "contact" theology actually looks forward to facing the kinds of obstacles to native piety that evolution implies. A theology that seriously (and not just half-heartedly) mulls over Darwinian evolution cannot remain completely the same as before. Evolution demands that we think out more carefully how God might influence the world. For, even though the God of evolution is not a dictator, and apparently does not interrupt the flow of natural causation, religious faith implies necessarily that there is still some significant way in which God does influence and interact with the natural world. The religious sense of a God who arrives out of the future, and who comes to meet the world in the mode of a repeatedly fresh promise of new life is, we think, a most appropriate framework for interpreting the data of evolutionary science.

In summary, the idea of God, taken in consort with (and not as an alternative to) evolutionary theory, can help us account for the increasing complexity and consciousness that evolution has brought about not only in life, but in culture and religion as well. Hence it is suggested that the idea of a transcendent divine mystery explains not only the fact that the universe has order to it, but also that it has a penchant for novelty and creativity, such as we see in evolution.

Divine creativity in terms of God's inviting (not forcing) the cosmos to express itself in increasingly more varied ways. God is the ultimate source not only of the order in the world, but also of the troubling novelty and diversity that always somehow disrupts the *status quo*. As novelty does come into the world, the present order has to give way. And what we confusedly refer to as "chance," instead of being a "cause" of evolution, may be understood as the consequence of a breakdown in present forms of order as novelty enters in.

The ultimate or remote origin of this novelty is one of the things we mean by God. God's role in evolution is not only that of being the stimulus that stirs the cosmos toward deeper novelty and beauty. "God's will" by this account, is to maximize evolutionary novelty and diversity.

Our religious faith tells us that the same God who creates the universe also promises to save it from all its travail, suffering, and death. This would mean then that the whole story of cosmic evolution, in all its detail and incredible breadth, is permanently taken into God's loving memory.

Our theology cannot tolerate a deity who merely creates and then abandons the world. For us the same God who invites the world to evolve is also intimately involved in the evolutionary process. God struggles along with all beings, participating in both their pain and enjoyment, ultimately redeeming the world by an infinite compassion so that in the end nothing is ever completely forgotten or lost.

This is only a brief account of how its encounter with evolutionary science is transforming contemporary theology. Many varieties of evolutionary theology exist today because of opposite theories and samples, and we have presented only a small piece of the rethinking going on in theology after Darwin. It is unfortunate though that much contemporary religious thought gets hung up in creationism or contrast. For although evolutionary theology is inevitably in need of constant revision—and we do not wish to enshrine for all time any particular version of it—we consider evolution to be, at least provisionally, a most appropriate and fruitful scientific framework within which to think about God today.

4. *Confirmation:* We fully endorse the attempts to construct an evolutionary theology. We would go even further in establishing the close connection between theism and evolution. Religious ideas provide much of the soil in which Darwinian ideas have taken root in the first place.

There are a number of recent studies that demonstrate theism's fundamental "confirmation" of evolutionary thinking, such as some Islamic thinkers, or rejected evolution theory, and we cannot discuss them all here.[48]

What some theologians (among others) have clarified, is that the infinite pours itself out in love to the finite universe for central idea of theistic.[49]

This is the fundamental meaning of "revelation". But if we think carefully about this central religious teaching, it should lead us to conclude that any universe related to the inexhaustible self-giving love of God must be an evolving one. In other words, it might endure what we know scientifically as a difficult and dramatic evolution towards increasing complexity, life, and consciousness. In the final analysis, it is as a consequence of the infusion of God's self-giving love that the universe is exited onto the path of self-transcendence, that is to say, evolution[50].

Viewed in this light, the evolution of the cosmos is more than just compatible with theism, as the contrast position argues, or "consonant" with it, as the contact approach might say. Rather, it would not be too much to say that faith in a god of self-giving love actually anticipates an evolving universe.

It would be very difficult for some theologians to reconcile the religious teaching about God's infinite self-giving love with any other kind of cosmos. In summary; by the close of the century, the fact of evolution was accepted by virtually all scientists, and by vast majority of theologians. The causes of biological change were the subject of continuing discussion at both scientific and philosophical levels, and the broader interpretations of the evolutionary process varied widely. At one extreme, there were still many average Christians, especially in rural areas, who rejected evolution completely; but most of the leaders of even the more conservative churches realized that there was overwhelming evidence in its favour. At the opposite extreme, naturalistic philosophies had relatively little popular support. The liberal middle position between traditionalism and modernism was gaining in strength.

Ian G. Barbour, regarding the influence of evolutionary thought on theology said that.[51]

Methods in Theology

(a) *Revelation*: Among reactions to both evolution and biblical literalism by some conservatives, and rejection of all forms of revelation by some modernists, in the emerging liberal view, the Bible was valued as the fallible human record of man's religious experience and also as witness to revelation, understood not as the dictation of a guaranteed text but as God's presence and activity in the life of Israel, the prophets, and Christ.

(b) *Natural Theology*: The argument from design, in the form Paley had popularized, was permanently undermined by the theory of evolution. In a reformulated version, which was never as widely used, purposeful design was to be seen in the laws and structures through which life and mind had emerged, and in the directionality of the total process.

(c) *Religious and Moral Experience*: The distinctive new element that became dominant in the nineteenth-century theological method was the appeal to human experience as the basis for theology.

Today there is one large group of phenomena which can be explained only on the wave theory, and another large group which can be explained only on the corpuscular theory. Scientists have to leave it at that, and wait for the future, in the hope of attaining some wider vision which reconciles both. We should apply these same principles to the questions in which there is a variance between science and religion.

According to Islamic philosophy it would in some ways to be compatible to theism and scriptures that will be explained in next chapter.

Conclusion

Under the headings of conflict, contrast, contact and confirmation, we can present the positions of each approach as it responds to the attractive questions that science is raising for religion today.

The conflict approach may at one moment have seemed the most compelling, but at other times we may have been attracted to the clarity of contrast, or to the cloudier experiments of contact, or even perhaps to the overtures of the confirmation approach. It is possible that anyone individual may be able to embrace aspects of several approaches at the same time. Indeed, after gaining some distance from them, the four ways seem to resemble less a fixed typology than differentiated phases of a single complex process. "Confirmation" could conceivably be included under the more generic category of "contact". However, there is a clear logical distinction between the two approaches. In a way that include easily be lost if we allow it simply to be absorbed into our third type, "confirmation" illustrates out how religion in some way nourishes science.

Another reason for keeping the categories distinct is that followers of a "contact" approach may not always wish to accept some of the more radical implications of confirmation.

Summary of Chapter Two

- Religions try to answer important but mysterious questions like "Where did the world come from?" and "What happens to us Hereafter?"
- Our understanding and interpretation of religion is that it is collection of doctrines or a specific system of belief that springs from revelation that has been brought by prophets to illustrate descriptive and normative statements, and to guide human beings in religious resources.
- It is not possible to separate man's way of thinking from his

way of living and his dealing in life. Religion bases its interpretation and viewpoint on believing that this universe, life and man have a Creator, a Lord, a God; and that man's existence on this earth is neither a meaningless nor aimless one, nor it is random happening. Life and man have their goals and values exceeding the time span of man's existence on the earth's surface.

- To illustrate the various possibilities, several different ways in which the sciences can be classified are first considered. Then the different ways in which the sciences have been classified—according to some interpretations—by certain key figures in the history of thought, are sketched with emphasis upon the classification proposed by St. Thomas Aquinas.
- The methods of careful observation and experiment have been in use from antiquity, but became more widespread after the seventeenth century. Developments in instrument making, in mathematics and statistics, in terminology, and in communication technology have altered the methods and the results of science.
- The goal of the sciences is to answer only those questions that are publicly testable. Science produces *useful models* which allow us to make often useful predictions.
- Scientific findings and religious beliefs are normally quite separate; the main battles between religion and science are in areas in which they overlap. Here, both often hold conflicting positions.
- The history of human thoughts further reveals that there has been constant conflict between the devotees of religion, philosophy and science. They are totally different worldviews and their outlook on life and of life is mostly antagonistic and conflicting.
- It seems there are four approaches and ways in which science and religion can be related to each other:
    1. *Conflict*: The conviction that science and religion are fundamentally irreconcilable.
    2. *Contrast*: The claim that there can be no genuine conflict since religion and science are each responding to radically different questions.
    3. *Contact*: An approach that looks for dialogue, interaction,

and possible "consonance" between science and religion, and especially for ways in which science shapes religious and theological understanding.

4. *Confirmation*: A somewhat quieter, but extremely important perspective that highlights the ways in which, at a very deep level, religion supports and nourishes the entire scientific enterprise.

Here are three examples of clash:

- Marx (1818-1883) says that religion is meant to create illusory fantasies for the poor; he also wrote that religion was, "an opiate of the people." This statement best describes his various views on religion. Marx wrote that there was a social relationship between the upper class or bourgeoisie and religion. The upper class that owned the means of production used religion as a tool to keep the working class or proletariat, oppressed and poor.
  But Marx doesn't spend much time looking at religion in general; instead he focuses on the religion with which he is most familiar. Another problem arises from his claim that religion is wholly determined by material and economic realities. This is not true. In Galileo (1564-1642) there is a bold commitment to the idea of unity (that there is one God behind both Scripture and nature). For Galileo, the same God who created the things that we discover through science also wrote all of the Scriptures. He did not ignore the *Bible*, but he knew very well that if his doctrine were proved, then it could not contradict the Scripture when they were rightly understood.
- Does Darwin (1809-1882)'s theory put the final nail in religion's coffin? Or can there be perhaps, a fruitful encounter of religion with evolutionary thought? Darwin observed that all living species produce more offspring than ever reach maturity. Evolution is a purely scientific theory that need not be cast in either materialist or religious terms. Our religious faith tells us that the same God who creates the universe also promises to save it from all its travail, suffering, and death. This would mean then that the whole story of cosmic evolution, in all its detail and incredible breadth, is

permanently taken into God's loving memory. According to Islamic philosophy, evolution would in some ways be compatible with theism and scriptures, as will be explained in the next chapter.

- The model or combination of models that a person adopts for relating science and religion is likely to depend strongly on his or her upbringing, as well as on the fundamental presuppositions he or she brings to the issue. When talking about scientific and religious issues, we should emphasize those competent and successful scientists today who can be found in all four categories. We should also avoid giving simplistic answers to questions about science and religion.
- In this research the discussion is not restricted to science and Christianity alone. It examines the relationships of science with both Islam and Hinduism, especially with regard to Marx and Darwin.
- Under the headings of conflict, contrast, contact and confirmation, we can present the positions of each approach as it responds to the attractive questions that science is raising for religion today. But in our understanding, religion, especially Islam, is not only not opposed to scientific and technological progress, on the contrary, it encourages it and the same will be explained further in the next chapter.

FOOTNOTES

1. Quotation from: The University of Cambridge, www. wikipedia.org/wiki/University_of_Cambridge.
2. Ward and Trent, *et al. The Cambridge History of English and American Literature*, New York: G.P. Putnam's Sons, 1907–21; New York: Bartleby.com, 2000.
3. ww.websters-online-dictionary.org
4. Encyclopaedia Britannica.
5. Webster's New World Dictionary (Third College Edition)
6. Winston King, *Encyclopaedia of Religion*, p. 7693.
7. Paul Edwards, The *Encyclopaedia of Philosophy*, and V.7 There are at least two different books titled "Encyclopaedia of Philosophy:" one by Paul Edwards, Paul Edwards and the other by Donal Borchedt.
8. *Ibid.*, p. 19.

9. Edeard H., Has Cotton, *Science Discovered God?*, Thomas Y. Crowell Company Publishers, New York. Second Printing 1931, p. 93.
10. Religion [First Edition]. Winston King. *Encyclopedia of Religion*, Ed. Lindsay Jones, Vol. 11. 2nd ed. Detroit: Macmillan Reference USA, 2005. pp. 7692-7701.
11. *Ibid., Encyclopedia of Religion.*
12. *Ibid., Encyclopedia of Religion.*
13. *Marx's Religion of Revolution*, J. North, Regeneration Through Chaos, p. 88, 1984.
14. *Ibid., Encyclopedia of Religion.*
15. *Ibid., Encyclopedia of Religion.*
16. Durkheim, *the Elementary Forms of the Religious Life*, (1912, English translation by Joseph Swain: 1915), The Free Press, 1965. *ISBN 0-02-908010-X,* new translation by Karen E. Fields 1995, *ISBN 0029079373.*
17. *Encyclopaedia Britannica* (2006) as quoted on *Religion Facts.* Retrieved on *2007-03-17.*
18. *The free Dictionary*, By Farl.
19. *The Oxford English Dictionary*, second edition 1998, Volume XIV.
20. *Definition of Science* from Amicus Curiae (Edwards *vs.* Aguillard).
21. William J. Good, P.K. Hatt; *Methods in Social Research* (McGraw Hill Book Company, Singapore, 1952), p. 7.
22. *Routledge Encyclopaedia of Philosophy*, Version 1.0, London: Routledge.
23. A.D. White, "*A History of the Warfare of Science with Theology in Christendom*", Prometheus Books, (1896; Reprinted 1993) *Read reviews or order this book safely from Amazon.com online book store*
24. Routledge *Encyclopaedia of Philosophy*, Version 1.0, London: Routledge.
25. Quotation from: John F. Haught *Religion and Science* Paulist Press, Mahwah, New Jersey, 1995 and Ian G. Barbour, *Issues in Science and Religion*, Harper & Row, Publishers, New York, Hagerstown and M. Peterson and other, *Reason and Religious Belief* trans by E. Soltani, Oxford University Press, 1991, p. 358.
26. John F. Haught, Edeard H., *Religion and Science*, Paulist Press, Mahwah, New Jersey 1995, p. 11.
27. William R. Shea, *Galileo's Intellectual Revolution*, second Edition, Neal Watson Academic Publications, inc. New York 1977, p. 188.
28. G. Roger, *Newton, Galileo's, Vinod Vasishtha*, New Delhi, 2005, p. 98.
29. Conflation, a term that appears often in the pages ahead simply means the collapsing of distinct items in such a way that their differences are apparently lost.

30. John F. Haught, *Religion and Science*, Paulist Press, Mahwah, New Jersey1995, p. 23.
31. Galileo Galilei (1564-1642) was an Italian scientist who formulated the basic law of falling bodies, which he verified by careful measurements. He constructed a telescope with which he studied lunar craters, and discovered four moons revolving around Jupiter and espoused the Copernican cause: www-history.mcs.st-andrews.ac.uk/ Mathematicians/Galileo.html
32. Dowl, Phil, "*Galileo, Darwin, and Hawking*", William B., Eerdmans Publishing Company, Grand Rapids, Michigan/Cambridge, U.K.
33. Karl Heinrich Marx (May 5, 1818, Trier, Germany – March 14, 1883, London, England) was an immensely influential German philosopher, political economist, and socialist revolutionary. While Marx addressed a wide range of issues, he is most famous for his analysis of history in terms of class struggles, summed up in the opening line of the introduction to the Communist Manifesto: "The history of all hitherto existing society is the history of class struggles".
At the same time as Engels, Marx took part in the political and philosophical struggle of his times, writing the Communist Manifesto a year before the Revolutions of 1848, although the two events had nothing to do with each other. Marx had broken with his university environment, German Idealism and the Young Hegelians, and took part in the debates of the European workers' movement, in particular in relation with the First International founded in 1864. He published the first tome of *Das Kapital* in 1867, a few years before the 1871 Paris Commune. The influence of his ideas, already popular during his life, was given added impetus by the victory of the Russian Bolsheviks in the 1917 October Revolution, and there are few parts of the world which were not significantly touched by Marxian ideas in the course of the twentieth century. The relation of Marx's own thought to the popular "Marxist" interpretations of it during this period is a point of controversy; he himself once said that "the only thing I know is that I'm not a Marxist"(In response to the views of a French Social-Democratic Party). While Marx's ideas have declined in popularity, particularly with the decline of Marxism in Russia, they are still very influential today, both in academic circles, some worker movements, and in political practice, and Marxism continues to be the official ideology of some Communist states and political movements.
→ Karl Marx: "*Critique of the Gotha Programme*" (Marx/Engels Selected Works, Volume Three, pp. 13-30), McLellan, D. (1973) *Karl Marx: His Life and Thought*, Basingstoke: Macmillan, p. 274.

34. *Ibid.*, p. 277, *www.about(atheism).com*
35. *Ibid.*, pp. 270-279.
36. *www.revision-notes.co.uk.*
37. J. North, *Marx's Religion of Revolution*, Regeneration Through Chaos, 1984, p. 144.
38. P. Masterson, *Atheism and Alienation*, Gil & Macmillan, 1971, p. 92.
39. *Ibid.*, p. 87.
40. *Ibid.*, p. 274, *www.about.com*
41. See chapter 3.
42. Charles Robert Darwin (12 February 1809 – 19 April 1882) was an eminent English naturalist who achieved lasting fame by convincing the scientific community that species develop over time from a common origin. His theories explaining this phenomenon through natural and sexual selection are central to the modern understanding of evolution as the unifying theory of the life sciences, essential in biology and important in other disciplines such as anthropology, psychology and philosophy. Darwin developed his interest in natural history while studying first medicine, then theology, at university. His five-year voyage on the Beagle established him as a geologist whose observations and theorising supported Charles Lyell's uniformitarian ideas, and the subsequent publication of his journal of the voyage made him famous as a popular author. Puzzled by the geographical distribution of wildlife and fossils he collected on the voyage; he investigated the transmutation of species and conceived his theory of natural selection in 1838. He had seen others attacked for such heretical ideas and confided only in his closest friends while carrying out extensive research to meet anticipated objections. However, in 1858, Alfred Russel Wallace sent him an essay describing a similar theory, forcing early joint publication of both of their theories. His 1859 book, On the Origin of Species, established evolution by common descent as the dominant scientific explanation of diversification in nature. Human origins and features without obvious utility such as beautiful bird plumage were examined in The Descent of Man, and Selection in Relation to Sex, followed by The Expression of the Emotions in Man and Animals. His research on plants was published in a series of books, and in his final book, he examined earthworms and their effect on soil. In recognition of Darwin's pre-eminence, he was buried in Westminster Abbey, close to John Herschel and Isaac Newton.
    → Edwards, A.W.F. 2004 Darwin, Leonard (1850–1943). In: *Oxford Dictionary of National Biography*, Oxford University Press, Bannister, Robert C. (1989) and *Social Darwinism: Science and Myth in Anglo-American Social Thought*., Philadelphia: Temple University Press,

ISBN 0-87722-566-4, Browne, E. Janet (2002) and Charles Darwin: Vol. 2 The Power of Place, London: Jonathan Cape, ISBN 0-7126-6837-3.

43. John F. Haught, *Religion and Science*, Paulist Press, Mahwah, New Jersey, 1995, p. 48.
44. *Ibid.*, p. 49.
45. Ernst Benz, *Evolution and Christian Hope* (Garden City, N.Y.: Doubleday, 1996) and also *New Theology* (in Percian), A. Khosro Panah, Qom, 2000, p. 150.
46. Jay Stephen Gould, *Ever Since Darwin* (New York: Washington Square Press, 1982), pp. 132-35.
47. Hans Kung, *Does God Exist*? trans. by Edward Quinn (New York: Doubleday, 1980), p. 347.
48. See for example, Ernst Benz, *Evolution and Christian Hope* (Garden City, N.Y.: Doubleday, 1996) and also *New Theology* (in Percian), A. Khosro Panah, Qom, 2000, p. 188.
49. Karl Rahner, S.J., *Hominization, trans.* by W.J. O'Hara (New York: Herder & Herder, 1965).
50. *Ibid.*, p. 96.
51. Ian G. Barbour, *Issues in Science and Religion*, Harper & Row, Publishers, New York, Hagerstown, San Francisco, London, 1971, p. 114.

3

Islam and Science

الَّذِينَ يَذْكُرُونَ اللَّهَ قِيَامًا وَقُعُودًا وَعَلَىٰ جُنُوبِهِمْ وَيَتَفَكَّرُونَ فِي خَلْقِ السَّمَاوَاتِ
وَالْأَرْضِ رَبَّنَا مَا خَلَقْتَ هَٰذَا بَاطِلًا سُبْحَانَكَ فَقِنَا عَذَابَ النَّارِ .

> "Men who celebrate the praises of Allah, standing, sitting, and lying down on their sides, and contemplate the (wonders of) creation in the heavens and the earth, (With the thought): "Our Lord! Not for naught Hast Thou created (all) this! Glory to Thee! Give us salvation from the penalty of the Fire."
>
> —*The Holy Quran* 3:191

Introduction to the Islamic View

There is a fundamental conflict between the religious approach and scientific approach about nature. In Islam, the total world is a unique and transcendent reality that has been created only by God and has been operated by him, and one soul attends it;

> "and Allah's is the East and the West. Therefore, whither you turn; thither is Allah's purpose"
>
> —*The Holy Quran*, chapter: 2.115

There is no difference between its exterior and interior, its beginning and end, body and soul. There is a relation among its various parts and a change in one part, influences all other parts. All creation comes from one centre and returns to that centre. There are also such beliefs in Hinduism and other Eastern religions. When we use the term "modern", we mean neither contemporary nor up-to-date nor successful in the conquest and domination of the natural world. Rather, for us "modern" means that which is cut off from the transcendent, from the immutable principles which in reality govern all things and which are made known to man through revelation in its most universal sense.

Ever since the dawn of human life on this planet, man has always sought to understand Nature, his own place in the scheme of creation and the purpose of life itself. In this quest for truth, spanning many centuries and diverse civilizations, some organized religions have been based on their sources, claimed by their adherents to be divinely inspired. Others have relied solely on human experience.

Al-Quran, the main source of the Islamic faith, is a book believed by Muslims to be of a completely Divine origin. Muslims also believe that it contains guidance for all mankind. Since the message of the *Quran* is believed to be for all times, it should be relevant to every age.

1. The basic statement of Islam is: "There is no god other than Allah" (*Quran*: Ch. 37 v. 35).

2. Everything is created, that is to say given its qualifications, and directed according to these qualifications by Allah and as long as He wishes.

> "And who makes (things) according to a measure, then directs." (ch. 87/v. 3)
>
> "He said who your Lord, Moses is? He answered, Our Lord is He who giveth all things their qualifications and directed them." (ch. 20/v. 49, 50)
>
> "Unto Him do all creatures in heaven and earth make petition; everyday is He in work." (ch. 55/v. 29)
>
> "Then let man look to his food: How He pours water in showers. Then split the earth in clefts, and causes the grain to grow therein, and grapes and green fodder. And the olive and the palm."
>
> (ch. 80/v. 25-29)

> "Say: He is Allah, the One! Allah is He on whom all depend. He begetteth not nor was begotten. And there is none comparable unto Him." (ch.112)

> "They said, burn him, and avenge your gods: If ye do this it will be well. We said O fire, be thou cold, and caused preservation unto Abraham. And they sought to lay a plot against him: but we caused them to be the sufferers." (ch. 21/v. 68-70)

3. So, according to the *Holy Quran*, nothing can be explained fully when Allah is not taken into account. In other words, everything needs Allah for existing. If you say that anything does not need Allah, or that you can explain something only by a factor which is not Allah, you will have assigned this factor to some extent a property of Allah, which in fact it has not. And anything which does not need Allah is assigned a status similar to Allah, a divine status. Many Quranic verses urge us to reflect and study and to observe the stars and galaxies. They impress upon us the Creator's magnificence, and exhort us to travel and observe the miraculous nature of our organs and of creation. The *Quran* places all of creation before our eyes. Touching upon a multitude of facts, it tells us that;

> "Those who truly fear God, among His servants, are those who have knowledge" (ch. 35/v. 28)

And so encourages us to seek knowledge, to reflect and research. However, it ought to be remembered that the first condition for all such activities is that they comply with the spirit of the *Quran*, lest we begin departing from it.

Our knowledge of science and its facts can and should be used within the limits of Islam, not to impress others or silence their arguments. Our primary aim must be to win the pleasure of God and make sure that our audience understands the points we are making. There is also other traditions that emphasize the importance of knowledge and science in Islam, for example, Imam Ali (A.S.) illustrates that: "good is not wealth progeny should be much but is that your knowledge should be much your forbearance should be great, and that you should vie with other people in worship of Allah". He also said that "knowledge is venerable estate: good manners are new dresses; and thinking is clear mirror"[1].

It is wrong to regard science as superior to religion and to seek to justify substantial Islamic issues and Islam as a whole through modern scientific facts.

Such attempts would show that we have doubts about Islam and thus need science to reinforce our own belief. It is also wrong to accept science or scientific facts as absolute, for such things are subject to change. At best, they only support what the *Holy Quran* says. In no way can the unchangeable and eternal *Quran* be confirmed by that which is changeable and temporary. Given this, Muslims should use science only as a tool to awaken sleeping or confused minds.

Even definitely established scientific facts cannot uphold the truths of faith; they can only be instruments to give us ideas or to trigger us to reflect. God, not science, establishes the truths of faith in our conscience, for faith comes only, and only by Divine guidance. Those who seek to acquire faith from science may never feel the existence of God within their own consciousness. In reality, they will be nature worshippers, not worshippers of God.

Mankind has often made the assignment that has been mentioned above, to gods such as the god of sun, the god of water, the god of love and so on. These were thought of as having partial authority on some parts of the world.

Today the same is true for some mathematical, geometrical, physical concepts and relations. An atheist probably says: Everything will explain or will be explained by science; so there is no need for a god. The first part of this argument is good and strong and the *Holy Quran* also favours this kind of reasoning. But there is a difference as to the second part: According to the *Quran*, science (or causal thinking) needs Allah in order to explain existence. Again, as you need Allah to explain existence, if He is not taken into account; then there must be godlike things that are assigned the post.

Many atheists suggest that we create our gods in our minds. But is it not interesting that some prophets also say the same to their people concerning their gods. According to the *Quran*: "Hud answered, now shall there suddenly fall upon you from your Lord vengeance and indignation. Will ye dispute with me concerning the names which ye have named, and your fathers; as to which God hath not revealed unto you any authority?" (ch. 7/v. 70) and that the atheists also may have given some things (as matter and its parts) the posts of god? So, the critical question is: "Whether Allah excludes godlike properties (as unity, coordination, execution, knowledge, predictability, absoluteness, creation of new entities and so on) of scientific entities (such as matter and energy), the media where these exist (dimensions), their states (as order, chaos), relations between all these (as of matter relating to space or energy; relevant formulations and so on) or whether these latter things leave no place for the existence of an active god.

These really constitute good subjects for debate, especially if you consider verses as “And (He is) who makes (things) according to a measure, then guides (them to their goal)” (ch. 87/v. 3) “He said ‘who is your Lord, Moses’? He answered, ‘Our Lord is he who giveth all things, their properties, and directed them.’ ” (Ch. 20/v. 49, 50)

The difference between the two approaches may be summarized as:

According to Islam: “The creatures which includes (includes everything) are given their qualifications (including the physical laws, equations, formulas [we may be unknowing everything, the real is known by Allah]) by God, and they are executed and may be changed by Allah whenever or wherever He wants.”

The (atheist) scientist says, “The properties (including the above mentioned laws and so on) of everything are intrinsic to them and absolute and not subject to change except for any specific conditions.”

And, therefore, there is no trade-off between Islam and Real-Science; both support each other. Islam is not only not opposed to scientific and technological progress; on the contrary, it encourages it, laying stress only on two points:

1. Scientific, technological and social progress shall not result in man waxing proud and thereby disregarding his Creator.
2. This endeavour and progress shall be utilized to better the condition of men and never be used in propagating sin or to buttress the foundations of cruelty and oppression.

The *Holy Quran*, however, does not aim at explaining certain laws governing the Universe; it has an absolutely basic religious objective. The descriptions of Divine Omnipotence are what principally incite man to reflect on the works of Creation.

Quranic Attitude towards Science

The relation between the *Holy Quran* and science is not easily identifiable and there is substantial discord between classical and modern Islamic views on this subject. All sources, both "classical and modern, agree that the *Quran* condones, even encourages the acquisition of science and scientific knowledge, and urges humans to reflect on the natural phenomena as signs of God's creation". Some scientific instruments produced in classical times in the Islamic world were inscribed with Quranic citations. Most Muslims agree that doing science is an act of religious merit, even a collective duty of the Muslim community.

There are, however, many disagreements traceable to interpretations of the *Holy Quran*. On the one hand, we have classical *Quran*, commentators who assigned to the *Quran* a separate and autonomous realm of its own. Al-Biruni (973-1048 CE), one of the most celebrated Muslim scientists of the classical period, held that the *Quran* does not interfere in the business of science nor does it infringe on the realm of science. The main arguments presented by this group of Muslims is the possibility of multiple scientific explanations of natural phenomena, the ever-changing nature of science and the considerable differences in the interpretation of the verses that may have a connection to science or natural phenomena. On the other hand, many contemporary Muslims, both amateurs and intellectuals, have gone as far as arguing that "Islam is a religion of science" urging others to explore the *Quran* for scientific truths which are now discoverable by modern science.

History of Science in the Islamic World

When the power of Greek civilization was eclipsed by the Roman Empire, many Greek doctors began to practice medicine for the Roman elite, but sadly the physical sciences were not so well supported. Following the collapse of the Roman Empire, Europe entered the so-called Dark Ages, and almost all scientific research ground to a halt. The rise of Christianity saw the suppression and destruction of most classical Greek philosophy (along with Greek and Roman art, literature and religious iconography) as heretical and pagan. In the Middle East, however, many Greek natural philosophers were able to find support in the newly created Arab Caliphate-Imam—(Empire), and the Islamic scholars built upon previous work in medicine, astronomy and mathematics while developing such new fields as alchemy (chemistry). For example, the scholar Muhammad ibn Musa al-Khwarizmi gave his name to what we now call an algorithm, and the word algebra is derived from *al-jabr*, the beginning of the name of one of his publications in which he developed a system of solving quadratic equations, thus beginning Al-gebra. The history of science in the Islamic World examines the full range of scientific investigation in the Islamic World, whether performed within a religious or secular context, or for religious or secular motives. From this perspective, it doesn't matter whether the particular scientist was a Muslim (e.g., al-Khwarizmi), a Sabian (e.g., Thabit ibn Qurra), a Christian (e.g., Hunain ibn Ishaq), or a Jewish (e.g., Hasdai ibn Shaprut), whether he advocated strict adherence to Muslim traditions (e.g., al-Ghazzali) or was he critical of tradition and open to the ideas of foreign philosophers (e.g., Averroës), or whether his patron was a Muslim (e.g., al-Ma'mun) or not (e.g., Hulagu Khan). If he studied natural phenomena and worked within the Islamic world, his work fits the historians' concern with science in the Islamic World, and there is a long story about Muslims' improvement in the world that needs extensive and independent research.

The Arrival of Modern Science in the Muslim World

At the beginning of the nineteenth century, modern science arrived in the Muslim world but it wasn't the science itself that affected Muslim scholars. Rather, it "was the transfer of various philosophical currents entangled with science that had a profound effect on the minds of Muslim scientists and intellectuals. Schools like Positivism and Darwinism penetrated the Muslim world and dominated its academic circles and had a noticeable impact on some Islamic theological doctrines "There were different responses to this among the Muslim scholars:

These reactions, in words of Professor *Mehdi Golshani*[2] were as follows:

1. "Some rejected modern science as corrupt foreign thought, considering it incompatible with Islamic teachings, and in their view, the only remedy for the stagnancy of Islamic societies would be the strict following of Islamic teachings.
2. Other thinkers in the Muslim world saw science as the only source of real enlightenment and advocated the complete adoption of modern science. In their view, the only remedy

for the stagnation of Muslim societies would be the mastery of modern science and the replacement of the religious worldview by the scientific worldview.

3. The majority of faithful Muslim scientists tried to adapt Islam to the findings of modern science; they can be categorized in the following sub-groups: (a) Some Muslim thinkers attempted to justify modern science on religious grounds. Their motivation was to encourage Muslim societies to acquire modern knowledge and to safeguard their societies from the criticism of Orientalists and Muslim intellectuals; (b) Others tried to show that all important scientific discoveries had been predicted in the *Quran* and Islamic tradition and appealed to modern science to explain various aspects of faith; (c) Yet other scholars advocated a re-interpretation of Islam. In their view, one must try to construct a new theology that can establish a viable relation between Islam and modern science. The Indian scholar, *Sayyid Ahmad Khan,* sought a theology of nature through which one could re-interpret the basic principles of Islam in the light of modern science; and (d) Then there were some Muslim scholars who believed that empirical science had reached the same conclusions that prophets had been advocating several thousand years ago. The revelation had only the privilege of prophecy.
4. Finally, some Muslim philosophers separated the findings of modern science from its philosophical attachments. Thus, while they praised the attempts of Western scientists for the discovery of the secrets of nature, they warned against various empiricist and materialistic interpretations of scientific findings. Scientific knowledge can reveal certain aspects of the physical world, but it should not be identified with the alpha and omega of knowledge. Rather, it has to be integrated into a metaphysical framework—consistent with the Muslim worldview—in which higher levels of knowledge are recognized and the role of science in bringing us closer to God is fulfilled".[3]

The Relation between Islam and Science

Islam has its own worldview system including beliefs about "ultimate reality, epistemology, ontology, ethics, purpose, etc". Muslims believe that the *Quran* is the literal word and the final revelation of God for the guidance of humankind.

Science in the broadest sense refers to any system of knowledge attained by verifiable means, and in a narrower sense to a system of acquiring knowledge based on observation, experimentation, and methodological naturalism, as well as to the organized body of knowledge humans have gained by such research. Scientists maintain that scientific investigation must adhere to the scientific method, a process for evaluating empirical knowledge that explains observable events in nature as results of natural causes, rejecting supernatural notions.

Modern science has greatly influenced thought in the Muslim world. There have been differing reactions to its arrival. Some Muslims have interpreted the *Quran* so as to support their belief that it makes statements about the universe that have only been discovered by science in modern times. Scientists and philosophers have tried to show logical fallacies in these arguments and some Muslim thinkers have decried efforts to prove the validity of the *Quran* using modern science, which is constantly changing and reevaluating its assumptions and conclusions.

On the other hand, there are specific references to human development and embryology in the *Quran* and *hadith*. Some scholars such as Jabir Ibn Haiyan (Geber)(*c*.721–*c*.815)[4], Faarabi (870-950)[5], Rumi (1207-1273 CE)[6], Raazi[7], Aveciena (980-1037)[8], Kharazmi (780-850)[9], Al-Ghazali (1058-1111)[10], Mulla Sadra (*c*. 1571–1640)[11], Allameh Tabatabaei (1892-1981)[12], Morteza Motahhari (1920-1979)[13] and others have found strong parallels between these statements and the positions of the ancient Greek thinkers such as Aristotle, Hippocrates, and Galen, whose writings were widely available in pre-Islamic Age.

Improving of Science in Islamic World

The modern advancement of science in the Islamic world can be seen as part of the broader movement of the Islamization of knowledge.

A Muslim engaged in this field is called a Muslim scientist. This is not the same as science as conducted by Muslims in the secular context. However, certain liberal movements in Islam eschew the practice of Islamic science, arguing that science should be considered separate from religion.

Fields

These are some of the fields in which Islamic scientists have dealt with these issues:

Scientific Method

During the Middle Ages, Islamic scholars made significant advances in mathematics, medicine, astronomy, engineering, and many other fields. During this time Islamic philosophy developed and was often pivotal in scientific debates—key figures were usually scientists and philosophers.

The prominent Iranian scientist Ibn Al-Haitham used the scientific method to obtain the results in his book *Optics*. In particular, he performed experiments and used the scientific method to show that the intromission theory of vision supported by Aristotle was scientifically correct, and that the emission theory of vision supported by Ptolemy and Euclid was wrong. It is known that Roger Bacon (who is usually erroneously given the credit for having founded the scientific method) was familiar with Ibn Al-Haitham's work.

Science was one of the most powerful areas of the Islamic culture of the period.

Mathematics

A Seljuk manuscript from the thirteenth century depicts Socrates *(Soqrt)* in discussion with his pupils.

In the history of mathematics, "Islamic mathematics" refers to the mathematics developed by mathematicians of the Islamic culture, from the beginning of Islam until the seventeenth century—mostly including Arab and Persian mathematicians, as well as other Muslims and non-Muslims that were a part of Islamic culture. Islamic mathematics (also known as Arabic mathematics since most of the texts are written in Arabic) is the main aspect of the greater history of Islamic science, and also an important part of the history of mathematics.

Islamic science and mathematics flourished under the Islamic Caliphate (also known as the Arab Empire or Islamic Empire) established across the Middle East, Central Asia, North Africa, Sicily, the Iberian Peninsula, and in parts of France and Pakistan (known as

India at the time) in the eighth century. Although most Islamic texts on mathematics were written in Arabic, they were not all written by Arabs, since—much like the status of Greek in the Hellenistic world—Arabic was used as the written language of non-Arab scholars throughout the Islamic world at the time. Many of the most important Islamic mathematicians were Persians.

Recent research paints a new picture of the debt that we owe to Islamic mathematics. Certainly many of the ideas which were previously thought to have been brilliant new conceptions due to European mathematicians of the sixteenth, seventeenth and eighteenth centuries are now known to have been developed by Arabic/Islamic mathematicians around four centuries earlier. In many respects, the mathematics studied today is far closer in style to that of Islamic mathematics than to that of Hellenistic mathematics.

Medicine

Prophetic Medicine (*al-tibb*) was a genre of medical writing intended as an alternative to the Greek-based medical system. It advocated the traditional medical practices of *Muhammad's* time (those mentioned in the *Quran*). *Al-tibb* therapy did not require the patient's undergoing any surgical procedures.

The "*Kitab fi al-jadari wa-al-hasbah*", with its introduction on measles and small pox was also very influential in Europe.

In referring to the pre-modern Islamic contribution to embryology, Joseph Needham writes that: "Arabic science, so justly famed for its successes in certain fields such as optics and astronomy, was not of great help to embryology".

Astrology

Islamic astrology, in Arabic *ilm al-nujum*, is, is the study of the heavens by early Muslims. In early Arabic sources, *ilm al-nujum* was used to refer to both astronomy and astrology. In medieval sources, however, a clear distinction was made between *ilm al-nujum* (science of the stars) and *ilm al-falak* (science of the celestial orbs), referring to astrology, and *ilm al-haya* (science of the figure of the heavens), referring to astronomy. Both fields were rooted in Greek, Persian, and Indian traditions. Despite consistent critiques of astrology by scientists and religious scholars, astrological prognostications required a fair amount of exact scientific knowledge and thus gave partial incentive for the study and development of astronomy.

Astronomy

Islamic astronomy closely parallels the genesis of other Islamic sciences in its assimilation of foreign material and the amalgamation of the disparate elements of that material to create a science that was essentially Islamic. These include *Indian* and *Sassanid* works in particular. Some *Hellenistic* texts were also translated and built upon as well.

Islamic interest in astronomy ran parallel to the interest in mathematics. Noteworthy in this regard was the Almagest of the Greek-speaking Egyptian scholar Ptolemy (A.D. *c*. 100-*c*. 178). The Almagest was a landmark work in its field, assembling, as Euclid's Elements had previously done with geometrical works, all extant knowledge in the field of astronomy that was known to the author. This work was originally known as *The Mathematical Composition*, but after it had come to be used as a text in astronomy, it was called *The Great Astronomer*. The Islamic world called it the Greatest prefixing the Greek work *megiste* (greatest) with the article al; and it has since been known to the world as *Al-megiste* or, after popular use in Western translation, *Almagest*. Ptolemy also produced other works such as, *Optics*, *Harmonica*, and some suggest he also wrote *Tetrabiblon*.

The *Almagest* was a specially unifying work for its exhaustive lists of sidereal phenomena. Ptolemy drew up a list of chronological tables of Assyrian, Persian, Greek, and Roman kings for use in reckoning the lapse of time between known astronomical events and fixed dates. In addition to its relevance to calculating accurate calendars, it linked far and foreign cultures together by a common interest in the stars and astrology.

The work of Ptolemy was replicated and refined over the years by Persian and Islamic astronomers and astrologers. The astronomical tables of *al-Khwarizmi* and of *Abu'l-Qasim Maslama b. Ahmad* (*al-Majriti*) served as important sources of information for latinized European thinkers rediscovering the works of astronomy, where extensive interest in astrology was discouraged.

Modern Islamic philosophy has, in response to challenges of secular science and concerns that secular society is unwilling or unable to limit its uses of "dangerous technology", especially nuclear weapon or biotechnology, begun to look at the origins of science to determine what ethics or limits can or should be imposed on science, and what goals or visions are appropriate for science[14].

The Miracle of Islamic Improvements in Science

The concept that the sciences are exclusively the products of Western minds remains unquestioned by most individuals. A review of any of the standard texts or encyclopedias regarding the history of science would support this view. As these books are perused, it becomes evident that the only contributors given significant mention are Europeans and/or Americans. It is hardly necessary to repeat the oft-mentioned names: Galileo, Copernicus, Kepler, Bacon, Newton, Da Vinci, Benjamin Franklin, etc. The unavoidable conclusion is that major contributions to the development of the modern sciences by other cultures are minimal. Most texts give little or no mention of the advancements made by ancient Indian, Chinese or, particularly, Muslim scholars.

Western civilization has made invaluable contributions to the development of the sciences. However, so have numerous other cultures. Unfortunately, Westerners have long been credited with discoveries made many centuries before by Islamic scholars. Thus, many of the basic sciences were invented by non-Europeans. For instance, George Sarton[15] states that modern Western medicine did not originate from Europe and that it actually arose from the (Islamic) orient.

The data in this section concerning dates, names and topics of Western advances has been derived from three main sources: *World Book Encyclopaedia, Encyclopaedia Britannica* and Isaac Asimov's[16] book, *Chronology of Science and Discovery*. Supportive data for the accomplishments of Islamic scholars is derived from the miscellaneous references listed in the bibliography of this book, and are mentioned here as examples:

What is taught: The first mention of man in flight was by Roger Bacon, who drew a flying apparatus. Leonardo da Vinci also conceived of airborne transport and drew several prototypes.

What should be taught: Ibn Firnas of Islamic Spain invented, constructed and tested a flying machine in the 800 A.D. Roger Bacon learned of flying machines from Arabic references to Ibn Firnas' machine. The latter's invention antedates Bacon by 500 years and Da Vinci by some 700 years.

What is taught: Glass mirrors were first produced in 1291 in Venice.

What should be taught: Glass mirrors were in use in Islamic Spain as early as the eleventh century. The Venetians learned the art of fine glass production from Syrian artisans during the ninth and tenth centuries.

What is taught: Until the fourteenth century, the only type of clock available was the water clock. In 1335, a large mechanical clock was erected in Milan, Italy. This was possibly the first weight-driven clock.

What should be taught: A variety of mechanical clocks were produced by Spanish Muslim engineers, both large and small, and this knowledge was transmitted to Europe through Latin translations of Islamic books on mechanics. These clocks were weight-driven. Designs and illustrations of epi-cyclic and segmental gears were provided. One such clock included a mercury escapement. The latter type was directly copied by Europeans during the fifteenth century. In addition, during the ninth century, Ibn Firnas of Islamic Spain, according to Will Durant, invented a watch-like device which kept accurate time. The Muslims also constructed a variety of highly accurate astronomical clocks for use in their observatories.

What is taught: In the seventeenth century, the pendulum was developed by Galileo during his teenage years. He noticed a chandelier swaying as it was being blown by the wind. As a result, he went home and invented the pendulum.

What should be taught: The pendulum was discovered by Ibn Yunus al-Masri during the tenth century, who was the first to study and document its oscillatory motion. Its value for use in clocks was introduced by Muslim physicists during the fifteenth century.

What is taught: Movable type and the printing press were invented in the West by Johannes Gutenberg of Germany during the fifteenth century.

What should be taught: In 1454, Gutenberg developed the most sophisticated printing press of the middle Ages. However, movable brass type was in use in Islamic Spain 100 years prior, and that is where the West's first printing devices were made.

What is taught: Isaac Newton's seventeenth century study of lenses, light and prisms forms the foundation of the modern science of optics.

What should be taught: In the eleventh century Al-Haytham determined virtually everything that Newton advanced regarding optics centuries prior and is regarded by numerous authorities as the "founder of optics. There is little doubt that Newton was influenced by him. Al-Haytham was the most quoted physicist of the middle ages. His works were utilized and quoted by a greater number of European scholars during the sixteenth and seventeenth centuries than those of Newton and Galileo combined.

What is taught: Isaac Newton, during the seventeenth century, discovered that white light consists of various rays of coloured light.

What should be taught: This discovery was made in its entirety by al-Haytham (eleventh century) and Kamal ad-Din (fourteenth century). Newton did make original discoveries, but this was not one of them.

What is taught: The concept of the finite nature of matter was first introduced by Antione Lavoisier during the eighteenth century. He discovered that, although matter may change its form or shape, its mass always remains the same. Thus, for instance, if water is heated to steam, if salt is dissolved in water or if a piece of wood is burned to ashes, the total mass remains unchanged.

What should be taught: The principles of this discovery were elaborated centuries before by Islamic Persia's great scholar, al-Biruni (d. 1050). Lavoisier was a disciple of the Muslim chemists and physicists and referred to their books frequently.

What is taught: The Greeks were the developers of trigonometry.

What should be taught: Trigonometry remained largely a theoretical science among the Greeks. It was developed to a level of modern perfection by Muslim scholars, although the weight of the credit must be given to al-Battani. The words describing the basic functions of this science, sine, cosine and tangent, are all derived from Arabic terms. Thus, original contributions by the Greeks in trigonometry were minimal.

What is taught: The use of decimal fractions in mathematics was first developed by a Dutchman, Simon Stevin, in 1589. He helped advance the mathematical sciences by replacing the cumbersome fractions, for instance, 1/2, with decimal fractions, for example, 0.5.

What should be taught: Muslim mathematicians were the first to utilize decimals instead of fractions on a large scale. Al-Kashi's book, *Key to Arithmetic*, was written at the beginning of the fifteenth century and was the stimulus for the systematic application of decimals to whole numbers and fractions thereof. It is highly probable that Stevin imported the idea to Europe from al-Kashi's work.

What is taught: Kerosene was first produced by an Englishman, Abraham Gesner, in 1853. He distilled it from asphalt.

What should be taught: Muslim chemists produced kerosene as a distillate from petroleum products over 1,000 years prior to Gesner[17].

The Situation of the Modern Science

It is clear that modern science is successful in telling us the weight and chemical structure of a red pine leaf, but it is totally irrelevant to what is the meaning of the turning of this leaf to red. The 'how' has been explained in modern science, the 'why' is not its concern. If you are a physics student and you ask the question, 'what is the force of gravitation?' the teacher will tell you the formula, but as to what the nature of this force is, he will tell you it is not a subject for physics. So [science] is very successful in certain fields, but leaves other aspects of reality aside.

Professor Nasr's View

Professor Seyyid Hossein Nasr[18], writing about the relationship between Islam and modern science, held that there are several important phenomena that are going on in the Islamic world:

First and most powerful, is the continuous flow and absorption of Western science and technology into all existing Islamic countries to the extent that [they] can absorb it. In every single Islamic country, whatever the political regime, whatever the economic policy, whatever the attitude towards the West [they may espouse], whether they are completely pro-Western or have demonstrations in the street against the West, the adoption of Western science and technology goes on. This is a very telling fact for the whole of the Islamic world. There are some places where some thought is being given to the consequences of this process. Now there are many questions to ask here. First of all is this [transfer of science and technology] going on successfully? Is it not going on successfully? If it is not successful, what is it not going on successfully? And if it is, why?

The second phenomenon that is going on [today] is the [gradual] attempt being made to study both the meaning and the history of

Islamic science. It seems that in this field that Muslims should really be ashamed of themselves, to put it mildly.

It is clear that it is not possible to bring all instances of clash between scientific point and some religious scripture here, so we try to investigate two of the most famous examples of this clash.

Galileo's clash with the Church concerning his view of the solar system is probably the best known example of the conflict model between science and religion although this particular issue was resolved many years ago. Creationists who maintain that the universe is only thousands of years old, when there is overwhelming evidence of its great antiquity, give credence to the idea that science and religion are invariably opposed. On the other side, well-known scientists who assert that science leaves no room for religion, also support this model.

It is important to note that most of the scientists, who laid the basis for the scientific age, including Boyle, Copernicus, Faraday, Galileo, Kepler, Maxwell, and Newton, believed in a personal God who revealed Himself in the Scriptures and answered prayer. For many people, therefore, there must be other plausible ways of relating science and religion.

Marx's View and Islamic Reaction

On the 13th day of 1367, Imam Khomeini sent a letter to Gorbachev, the leader of the Union of Socialist Soviet Republics, explained Islam and invited him to accept it. He wrote:

"Mr. Gorbachev!

With a rather freedom for religious ceremonies in some Republics, you showed not regarding religion as an opiate to society. Indeed, can we call the religion which saves Iran against superpowers, an opiate? Is the religion that wants justice and freedom for people, an opiate[19]?

The concept of religion may be viewed from two perspectives: the human or the Divine. The followers of the great world religions take religion to be God-revealed principles, values and commandments and therefore, do not, in explaining the origin of religion, refer to man. By contrast, the modern Western world imputes the origin of religion to man and then seeks to explain it away according to the different sciences of man—anthropology, sociology or psychology.

In order to illustrate the differences of opinion that arise among those who, from ignorance or from limitations, offer their definition of a matter, Jalal al-Din al-Rumi (1207-1273 CE), a famous Muslim scientist of the thirteenth century, made this analogy: some blind persons encounter an elephant and, on touching different parts of the animal's body, offer their partial, inept and contradictory definitions of an elephant: one finds it to be a heavy, thick column, another a hard, flexible pipe, and so on. This is what those who try to explain the origin of religion have achieved in the West. Just as the anthropologists drew different conclusions, sociologists also put forward different opinions about the origin of religion.

In chapter Two we have seen that religion according to Marx (1818-1883), as the opiate of the masses, will inevitably become a thing of the past. He also illustrated that revolution would be created by the alliance of middle class intellect and labour.

For a criticism of this viewpoint according to Islam, we have to pay attention to the point that they (positivists, Marx and the others) make when they say that religion is a means contrived by mankind to cover up problems that man could not solve but which, with further advances in civilization, will one day be solved. And so, they ask, will religion then no longer be needed? They argue that religion was put together as a kind of outpouring of man's feeling of powerlessness in the world or of his feelings of relief and gratitude when rescued from powerlessness.

Sometimes "Religion is the sigh of the oppressed creature" is included. If we compare these with the full quotation, it is clear that a great deal more is being said than what most people are aware of.

In the above quotation Marx is saying that the purpose of religion is to create illusory fantasies for the poor. Economic realities prevent them from finding true happiness in this life, so religion tells them that this is acceptable because they will find true happiness in the next life. Although this is a criticism of religion, Marx is not without sympathy: people are in distress and religion provides solace, just as people who are physically injured receive relief from opiate-based drugs. For all its problems, religion doesn't matter so much. It is not the real problem. Religion is a set of ideas, and ideas are expressions of material realities. Religion can be a sign of an illness, not the illness itself.

Still, it would be a mistake to think that Marx is uncritical towards religion—it may try to provide heart, but it fails. For Marx, the problem lies in the obvious fact that an opiate drug fails to fix a physical injury—it merely helps you forget pain and suffering. This may be fine up to a point, but only as long as we are also trying to solve the underlying problems causing the pain. Similarly, religion does not fix the underlying causes of people's pain and suffering—instead, it helps them forget why they are suffering and gets them to look forward to an imaginary future when the pain will cease.

Marx did not make religion the primary enemy of workers and communists, regardless of what might have been done by twentieth century communists. Had Marx regarded religion as a more serious enemy, he would have devoted more space to it in his writings. Instead, he focused on economic and political structures that in his mind served to oppress people.

For this reason, some Marxists could be sympathetic to religion. Karl Kautsky, in his Foundations of Christianity, wrote that early Christianity was, in some respects, a proletarian revolution against privileged Roman oppressors.

Marx's relationship with, and his ideas about religion are more complex than most realize. He argues that religion is not so much an independent "thing" in society but, rather, a reflection or creation of other, more fundamental "things" like economic relationships. That is not the only way of looking at religion, but it can provide some interesting illumination on the social conditions.

Whatever one's final conclusion about the accuracy or validity of Marx's ideas on religion, we should recognize that he provided an invaluable service by forcing people to take a hard look at the social web in which religion always occurs. Because of his work, it has become impossible to study religion without also exploring its ties to various social and economic forces, but his viewpoint cannot answer to all cases. He also showed that people's spiritual lives can no longer be assumed to be totally independent of their material lives. There is another historical example that shows religion has the potentiality to create social reforms for social justice and goodness:

In 1891, the Tobacco concession was awarded to the British by Nasereddin Shah Qajar (Iranian King); however, the following turns of events foiled the British attempts to follow through with this.

Nasereddin Shah liked going to Europe and used to travel there for three times a year. In his last trip dated 1889 he travelled to Britain. Due to the Shah's extravagance during the trip, which was encouraged by Aminossoltan, Nasereddin Shah's chancellor, he was left with no money for spending and leading his Epicurean life style. Therefore, he gave the concession of Tobacco products to a Britisher called Major Talbot and in turn received some money to continue his extravagance.

Talbot was one of the advisors to the British Prime Minister. The two sides sat around the table of negotiations in Berating City where Talbot, through bribing courtiers such as Aminossoltan was able to win the agreement of the Shah on the issue. The promised price was 25,000 Liras. After the Shah's return, Talbot came to Iran to get the project started. According to the agreement, the company called Regie was to pay 15,000 Liras yearly to Iran and would enjoy the possession of the products of the tobacco plantations under a sale concession. It ensured that the products would be cheaply bought and expensively sold.

After the agreement was signed, the staff of the British company came to Iran and went to different cities of Iran. However; people did not let them in. The people of the major cities like Shiraz, Tabriz, Isfahan and Tehran showed their opposition to the deal. Finally, for these reasons. Ayatollah Mirza Shirazi issued the abolition of the tobacco concession and Britain could not succeed in this action.

Brigadier General Sir Percy Sykes, wrote the following passage in his book, *History of Persia* (3rd edition, printed 1930), regarding the futile formation of the Tobacco Corporation in Iran.

"Less fortunate than the Imperial Bank of Persia was the fate of the Tobacco Regie. This ill-judged concession gave full control over the production, sale, and export of all tobacco in Persia. In return for these rights a sum of £15,000 was to be paid annually to the Shah; in addition, after the working expenses and 5 per cent had been set aside, His Majesty was to receive one quarter of the profits. The concession affected the position of tobacco growers, sellers, and smokers alike; and in Persia both men and women smoke regularly. Its gross unfairness was aggravated by the fact that many of the employees were drawn from a somewhat low class and by the lack of tact displayed in dealing with Persian rights. In short, first public indignation and then fanaticism was aroused. Haji Mirza Hasan Shirazi, the leading Mujtahid, placed an interdict on smoking, and the order was obeyed throughout the land, the royal palace being no exception. Finally, after disturbances had broken out and intense hostility had been displayed towards Europeans, the Shah cancelled the concession and agreed to pay compensation to the extent of half million sterling. This sum was borrowed from the Imperial Bank of Persia and may be considered to constitute the beginning of the Persian National Debt."

The Issue of Tobacco Sanction by Ayatollah Shirazi. Ayatollah Shirazi wrote a letter to the Shah, asking him to abolish the concession but he ignored Mirza's order. Thus, Mirza issued a *fatwa*: "In the name of God, the beneficent, the merciful; today, the use of tobacco is the same to war with Imam Mahdi, that means not allowed".

This *fatwa* caused a semi-revolution among people; they stopped using tobacco, the tobacco shops were closed and everybody broke the *hookahs*. They stop dealing with the Regie Corporation. This continued till an announcement was stuck to city walls: "according to Ayatollah Mirza Shirazi, within 48 hours the concession must be abolished or people would get ready for *jihad* on Monday."

The Shah resorted to force and tried to threaten the scholars and people by exiling. The manager of Regie Company asked Aminossoltan to persuade the scholars and even wanted him to exile Mirza Ashtiani, the great Marja out of Tehran. Shah wrote to Mirza Ashtiani: "stay in Tehran and use the *hookah* or leave".

Mirza asked for a day to be prepared. The next day morning, Monday people went protesting in the streets and headed towards Mirza's house. Shah sent somebody there and asked Mirza about his conditions to stop this saga. Mirza Ashtiani replied: "we want the concession to be abolished and the foreigners to lose access to our sources."

However, the protests continued and a number of people were killed and injured. Mirza told people to go back to their work.

Aminossoltan brought the Shah's verdict about the abolition to Mirza Shirazi. He said the *fatwa* is valid till Mirza Ashtiani's letter about this abolition is sent to me. When he saw the announcement on the abolition, he declared his *fatwa* was finished[20].

On Tuesday, there was an announcement that people are allowed to use *hookahs* and tobacco. On 5 April, 1891, Shah signed the official abolition of the Tobacco concession. Since then, in Iranian history, this has been called the Tobacco revolution, which showed the power of religion, and which, therefore, should not be considered an opiate.

Islam and Evolution (Darwinian Theory)

What is Islam's view on evolution? There are many theories of evolution. Some of them are acceptable according to Islam, while there are others that are not acceptable. If by evolution one means the development and growth that Allah Almighty has placed in the nature of His creation, then this is acceptable and the *Quran* itself talks about it. According to the Islamic view, human beings are a special creation of Allah. Allah created the body of Adam and his wife Eve from the soil and their soul from himself, and then through them created many men and women.

It could not accept the theory which says that all living organisms came from matter and man evolved from lower living organisms. There is a link between the human body and other living organisms, but this does not prove that one evolved from the other. Does that mean that the prophet Adam also looked like a lower living organism? In the question asked, if 'evolution' implies that man is actually an evolved form of some other creature, then Islam does not affirm such a standpoint. Darwin's theory of Evolution has influenced the minds of people and their character has been influenced as well. Such people do not believe in divine morals and values. They do not believe in God, soul and the Hereafter. Islam says that God has created this universe and Humans with a specified goal. The evolutionists' claim that the universe started from the first atom and life started from the "first cell". The evolutionists cannot answer the question as to who created the atom and cell. In the belief of the evolutionists, inanimate matter must have produced a living cell as a result of coincidence. Many modern biologists have rejected this claim. Great evolutionists like the Russian biologist Alexander Oparin and the American chemist Stanley Miller experimented to prove that a living cell could originate by coincidence but failed and they admitted their failure. Oparin in *Origin of Life* and Stanley Miller in *Molecular Evolution of Life* discuss the issue in detail. Jeffery Bada in his book *Earth Admits*, "we still face the biggest unsolved problem that we had when we entered the twentieth century: how did life originate on earth."[21] The conditions required for the formation of the cell are too great in quantity to be explained away by coincidences. The DNA molecule is so complex that it cannot be accidental or coincidental. The mechanism of evolution has been also rejected. No deer becomes a horse and no ape becomes a man. It is a fallacious theory having no historical and scientific evidence.

There is another Islamic viewpoint for Human Embryonic Development[22]:

> We created man from an extract of clay. Then we made him as a drop in a place of settlement, firmly fixed. Then we made the drop into an *alaqah* (leech, suspended thing, and

> blood clot), then we made the *alaqah* into a *mudghah* (chewed substance). *(Quran,* 23:12-14)

Literally, the Arabic word *alaqah* has three meanings: (1) leech, (2) suspended thing, and (3) blood clot.

In comparing a leech to an embryo in the *alaqah* stage, we find similarity between the two as we can see in Fig. 3.1. Also, the embryo at this stage obtains nourishment from the blood of the mother, similar to the leech, which feeds on the blood of others.

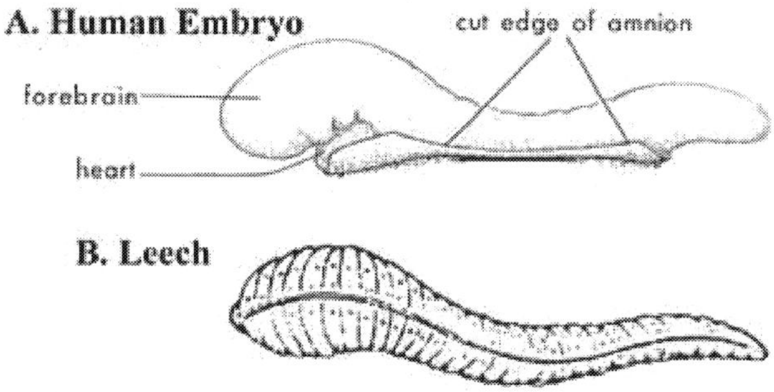

Fig 3.1: Drawings illustrating the similarities in appearance between a leech and a human embryo at the *alaqah* stage. (Leech drawing from Human Development as described in the *Quran* and *Sunnah*.

The second meaning of the word alaqah is suspended thing. This is what we can see in Fig. 3.2 and Fig. 3.3, the suspension of the embryo, during the *alaqah* stage, in the womb of the mother.

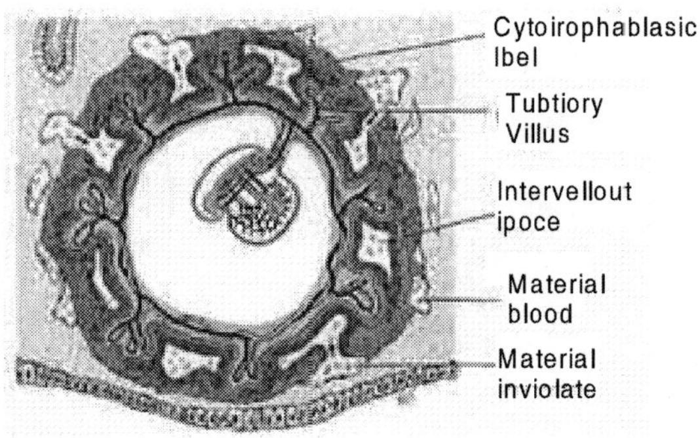

Fig. 3.2: We can see in this diagram the suspension of an embryo during the *alaqah* stage in the womb (uterus) of the mother.

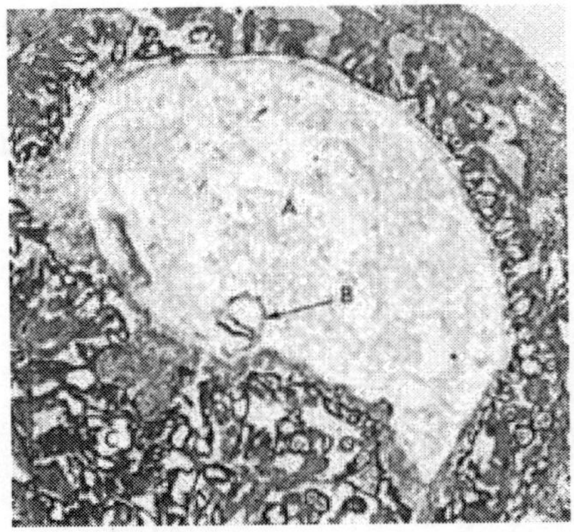

Fig. 3.3: In this photomicrograph, we can see the suspension of an embryo (marked B) during the *alaqah* stage (about 15 days old) in the womb of the mother. The actual size of the embryo is about 0.6 mm.

The third meaning of the word *alaqah* is blood clot. We find that the external appearance of the embryo and its sacs during the *alaqah* stage is similar to that of a blood clot. This is due to the presence of relatively large amounts of blood present in the embryo during this stage (see Fig. 4). Also during this stage, the blood in the embryo does not circulate until the end of the third week. Thus, the embryo at this stage is like a clot of blood.

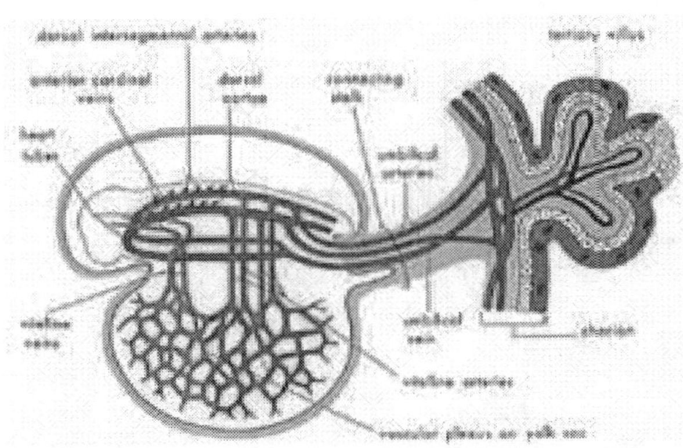

Fig. 3.4: Diagram of the primitive cardiovascular system in an embryo during the *alaqah* stage. The external appearance of the embryo and its sacs is similar to that of a blood clot, due to the presence of relatively large amounts of blood present in the embryo.

So the three meanings of the word *alaqah* correspond accurately to the descriptions of the embryo at the *alaqah* stage.

The next stage mentioned in the verse is the *mudghah* stage. The Arabic word *mudghah* means "chewed substance." If one were to take a piece of gum and chew it in his or her mouth and then compare it with an embryo at the *mudghah* stage, we would conclude that the embryo at the *mudghah* stage acquires the appearance of a chewed substance. This is because of the somites at the back of the embryo that "somewhat resemble teethmarks in a chewed substance." (See Figs. 3.5 and 3.6).

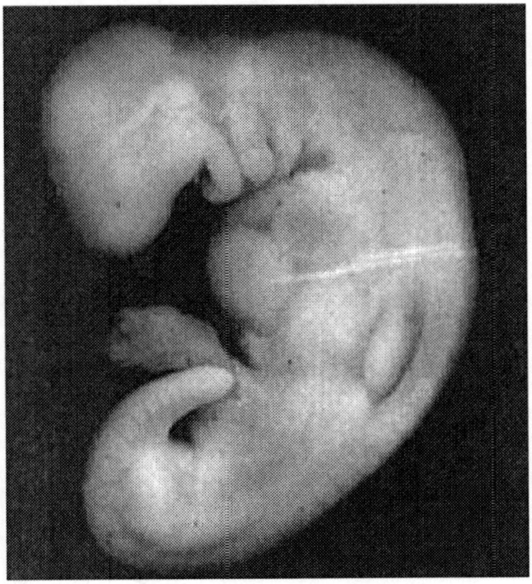

Fig. 3.5: Photograph of an embryo at the *mudghah* stage (28 days old). The embryo at this stage acquires the appearance of a chewed substance, because the somites at the back of the embryo somewhat resemble teeth marks in a chewed substance. The actual size of the embryo is 4 mm. (*The Developing Human*, Moore and Persaud, 5th ed., p. 82, from Professor Hideo Nishimura, Kyoto University, Kyoto, Japan.)

How could Prophet Muhammad have possibly known all this 1400 years ago, when scientists have only recently discovered this using advanced equipment and powerful microscopes which did not exist at that time? Hamm and Leeuwenhoek were the first scientists to observe human sperm cells (spermatozoa) using an improved microscope in 1677 (more than 1000 years after Prophet Muhammad).

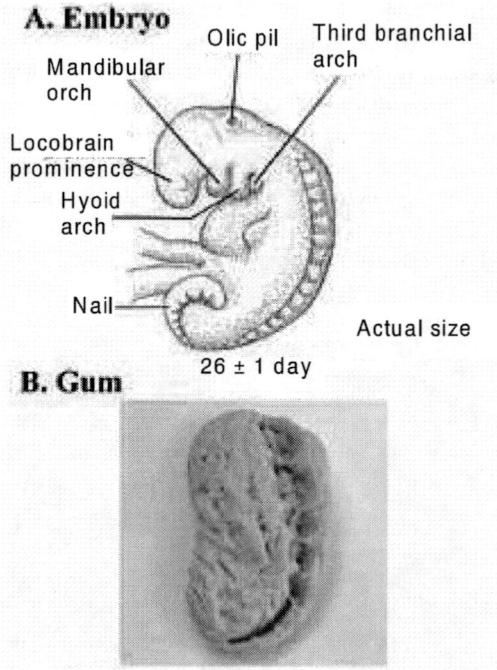

Fig. 3.6: When comparing the appearance of an embryo at the *mudghah* stage with a piece of gum that has been chewed, we find similarity between the two. (A) Drawing of an embryo at the *mudghah* stage. We can see here the somites at the back of the embryo that look like teeth marks. (*The Developing Human*, Moore and Persaud, 5th ed., p. 79.) (B) Photograph of a piece of gum that has been chewed.

They mistakenly thought that the sperm cell contained a miniature preformed human being that grew when it was deposited in the female genital tract.

Professor Emeritus Keith L. Moore is one of the world's most prominent scientists in the fields of anatomy and embryology and is the author of the book entitled *The Developing Human*, which has been translated into eight languages. This book is a scientific reference work and was chosen by a special committee in the United States as the best book authored by one person. Dr. Keith Moore is Professor Emeritus of Anatomy and Cell Biology at the University of Toronto, Toronto, Canada. There, he was Associate Dean of Basic Sciences in the Faculty of Medicine and for 8 years was the Chairman of the Department of Anatomy. In 1984, he received the most distinguished award presented in the field of anatomy in Canada, the J.C.B. Grant Award from the Canadian Association of Anatomists. He has directed many international associations, such as the Canadian and American Association of Anatomists and the Council of the Union of Biological Sciences.

In 1981, during the Seventh Medical Conference in Dammam, Saudi Arabia, Professor Moore said: It has been a great pleasure for me to help clarify statements in the *Quran* about human development. It is clear to me that these statements must have come to Muhammad from God, because almost all of this knowledge was not discovered until many centuries later. This proves to me that Muhammad must have been a messenger of God.

Darwin was well aware that his theory faced lots of problems. He confessed these in his book in the chapter 'Difficulties of the Theory'. These difficulties primarily consisted of the fossil record, complex organs of living things that could not possibly be explained by coincidence (e.g., the eye), and the instincts of living beings. Darwin hoped that these difficulties would be overcome by new discoveries; yet this did not stop him from coming up with a number of very inadequate explanations for some. The American physicist Lipson made the following comment on the 'difficulties' of Darwin:

> "On reading The Origin of Species, I found that Darwin was much less sure himself than he is often represented to be; the chapter entitled 'Difficulties of the Theory' for example, shows considerable self-doubt. As a physicist, I was particularly intrigued by his comments on how the eye would have arisen."[23]

Lamarck and Darwin believed in the transferring of traits of one species to the other. They maintain that living creatures passed on the traits they acquired during their lifetime to the next generation. Giraffes evolved from antelopes and bears transformed into whales. However, the laws of inheritance discovered by Gregor Mendel (1822-1884) and verified by the science of genetics have nullified the theory of evolutionary mechanism. Neo-Darwinism advances the "Modern Synthesis Theory". Mutations, i.e., genetic disorders do not cause living beings to develop; on the contrary they are always harmful. The fossil record theory of Darwin, which was a basic contention, has been rejected on scientific grounds. According to this theory, every living species has sprung from a predecessor. No "Transitional Forms" have yet been uncovered. On the contrary, the British Paleontologist, Derek V. Ager in *The Nature of the Fossil Record* admits that the fossil records show not gradual evolution but the sudden explosion of one group at the expense of another. This is just the opposite of Darwin's assumptions. Douglas J. Futuyma, an eminent evolutionist biologist in his book, *Science of Trail* declares that the organism is the creation of some omnipotent intelligence. Fossils show, writes Harun Yahua, in his book, *The Importance of Conscience in the Quran*, that living beings emerged fully developed and in a perfect state on the earth. That means that the Origin of Species, contrary to Darwin's suppositions, "is not evolution, but creation". On the wonders of creation the *Quran* in Sura Rehman aptly announces: "He has created man. He has taught him an intelligent speech". Then in the same Sura in verse 13 God announce: "Then which of the favours of your Lord will ye deny".

Darwinism maintains that living things were not created but came into being by chance. Darwinism, materialism and communism believe in matter, not in spirit. Darwin himself regarded his theory based on assumptions. The above discussions on Darwinism can be reviewed under three basic topics:

1. The Darwinism theory cannot scientifically explain how life originated on Earth.
2. No scientific finding shows that the "evolutionary mechanism" proposed by the theory has any evolutionary power at all.
3. The fossil record provided proves the exact opposite of what the theory suggests.

According to the *Quran,* Adam—the first man—was a direct creation of God, as a man. The Quran does not support that Adam evolved from another species.

However, it may be of some interest to note that in *Al-Sajadah* 32: 7-9, the *Quran* has referred to three different stages involved in the creation of man in such words that a slightly varied version of 'evolution' may be derived from it. *The Quran* says:

> He, who perfected everything that He created—He started the creation of man from clay then he inculcated in him [i.e. man] the potential to reproduce through a drop of humble fluid then He embellished and fashioned him in due proportion; and breathed into him of His spirit and [thereby] developed in you [the abilities of] listening, vision and feeling.

The above verses clearly tell us that in the beginning man was created from clay. The words 'creation from clay', obviously, does not necessitate that God created an effigy of man from clay and then gave life to it. It may, as we know, imply that in the beginning man came into existence out of the earth. In other words, God inculcated in earth—mixed with water—the potential to produce life. Over centuries or even millennia, the life-bearing potential of the earth materialized and a species quite similar to, yet somewhat different from man was born. This was the first stage in the creation of man, as is evidenced by the words: "He started the creation of man from clay".

In the second stage, the potential of reproducing life—of bearing offspring—through sexual contact between the male and the female genders was inculcated in this species. This stage is mentioned in the words: "then he inculcated in him the potential to reproduce through a drop of humble fluid".

In the third stage, the species was physically fashioned into proportion and with that God also breathed into it of His spirit, which developed in it the abilities of listening, vision and feeling. The words: "then He embellished and fashioned him in due proportion; and breathed into him of His spirit and [thereby] developed in you [the abilities of] listening, vision and feeling", point to this final stage in the development of the human species.

It may be interpreted from the above explanation that it was only the first pair of near-humans, i.e. Adam and Eve, who went through the three stages explained above. Adam's (and Eve's) creation was initiated from clay—that is, they were produced through the life-generation potential inculcated in the earth. Later on, the potential of reproduction through sexual contact was inculcated in Adam (and Eve). In the third stage, Adam (as well as Eve) was physically fashioned into due proportion and God breathed into them of His spirit and thereby developed the higher sapiential abilities in them.

The Renaissance led to the separation of philosophy from theology, reason from faith, and mysticism from gnosis. (The latter term S.H. Nasr uses not to designate a secret knowledge based on mystic revelation but to refer broadly to "illuminated knowledge"). In medieval times Christianity, like Islam, was steeped in tradition. But as the West emphasized the rigid logic of Aristotelian thinking, the sense of the sacred diminished. By the seventeenth century the science of the cosmos was secularized. The scientific revolution mechanized the Western worldview, and, with the appearance of the nineteenth century sociologist Auguste Comte, led to examining the person and society as elements that could be measured with the aim of manipulation and predictability.

Believing in Darwin's prophecy, evolutionist paleontologists have been digging up fossils and searching for missing links all over the world since the middle of the nineteenth century. Despite their best efforts, no transitional forms have yet been uncovered. All the fossils unearthed in excavations have shown that, contrary to the beliefs of evolutionists, life appeared on earth all of a sudden and fully-formed. Trying to prove their theory, evolutionists have instead unwittingly caused it to collapse.

A famous British paleontologist, Derek V. Ager, admits this fact even though he is an evolutionist:

> The point emerges that if we examine the fossil record in detail, whether at the level of orders or of species, we find, over and over again, not gradual evolution, but the sudden explosion of one group at the expense of another.[24]

Concerning Darwin's theory, S.H. Nasr attacks what he calls the "hypothesis" of evolution. He uses the term not to mean modifications within a particular species (which do occur, he says, as a species adapts itself to changed natural conditions) but the belief that through natural processes one species is actually transformed into another. Nasr passionately criticizes this on a wide variety of grounds—metaphysical, cosmological, religious, logical, mathematical, physical, biological, and paleontological—building arguments too complex to recapitulate here. His central concern is that what he calls "the deification of historical process" has become so powerful that in many souls it has replaced religion and veils the archetypal realities.[25]

Among his arguments is the contention that there is a remarkable unanimity that humankind descends from a celestial archetype but does not ascend from the ape or any other creature. Hinduism, Jainism,

Buddhism, Islam, and many other traditions do demonstrate awareness that other creatures have preceded humankind on earth and that the earth's geological configuration has changed. For example, over a thousand years ago Muslim scientists knew that sea shells on top of mountains meant that mountains had turned into seas and seas into mountains, and that land animals had preceded humans on earth. But no sacred scriptures, whether they speak of creation in six days or of cosmic cycles enduring over vast expanses of time, speak of higher life forms as evolving from lower ones.

However, contrary to the above interpretation, another theory that may be developed on the basis of the information given in the referred verses may be as follows:

- Man's creation, in the first stage, was initiated by the production of a like species from the earth. In this stage, a number of near—human pairs—male and female—were produced directly from the earth.
- In the second stage, the near-human pairs were inculcated with the ability of reproducing life through sexual interaction between the male and the female gender of the species.
- In the third stage, one of the directly produced pairs (as in the first stage)]—i.e. Adam and Eve—were physically fashioned into due proportion and were inculcated with the advanced human abilities. It was at this stage that Adam and Eve became complete humans.
- Over subsequent centuries, the other directly produced pairs (in the first stage) and their offspring became extinct. The only pair that survived, through its offspring was that of Adam and Eve.
- The whole human race that populates the planet is the offspring of the one directly produced pair, which was physically fashioned into due proportion and inculcated with the advanced human faculties.

In view of the information provided by the *Quran* and the human knowledge that has developed over time, one may subscribe to any explanation that seems correct to him. However, if the latter theory is accepted to be correct, it also helps explain the existence of the slightly different fossil bones. It seems that these bones are of the near-humans that, in contrast to Adam and Eve and their subsequent generations, were not physically fashioned into proportion or inculcated with the advanced human faculties and which became extinct over time.

It should be stressed here that the above is a development of a somewhat detailed scenario, on the basis of some vague indications of the *Quran* and the general knowledge that has become available to man. The scenario may or may not be completely accurate.

And, finally, it should also be stressed, that though we know Darwin's theory is opposed of Christianity scriptures, we cannot say the same about the Islamic scriptures. In the *Bible* the emphasis on creation by God is greater. For instance, we do not find in the *Holy Quran* that God created all animals, the earth and sky directly but in *Bible* we do, so whether evolution theory is opposed of the creation of Adam and Eve and scriptures or not? It should be stated that it is not contrast of religion. In fact there are different interpretations:

1. The evolution theory is opposed to Quranic scriptures especially in the Adam and Eve story.
2. There is no contrasting because some interpretations indicated that some men or creatures similar to him, were living before Adam.
3. According to religious language, it could be said that while these verses want to state that this Adam was created by God and belong to him, it also means they don't want to explain the details of creation.
4. Suppose this is different of scriptures; we can response there is contrast between this theory and Christianity scripture not all religion.

Summary of Chapter Three

- Islam is not only opposed to scientific and technological progress, on the contrary, it encourages it, laying stress only on two points:
    1. Scientific, technological and social progress shall not result in man waxing proud and thereby disregarding his Creator.
    2. This endeavour and progress shall be utilized to better the condition of men and should never be used in propagating sin or to buttress the foundations of cruelty and oppression.

- The *Quran* does not aim at explaining certain laws governing the Universe, however, it has an absolutely basic religious objective. The descriptions of Divine Omnipotence are what principally encourage man to reflect on the works of Creation.
- Even definitely established scientific facts cannot uphold the truths of faith; they can only be instruments to give us ideas or to trigger us to reflect. God, not science, establishes the truths of faith in our conscience, for faith comes only by Divine guidance. Those who seek to acquire faith from science may never feel the existence of God within their own consciousness. In reality, they will be nature worshippers, not worshippers of God.
- It is clear that it is not possible to bring all instances of the clash between the scientific view point and religious scriptures here, so we try to investigate two of most notorious clashes.
- Galileo's clash with the Church concerning his view of the solar system is probably the most well known example of the conflict model between science and religion. Although this particular issue was resolved many years ago, creationists who maintain that the universe is only thousands of years old, when there is overwhelming evidence of its great antiquity, give credence to the idea that science and religion are invariably opposed. On the other hand, well-known scientists who assert that science leaves no room for religion also support this model.
- Marx argues that religion is not so much an independent "thing" in society but, rather, a reflection or creation of other, more fundamental "things", like economic relationships. That is not the only way of looking at religion, but it can provide some interesting illumination on the social aspects.
- According to Marx it has become impossible to study religion without also exploring its ties to various social and economic forces, but his viewpoint cannot answer to all cases. Also, people's spiritual lives can no longer be assumed to be totally independent of their material lives. For Marx, the problem lies in the obvious fact that an opiate drug fails to fix a physical injury—it merely helps you forget pain and suffering. For this reason, some Marxists could be sympathetic to religion.

- There are many theories of evolution. Some of them are acceptable according to Islam, while there are others that are not acceptable. If by evolution one means the development and growth that Allah Almighty has placed in the nature of His creation, then this is acceptable. Darwin's theory of Evolution has influenced the minds of people and their character has been influenced as well. Such people do not believe in divine morals and values. They do not believe in God, soul and Hereafter.
- And finally, it should also be stressed, that though we know Darwin's theory is opposed of Christianity scriptures, we cannot say the same about the Islamic scriptures. In the *Bible* the emphasis on creation by God is greater. For instance, we do not find in the *Holy Quran* that God created all animals, the earth and sky directly but in *Bible* we do, so whether evolution theory is opposed of the creation of Adam and Eve and scriptures or not? It should be stated that it is not contrast of religion. In fact there are different interpretations:
- As a last point, many Islamic philosophers like Allameh Tabatabaei (1892-1981) believe that modern science can be used for the interpretation of the *Quran*.

FOOTNOTES

1. Imam Ali ibn Abu Talib, *Nahjul Balagha (Peak of Eloquence)*, Islamic Foundation Press, Kerala, India, 1990, p. 560.
2. Mehdi Golshani, *Holy Quran and the Sciences of Nature,* paperback ed., Studies in Contemporary Philosophical Th., 1997.
3. Professor Mehdi Golshani (Persian: مهدی گلشنی b. 1939 Isfahan, Iran) is a contemporary Iranian theoretical physicist and Philosophy. He received his B.Sc. in Physics from Tehran University in 1959 and his Ph.D. in Physics with a specialization in Particle Physics in 1969 from the University of California, Berkeley. The title of his doctoral dissertation is "Electron impact excitation of heavily ionized atoms". Golshani is a distinguished lecturer and researcher. His main research areas include Foundational Physics, Particle Physics, Physical Cosmology and Philosophical Implications of Quantum Mechanics. He is well known for his writings on science, religion and their interrelation. It has been said that Golshani wants to be a Muslim scientist and thinker who has deep roots in both science and religion.

He has been among the winners of the first year of the Templeton Science and Religion course programme [Progress in Theology, September 1995, Volume 3, Number 3, and Page 7] and also among the Former Judges of The Templeton Prize. Golshani is the founder and chairman of the Faculty of the Philosophy of Science at the Sharif University of Technology. He is also director of the Institute of Humanities and Cultural Studies, Tehran, Iran, and Professor of Sharif University of Technology, Physics Department and Senior Fellow of the Institute for Studies in Theoretical Physics and Mathematics (IPM), School of Physics. Golshani is a member of the American Association of Physics Teachers—Centre for Theology and Natural Science and Senior Associate of the International Centre for Theoretical Physics, Trieste, Italy. He is also a Member of the Philosophy of Science Association, Michigan, USA and European Society for the Study of Science and Theology. See: Golshani, Mehdi. *Holy Quran and the Sciences of Nature.* Paperback ed. Studies in Contemporary Philosophical Th., 1997. Golshani, Mehdi. *Can Science Dispense with Religion?* Hardcover ed. I.H.C.S., 1998.

4. Abu Musa Jabir ibn Hayyan (Arabic: جابر بن حيان) (*c*.721-*c*.815), known also by his Latinised name Geber, was a prominent Islamic alchemist, pharmacist, philosopher, astronomer, and physicist. Jabir was born in Tus, Khorasan, in Iran, Jabir's father's profession may have contributed greatly to his interest in alchemy. In Kufa he became a student of the celebrated Islamic teacher and sixth Imam Ja'far al-Sadiq. He has also been referred to as "the father of chemistry" by Europeans. His ethnic background is not clear; although most sources state he was an Arab, others describe him as Persian. Ibn Hayyan is widely credited with the introduction of the experimental method into alchemy, and with the invention of numerous important processes still used in modern chemistry today, such as the syntheses of hydrochloric and nitric acids, distillation, and crystallisation. His original works are highly esoteric and probably coded, though nobody today knows what the code is. On the surface, his alchemical career revolved around an elaborate chemical numerology based on consonants in the Arabic names of substances and the concept of *takwin*, the artificial creation of life in the alchemical laboratory.
   →from the *Encyclopedia Britannica,* E.J. Holmyard (ed.) *The Arabic Works of Jabir ibn Hayyan,* translated by Richard Russel in 1678. New York, E.P. Dutton (1928); Also Paris, P. Geuther.
5. Abū Nasr Muhammad ibn al-Farakh al-Frbi (Persian: محمد فارابی) or Abū Nasr al-Fārābi (in some sources, known as Muhammad ibn Muhammad ibn Tarkhan ibn Uzalagh al-Farabi), also known in the

West as Alpharabius, Al-Farabi, Farabi, and Abunaser *(b.* 870, *d.* between 14 December 950 and 12 January 951 CE) was an Islamic philosopher and one of the greatest scientists and philosophers of his time. The main influence on al-Fārābi's philosophy was the neo-Aristotelian tradition of Alexandria. A prolific writer, he is credited with over one hundred works. In contrast to al-Kindi, who considered the subject of metaphysics to be God, al-Farabi believed that it was concerned primarily with being *qua* being (that is, being of itself), and this is related to God only to the extent that God is a principal of absolute being. Al-Kindi's view was, however, a common misconception regarding Greek philosophy amongst Muslim intellectuals at the time, and it was for this reason that Avicenna remarked that he did not understand Aristotle's Metaphysics properly until he had read a prolegomena written by al-Farabi. The practical application of philosophy is a major concern expressed by al-Farabi in many of his works, and while the majority of his philosophical output has been influenced by Aristotelian thought, his practical philosophy is unmistakably based on that of Plato.[31] In a manner similar to *The Republic* (Plato), al-Farabi emphasizes that philosophy is both a theoretical and practical discipline; labelling those philosophers who do not apply their erudition to practical pursuits as "futile philosophers". The ideal society, he says, is one directed towards the realization of "true happiness" (which can be taken to mean philosophical enlightenment) and as such, the ideal philosopher must have all the necessary arts of rhetoric and poetics to communicate abstract truths to the ordinary people, as well as having achieved enlightenment himself. Al-Farabi compares the philosopher's role in relation to society with a physician in relation to the body; the body's health is affected by the "balance of its humours" just as the city's is determined by the moral habits of its people. The philosopher's duty, he says, is to establish a "virtuous" society by healing the souls of the people, establishing justice and guiding them towards "true happiness". Of course, al-Farabi realizes that such a society is rare and will require a very specific set of historical circumstances in order to be realized, which means very few societies will ever be able to attain this goal. He divides those "vicious" societies, which have fallen short of the ideal "virtuous" society, into three categories: ignorant, wicked and errant. *Ignorant* societies have, for whatever reason, failed to comprehend the purpose of human existence, and have supplanted the pursuit of happiness for another (inferior) goal, whether this be wealth, sensual gratification or power. It is interesting to note that democratic societies also fall into this category, as they too lack any guiding principal. Both *wicked* and *errant* societies have understood the true human end, but they have failed to follow it. The former because they have wilfully abandoned it, and the latter because their leaders have deceived and misguided them. Al-Farabi also makes mention of "weeds" in the virtuous society; those people who try to undermine its progress towards the true human end. Henry Corbin, who considers al-Farabi to be a crypto-Shi'ite, says that his ideas should be understood as a "prophetic philosophy" instead of being interpreted politically.

→ from the *Encyclopaedia Britannica,* Corbin, H. (1993). *History of Islamic Philosophy.* London: Keagan Paul International and Majid Fakhry, *Al-Farabi, Founder of Islamic Neoplatonism: His Life, Works, and Influence,* Oxford: Oneworld Publications, (2002), ISBN 1-85168-302-X.

6. *Mevlânâ* Jalâl ad-Dîn Muhammad R kmî (Persian: مولانا جلال الدین محمد رومی, Turkish: *Mevlânâ Celâleddin Mehmed Rumi),* also known as Mâwlânâ Jalâl ad-Dîn Muhammad Balkhî (Persian: محمد بلخی), but known to the English-speaking world simply as Rumi (1207-1273 CE) was a 13th century Persian *(Tâjîk)* poet, jurist, and theologian. His name literally means *"Majesty of Religion", Jalal* means *"majesty"* and *Din* means *"religion"*. Rumi was born in Balkh (then a city of Greater Khorasan in Persia, now part of Afghanistan) and died in Konya (in present-day Turkey). His birthplace and native tongue indicate a Persian heritage. He also wrote his poetry in Persian and his works are widely read in Iran, Afghanistan, Tajikistan, and in translation in Turkey, Azerbaijan, the US, and South Asia. He lived most of his life and produced his works under the Seljuk Empire. Rumi's importance is considered to transcend national and ethnic borders. Throughout the centuries he has had a significant influence on Persian as well as Urdu and Turkish literatures. His poems are widely read in the Persian speaking countries of Iran, Afghanistan and Tajikistan and have been widely translated into many of the world's languages in various formats. After Rumi's death, his followers founded the Mevlevi Order, better known as the "Whirling Dervishes", who believe in performing their worship in the form of dance and music ceremony called the sema.

   → See: Majid M. Naini, *The Mysteries of the Universe and Rumi's Discoveries on the Majestic Path of Love,* Universal Vision and Research, 2002, ISBN 0-9714600-0-0 and *Rumi's Thoughts,* edited by Seyed G. Safavi, London: London Academy of Iranian Studies, 2003.

7. Muhammad ibn (Persian: زکریای رازی *Zakaria ye Razi;* Arabic: ابو بکر محمد بن زکریا الرازی; Latin: Rhazes or Rasis). According to

al-Biruni he was born in Rayy, Iran in the year 865 AD (251 AH), and died there in 925 AD (313 AH). Razi was a versatile Persian physician, philosopher, and scholar who made fundamental and enduring contributions to the fields of medicine, alchemy, and philosophy, recorded in over 184 books and articles in various fields of science, his most important accomplishment being the discovery of alcohol. He was well versed in Greek medical knowledge and added substantially to it from his own observations.
→ See: Walker, P. *"The Political Implications of al-Razi's Philosophy"*, in C. Butterworth (ed.) *The Political Aspects of Islamic Philosophy,* Cambridge, MA: Harvard University Press, 61-94 (1992).

8. Avicenna (Latinized from Arab Ibn Sina; full name ابوعلی سینا/پورسینا; arabicized الحسين بن عبد الله بن سينا أبو علي; born 980, dead 1037) was a Persian physician, and a philosopher, scientist. Avicenna, whose name means "the son of Sina", was of Persian ethnicity. He was born in 980 (370 AH) in Afshana near Bukhara in Persia (now part of Uzbekistan) and died in 1037 (428 AH) in Hamadan (now in Iran). Avicenna authored some 450 books on a wide range of subjects, many of which concentrated on philosophy and medicine. His most famous works are *The Book of Healing* and *The Canon of Medicine,* which was for almost five centuries a standard medical text at many European universities. Avicenna's medical system was based on that of Galen which he combined with Aristotelian metaphysics as well as traditional Persian and Arab lore.
→from the *Encyclopaedia Britannica and Ibn Sina from the Encyclopaedia of Islam.*
9. Muhammad ibn (Arabic: محمد بن موسى الخوارزمي. was a Persian (and geographer mathematician, astronomer, astrologer). He was born around. 780 Khiva, Uzbekistan 850 and died around. He worked most of his life as a scholar in the House of Wisdom in Baghdad. His *Algebra* was the first book on the systematic solution of linear and quadratic equations. Consequently he is considered to be the father of algebra, a title he shares with Diophantus. Latin translations of his *Arithmetic,* on the Indian numerals, introduced the decimal positional number system to the Western world in the twelfth century. He revised and updated Ptolemy's *Geography* as well as writing several works on astronomy and astrology. His contributions not only made a great impact on mathematics, but on our language as well. The word algebra is derived from *al-jabr,* one of the two operations used to solve quadratic equations, as described in his book. The words *algorism* and *algorithm* stem from *algoritmi,* the Latinization of his name. His name is also the origin of the Spanish word *guarismo* and of the Portuguese word *algarismo,* both meaning digit.

→from *the Encyclopaedia Britannica and* Berggren, J. Lennart (1986). *Episodes in the Mathematics of Medieval Islam.* New York: Springer-Verlag, ISBN 0-387-96318-9.

10. Mohammad ibn Mohammad (1058-1111) (Persian: حامد محمد ابن محمد غزالی ابو, known as *Algazel* to the Western medieval world, born and died in Tus, in the Khorasan province of Persia (modern day Iran). He was a Muslim theologian, philosopher, and mystic of Persian origin and remains as one of the most celebrated scholars in the history of Islamic thought. Al-Ghazali contributed significantly to the development of a systematic view of Sufism and its integration and acceptance in mainstream Islam. He was a scholar of orthodox Islam, belonging to the Shafi'i school of legal thought of Sunnite Islam and to the Asharite school of theology.
    See: R.M. Frank, *Al-Ghazali and the Ash'arite School*, Duke University Press, London 1994. Campanini, M.: Al-Ghazzali, in S.H. Nasr and O. Leaman, History of Islamic Philosophy 1996.
11. Mulla Sadra (ملاصدرا; also spelt Molla Sadra or Mollasadra) also called Sadr al-Din al-Shirazi (*c.* 1571-1640) was a Persian philosopher, who led the Iranian cultural renaissance in the seventeenth century.
    The foremost representative of the illuminationist, or Ishraghi school of philosopher-mystics, he is commonly regarded by Iranians as the greatest philosopher their country has ever produced. His school of philosophy is called Transcendent Theosophy or al-hikmat al-muta'liyah. Born in Shiraz, Iran, the son of a notable Shirazi family, Mulla Sadra completed his education at Isfahan, which was the leading cultural and intellectual centre of his day. He was trained under the supervision of Mir Damad. After his studies with scholars there, he produced several works, the most famous of which was his *Asfar* (Journeys). *Asfar* contains the bulk of his philosophy, which was influenced by a personal mysticism bordering on the ascetic, that he experienced during a fifteen-year retreat at Kahak, a village near Qom, Iran. Expounding his theory of nature, Mulla Sadra argued that the entire universe—except God and his knowledge—was originated both eternally and temporally. Nature, he asserted, is the substance of all things and is the cause for all movement. Thus, nature is permanent and furnishes the continuing link between the eternal and the originated. Much of his philosophy was also existentialist in nature. Toward the end of his life, Mulla Sadra returned to Shiraz to teach. His teachings, however, were considered heretical by the orthodox Shiite theologians of his day, who persecuted him, though his powerful family connections permitted him to continue to write. He died in Basra, on a pilgrimage to Mecca, and was buried in present day Iraq.

→See: www.mullasadra.org and related Books as, Mircea, Eliade *The Encyclopedia of Religion,* Volume 15, Macmillan Publishing Company, New York, 1986.

12. Allameh Seyyed Muhammad Husayn Tabataba'i (علامه سید محمد حسین طباطبائی) (1892-1981) is one of the most prominent thinkers of contemporary Shia Islam. He is famous for the historical landmark work *Tafsir al-Mizan.* Tabatabaei was a philosopher, a prolific writer, and an inspiring teacher to his students who devoted much of his life to non-political Islamic studies. Many of his students were among the ideological founders of the Islamic Republic of Iran, namely Morteza Motahhari, Dr. Beheshti, Dr. Mohammad Mofatteh, Ayatollah Javadi Amoli and Ayatoolah Mesbah. Others like Nasr and Hasanzadeh Amuli remained and continued their studies in the intellectual non-political sphere. His other major philosophical work is a voluminous commentary of *Asfâr al-'arba'eh,* the magnum opus of Mulla Sadra who was the last of the great Persian (Iranian) Muslim thinkers of the medieval age. Apart from these he also wrote extensively on philosophical topics. His humanist approach is underlined by his three books on: the nature of man-before the world, in this world, and after this world. His philosophy is focused upon the sociological treatment of human problems. His two other works, *Bidâyat al-hikmah* and *Nihyât al-hikmah,* are considered among works of high order in Islamic philosophy.
13. Ayatollah Morteza Motahhari (نصر سید حسین; February 3, 1920—May 1, 1979) was an Iranian scholar, cleric, University lecturer, and politician. Motahhari is considered among the important influences on the ideologies of the Islamic Republic, and was a co-founder of Hosseiniye Ershad and the Militant Clergy Association *(Jâme'e-ye Rowhâniyat-e Mobârez).* Motahhari also was the person who formed the Council of Revolution of Iran, according to an order from Ayatollah Khomeini, who was his teacher during the Shah's reign. Motahhari also wrote several books on Islam, Iran, and historical topics. He taught philosophy at Tehran University. "Teachers Day" in Iran is celebrated on Ordibehesht 12 (2 May), the Persian date on which Motahhari was assassinated after leaving a late meeting at the house of Yadollah Sahabi. He was assassinated by gunshot, from a member of the Furqan Militia Group. Motahhari is the father-in-law of Iran's top nuclear negotiator Ali Larijani. It was by Motahhari's advice that Larijani switched from Computer Science to Western philosophy for graduate school. In honour of Motahhari, a major street in Tehran was named after him shortly after the Iranian revolution in 1979.

14. J.P. Hogendijk. *Bibliography of Mathematics in Medieval Islamic Civilization,* January 1999.
15. George Sarton Published 1927 Published for the Carnegie Institution of Washington by the Williams & Wilkins, Co. Original from the University of Michigan Digitized June 9, 2006.
16. Isaac Asimov, *Howard Freedman*, Published 2005, University Press of Mississippi ISBN 1578067383.
17. See: *Encyclopaedia Britannica* under the heading, Petroleum, and www.islaam.net.
18. Professor Syed Hossein Nasr (Persian: نصر سید حسین) was born in Tehran (1933). After receiving his early education in Iran, Nasr studied physics and mathematics at Massachusetts Institute of Technology (MIT) and received his doctorate from Harvard University in 1958 with specialization in Islamic cosmology and science. From 1958 until 1979, he was professor of the history of science and philosophy at Tehran University.

    In 1962 and 1965, he was visiting professor at Harvard University and in 1964-65 the first Agha Khan Professor of Islamic studies at the American University of Beirut. He was the founder and first president of the Iranian Academy of Philosophy. In 1979, he migrated to the United States and taught at several American universities before finally joining the George Washington University, Washington DC in 1984 where he is currently the University Professor of Islamic Studies. In 1981, Nasr gave the Gifford lectures at the University of Edinburgh, which was published the same year as Knowledge and the Sacred. In 1999, he was chosen to be the first Muslim scholar to receive the Templeton Religion and Science Course Award. Most recently, a volume on Nasr in the Library of Living Philosophers Series has been edited, which includes several studies on his views of science.

    Nasr has written a number of books and articles on the relation between religion and science in general and Islam and science in particular. His doctoral dissertation, which appeared first in 1964 under the title *An Introduction to Islamic Cosmological Doctrines*, is the first modern book devoted to the study of Islamic cosmology. In the Introduction, Nasr discusses three prominent figures of Islamic science and their approach to the study of nature. His next book Science and Civilization in Islam, first published in 1968, brought the concept of 'Islamic science' to the fore with full force. In this work, Nasr discussed the meaning of science within the context of Islamic religious worldview and analyzed the achievements of Islamic scientific tradition in such fields as medicine, astronomy, mathematics, algebra, chemistry, physics, geography, and natural history. The book is based on the original sources and remains one of the best compendia of science in the Islamic civilization.

Nasr's next work in the field of Islamic science is a huge scholarly enterprise that has unfortunately remained incomplete. An Annotated Bibliography of Islamic Science, compiled in three volumes with William Chittick, is a tour de force presentation of the available material on the history of Islamic science in Western languages. The first volume appeared in 1975, the third in 1991.

Nasr's most famous work on Islamic science is *Islamic Science: An Illustrated Study* (1976). It is the first of its kind in presenting Islamic science, its philosophical premises, its history and development with beautiful visual material, pictures, and diagrams. In addition, Nasr has dealt with the relation between Islam and science in his other writings such as Islamic Life and Thought (1981), The Young Muslim's Guide to the Modern World (1993), and The Islamic Intellectual History in Persia (1994).

Nasr has also been a pioneering figure on the relation between religion, science, and the environmental crisis. His early work *The Encounter of Man and Nature: The Spiritual Crisis of Modern Man*, first appeared in 1968, was one of the first books to predict the disastrous consequences of the environmental crisis. The book is a philosophical critique of the modern conception of nature as inert matter to be conquered and usurped by modern science and technology. This is also the first book in which Nasr takes up the challenge of modern science and its secular outlook. The second important book to appear in this line of writings is Religion and the Order of Nature, published in 1996, in which Nasr gives an account of the rise of modern science on the one hand, and the critique of secular and reductionist philosophies concerning nature, on the other. The book also attempts to revive the sacred notion of nature and traditional cosmology with which Nasr has been occupied throughout his intellectual career. As a prominent spokesman of the traditionalist school, Nasr has also dealt with science in its traditional and sacred sense. In this regard, *Knowledge and the Sacred* (1981) and *The Need for a Sacred Science* (1993) are the two most important books in which Nasr has tried to revive scientia sacra by showing the underlying unity and interrelatedness of the transmitted, intellectual, and physical sciences under the umbrella of metaphysics.

In his intellectual career, Nasr has dealt with all of the major aspects of the relation between religion and science. The Islamic sciences of nature, just like their traditional Christian or Hindu counterparts, look upon the order of nature as *vestigia Dei* or signs of God (ayat Allah), pointing to the Divine origin of things. This suggests that the order of nature has an essential (al-'aql), which makes it both sacred and essentially meaningful. Within this framework, the natural order is construed as having an intrinsic intelligibility that can be discovered and grasped by the intellect (al-'aql). The analytical function of logical reasoning is complemented by the synthesizing power of the intellect. The natural phenomena, dissected and analyzed into their constitutive elements by reason, are integrated into a coherent whole by the intellect that occupies a higher epistemological position because of its intuitive and synthetic ability. Thus Nasr presents a holistic view of the universe and a holistic epistemology for its scientific study.

The teleological nature of the Islamic sciences of nature also envisages a hierarchic order in nature. To explain this, Nasr uses the metaphysical language of traditional Islamic philosophy, whose first premise is to make a distinction between the Principle, i.e., God in His aspect of absoluteness, and manifestation, i.e., the world of creation. Just as the generation of the world of multiplicity from the One implies an ontological hierarchy, various levels of existence are also structured in hierarchic units, the cosmos being a special case in point. Since every level of reality has its own meaning and place in the total economy of Divine creation, none of them can be reduced to one single element, viz., and the so-called ultimate building block of things. According to Nasr, it is the teleological and hierarchic view of the universe that has prevented the Islamic sciences of nature from falling into the trap of reductionism and materialism.

In a similar way, the Muslim scientists, nearly all of them also accomplished philosophers, developed highly advanced methods of scientific experimentation without giving into physicalism and/or scientism. For Nasr, the greatest achievement and relevance of the Islamic scientific tradition lies not merely in its ability to find the direction of the *Ka'bah* but in its comprehensive outlook based on the metaphysical principles of Islam. In this regard, Islamic science is not just science developed and cultivated by people who happened to be Muslim. Rather, it is the scientific study of natural phenomena within the matrix of the worldview of the Islamic revelation.

The second aspect of Nasr's work on religion and science pertains to the critique of modern science. Nasr has been one of the most outspoken critics of Western secular science and its effect on the non-Western world. In a number of studies, he has shown that the roots of modern science are traceable to a set of philosophical assumptions that mark the demarcation line between the medieval Christian and the modern West.

Taking the Scientific Revolution of the sixteenth and seventeenth centuries to be a turning point in the history of Europe, Nasr focuses on the process of the gradual demise of Christian thought and the rise of the secular view of the universe, and argues that the rise of modern science is not the result of some groundbreaking discoveries in scientific measurement and instruments but rather of a radical change in the worldview of modern man that emerged in Europe after the sixteenth century. To substantiate this claim, Nasr identifies six dominant traits of modern science.

The first is the secular view of the universe that sees no traces of the Divine in the natural order on the one hand, and denies any telos or purpose to the universe on the other. Consequently, the teleological view of the universe, shared by all traditional civilizations, is rejected by modern science.

The second is the mechanization of the world-picture upon the model of machines and clocks the favourite image of the deists of the eighteenth and nineteenth centuries. Since modern science and philosophy claim to explain everything away in terms of scientific and rational analysis, the universe had to be constructed as a machine so that it would lend itself to the precise methods of analysis and measurement of modern physical sciences.

The third is rationalism and empiricism as the only reliable methods of arriving at truth. In spite of deep contradictions between the two, the secular and reductionist methods of philosophical analysis are shared by both schools.

The fourth is the legacy of Cartesian dualism that presupposes a complete separation between res cogitans and res extensa, viz., between the knowing subject and the object to be known. One of the conspicuous results of this separation is the epistemological and spiritual alienation of man from his natural environment and, in fact, from everything that may become the object of his knowledge.

The fifth is what Nasr calls the "Promethean view of man", which construes man as the measure of all things, and which Nasr contrasts with what he calls the "Pontifical man", i.e., man as a bridge between heaven and earth.

The last trait of modern secular science is the exploitation of nature as a source of power and domination, which was the driving force behind the Industrial Revolution and the rise of capitalism. Taken together, these six postulates constitute the philosophical framework of modern secular science, which has led to scientism and demise of the sacred view of the cosmos on the one hand, and to such modern disasters as the environmental crisis and nuclear warfare on the other.

In so far as the relationship between religion and science is concerned, Nasr is opposed to the modernist-puritanical view that an ethical dimension grafted to the practice of science will undo the misdeeds of modern secular science. Instead of confining the role of religion and ethics to the level of policy decisions, Nasr proposes a radical deconstruction of the philosophical foundations of modern science and attempts to revive the religious view of the universe. A sound metaphysical framework rooted in the perennial teachings of the great religions of the world is, for Nasr, a *sine qua non* for an authentic and veritable relationship between religion and science.

19. www.tebyan.net
20. Ayatollah Haj Mirza Mohammad Hasan Shirazi was one of Shi'ite scientists. In 1248 AH, as a youth, he left his hometown for Shiraz City where he studied both rational and traditional sciences. In 1295 AH, he left for the sacred thresholds in Iraq where he enjoyed Sheikh Morteza Ansari's guidance. In 1291 AH, he settled down in Samarra and he taught till he passed away in 1312 AH. His body was taken to Najaf Ashraf and buried there. The historic verdict of this honourable clergyman on Tobacco abolishing nipped the disaster of the year 1309 AH in the bud.
21. www.irfi.org, Charles Darwin, The Origin of Species: A Facsimile of the First Edition, Harvard University Press, 1964, p. 179.
22. See: Modified from Integrated Principles of Zoology, Hickman and others. Embryo drawing from *The Developing Human*, Moore and Persaud, 5th Ed., p. 73.
23. David Raup, *Conflicts Between Darwin and Paleontology*, Bulletin, Field Museum of Natural History, Vol. 50, January 1979, p. 24. Richard Monastersky, 'Mysteries of the Orient', *Discover*, April 1993, p. 40.
24. Derek V. Ager, *The Nature of the Fossil Record*, Proceedings of the British Geological Association, Vol. 87, 1976, p. 133, and also, see:.www.imanway.com.
25. See: *Man and Nature*: *The Spiritual Crisis of Modern Man*, (London: George Allen and Unwin Ltd., 1968); and *Science and Civilization in Islam* (Cambridge: Harvard University Press, 1968). Charles Darwin, the Origin of Species: A Facsimile of the First Edition, Harvard University Press, 1964, p. 302 and: Stefan Bengston, *Nature*, Vol. 345, 1990, p. 765.

4

Hinduism and Science

"Truth is my God."

—*Mahatma Gandhi*

Hinduism (known as *Hindu Dharma* in some modern Indian languages[1]) is a religion that originated on the Indian subcontinent. In contemporary usage Hinduism is also referred to as *Sanâtana Dharma* (सनातन धर्म), a Sanskrit phrase meaning "eternal law".[2]

During the fourth century B.C., Aryans—the same people that developed Greek culture—conquered much of present-day India. Their pantheon of gods, similar to that of the Greeks, combined with indigenous Indian traditions of meditation to form a loose combination of beliefs and practices that came to be known as Hinduism. "Orthodox" Hindus can be either pious worshippers of a god or atheists, self-negating ascetics or men of the world.[3]

The word *Hindu* is not a religious word. It is secular in origin. It is derived from the word *Sindhu*, which is the name of a major river that flows in the northwestern region of the Indian subcontinent. The ancient Greeks and Armenians used to refer the people living beyond the river Sindhu as Hindus and gradually the name struck. When the Muslims came to the subcontinent they called the people living in the region Hindustanis to distinguish them from the foreign Muslims. Subsequently when the British established their rule, they started referring to the local religions collectively under the name of Hinduism.[4]

The other point[5] that should be noted is that the word is neither Sanskrit nor Dravidian and did not originate in India. It was not used by Indians in their descriptions or writings till the seventeenth century.

If we go by the original definition of the word Hindu, anyone who lives in the subcontinent is a Hindu and whatever religion he or she practices is Hinduism. The word Hindu is secular word and literally translated it means Indian and the word Hinduism denotes any religion or religions that are practiced by the multitude of people living in the land beyond the river Indus.

Sometimes it was said that the Persian term *Hindu* comes from the Sanskrit *Sindhu*, i.e., the Indus River. In the *Rig Veda*, the Indo-Aryans mention their land as Sapta Sindhu (the land of the seven rivers of the northwestern Indian subcontinent, one of them being the Indus). This corresponds to Hapta-Hendu in the *Avesta* (Vendidad: Fargard 1.18)—the sacred scripture of Zoroastrianism of Iran. The term was used for people who lived in the Indian subcontinent beyond the "Sindhu."

With its origins in the Indus Valley Civilization and Vedic civilization, it has no known founder,[6] being itself a conglomerate of diverse beliefs and traditions. It is considered the world's oldest extant religion,[7] and has approximately a billion adherents, of whom about 890 million live in India,[8] placing it as the world's third largest religion after Christianity and Islam. Hinduism originates from the ancient Vedic tradition and other indigenous beliefs, incorporated over time. Prominent themes in Hinduism include Dharma (ethics and duties), Samskâra (The continuing cycle of birth, life, death and rebirth), *Karma* (action and subsequent reaction), and *Moksha* (liberation from the cycle of samskâra). Buddhism, Jainism and Sikhism share traits with Hinduism, because these religions originated in India and are created after Hinduism and focus on self-improvement with the general aim of attaining personal (first hand), spiritual experiences. They along with Hinduism are collectively known as *Dharmic* religions.

Hindu Philosophy

Like other religions, Hinduism has a special philosophy for itself and various schools. It divides into two main branches; *Astika* (Sanskrit: आस्तिक) and *Nastika* ("heterodox"). These are technical terms in Hinduism used to classify philosophical schools and persons, according to whether they accept the authority of the Vedas as supreme revealed scriptures, or not. By this definition, *Nyaya*, *Vaisheshika*, *Samkhya*, *Yoga*, *Purva Mimamsa* and *Vedanta* are classified as *astika* schools; while Charvaka, Jainism and Buddhism are considered *nastika* schools.[9] Hindu philosophy is divided into six orthodox schools of thought, or *darshanas*, listed below.

Philosophical Schools of Hinduism[10]

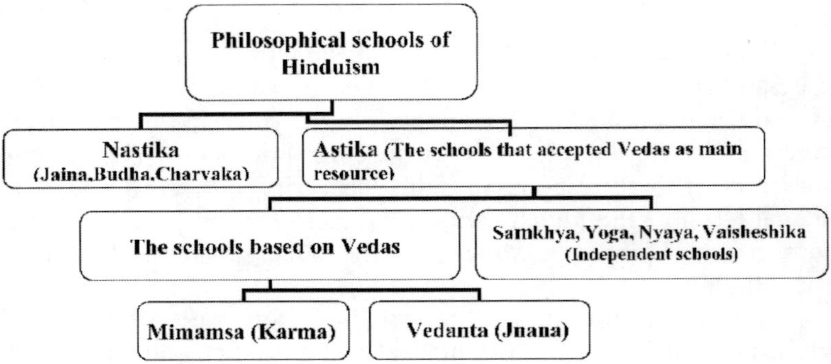

Fig. 4.1: The Philosophical Schools of Hinduism

A. Astika Schools

1. *Samkhya*
2. *Yoga*
3. *Nyaya*
4. *Vaisheshika*
5 *Purva Mimamsa*
6. Vedanta

These schools can be briefly described as follows:

1. Samkhya

Samkhya is one of the oldest of the orthodox philosophical systems in Hinduism. *Samkhya* postulates that everything in reality stems from *purusha* (Self or soul) and *prakriti* (matter, creative agency, energy). There are many souls and they possess consciousness, but they are devoid of all qualities. *Prakriti*/Matter consists of three dispositions: steadiness (*sattva*), activity (*rajas*), and dullness (*tamas*), known as the three *gunas* or qualities. Because of the intertwined relationship between the soul and these dispositions, an imbalance in disposition causes the world to evolve. Liberation occurs with the realization that the soul and the dispositions are different. *Samkhya* is a dualistic philosophy, but there are differences between *Samkhya* and other forms of dualism. In the West, dualism is between the mind and the body, whereas in *Samkhya* it is between the self and matter. The concept of the self is roughly equivalent to the Western concept of our consciousness. *Samkhya* was originally not theistic, but in confluence with *Yoga* it developed a theistic variant.

2. *Yoga*

Yoga is somewhat different from *Samkhya*. Its primary text is the *Bhagavad Gita*, which explores the four primary systems: *Karma Yoga, Raja Yoga, Jnana Yoga*, and *Bhakti Yoga*. In the *Bhagavad Gita* itself, *Yoga* is described as being many millions of years old, and is essentially a universal method of union with the Supreme. For many centuries *yoga* practitioners have debated about the specific nature of this Supreme (i.e., personal or non-personal), and according to the different traditions describe the Supreme as *Brahman*, *Paramatma*, or *Bhagavan* respectively.

The most significant difference from *Samkhya* is that *Yoga* incorporates the concept of a personal god, *Ishvara*, but also upholds *Ishvara* as the ideal upon which to meditate. This is either because *Ishvara* is the only aspect of the soul that has not become entangled with nature, or because *Ishvara* is the Supreme God himself (depending on one's point of view). *Yoga* also utilizes the concepts of *Brahman* and *Atman* found in the *Upanishads*, thus breaking from the *Samkhya* School by adopting concepts of Vedantic monism.

Yoga lays down elaborate prescriptions for gradually obtaining physical and mental control over the personal self. This grows until one's consciousness becomes aware of one's authentic self, or *atman*, as distinct from one's feelings, thoughts, and actions. Realisation of the goal of *Yoga* is known as *moksha, nirvana*, and *samadhi*, all of which hold that the *atman* is of the same quality as the infinite *Brahman*. Patanjali wrote an influential text on *Raja Yoga* entitled *Yoga Sutra* and is often quoted as an authority on the *Yoga* process.

3. *Nyaya*

The *Nyaya* school is based on the *Nyaya Sutras*. They were written by Aksapada Gautama, probably in the second century B.C. The most important contribution made by this school is its methodology. This methodology is based on a system of logic that has subsequently been adopted by the majority of the Indian schools. This is comparable to the relationship between Western science and philosophy, which was derived largely from Aristotelian logic.

Nevertheless, *Nyaya* was seen by its followers as more than logical in its own right. They believed that obtaining valid knowledge was necessary to gain release from suffering, and they took great pains to identify valid sources of knowledge and distinguish these from mere false opinions. According to *Nyaya*, there are exactly four sources of knowledge: perception, inference, comparison, and testimony. Knowledge obtained through each of these is either valid or invalid. *Nyaya* developed several criteria of validity. The later *Naiyanikas* gave logical proofs for the existence and uniqueness of *Ishvara* in response to Buddhism, which, at that time, was fundamentally non-theistic. An important later development in *Nyaya* was the system of *Navya-NyÄ* ya.*

4. Vaisheshika

The *Vaisheshika* school was founded by Kanada and postulates an atomic pluralism. All objects in the physical universe are reducible to certain types of atoms.

Although the *Vaisheshika* school developed independently from the *Nyaya*, the two eventually merged because of their closely related metaphysical theories. In its classical form, however, the *Vaisheshika* School differed from the *Nyaya* in one crucial respect: where *Nyaya* accepted four sources of valid knowledge, the *Vaisheshika* accepted only two, perception and inference.

5. Purva Mimamsa

The main objective of the *Purva Mimamsa* school was to establish the authority of the *Vedas*. Consequently, this school's most valuable contribution to Hinduism was its formulation of the rules of *Vedic* interpretation. Its adherents believe that one must have unquestionable faith in the *Vedas* and perform the *yajñas*, or fire-sacrifices, regularly. They believe in the power of the *mantras* and *yajñas* to sustain all the activity of the universe. In keeping with this belief, they place great emphasis on *dharma*, which consists of the performance of *Vedic* rituals.

The *Mimamsa* accepted the logical and philosophical teachings of the other schools, but felt they did not sufficiently emphasize attention to right action. They believed that the other schools of thought that aimed for release (*moksha*) did not allow for complete freedom from desire and selfishness, because the very striving for liberation stemmed from a simple desire to be free. According to *Mimamsa* thought, only by acting in accordance with the prescriptions of the *Vedas* may one attain salvation.

The *Mimamsa* school later shifted its views and began to teach the doctrines of *Brahman* and freedom. Its adherents then advocated the release or escape of the soul from its constraints through enlightened activity. Although *Mimamsa* does not receive much scholarly attention, its influence can be felt in the life of the practising Hindu, because all Hindu ritual, ceremony, and law are influenced by this school.

6. Vedanta

The *Vedanta*, or later *Mimamsa* school, concentrates on the philosophical teachings of the *Upanishads* rather than the ritualistic injunctions of the *Brahmanas*.

While the traditional *Vedic* rituals continued to be practised as meditative and propitiatory rites, a more knowledge-centred understanding began to emerge. These were ethical and aspects of *Vedic* religion that focused on meditation, self-discipline, and spiritual connectivity, more than traditional ritualism.

The more abstruse *Vedanta* is the essence of the *Vedas*, as encapsulated in the *Upanishads*. *Vedantic* thought drew on *Vedic* cosmology, hymns and philosophy. The *Brihadaranyaka Upanishad* appeared as far back as 3,500 years ago. While thirteen or so *Upanishads* are accepted as principal, over a hundred exist. The most significant contribution of *Vedantic* thought is the idea that self-consciousness is continuous with and indistinguishable from consciousness of *Brahman*.

The aphorisms of the *Vedanta sutras* are presented in a cryptic, poetic style, which allows for a variety of interpretations. Consequently, the *Vedanta* separated into six sub-schools, each interpreting the texts in its own way and producing its own series of sub-commentaries.

B. Nastika Schools

Astika is a Sanskrit adjective (and noun) that is derived from *Asti* ("it is or exists") meaning "believing" or "pious"; or "one who believes in the existence (of God, of another world, etc.)." *Nastika* [Na (not) + âstika] is its negative, literally meaning "not believing" or "not pious". As used in Indian philosophy *nastika* refers to non-belief in Vedic authority, not belief or lack of belief in theism[11].

As N.N. Bhattacharyya writes:

The followers of *Tantra* are often branded as *Nâstika* by the upholders of the *Vedic* tradition. The term Nâstika does not denote an atheist. It is applied only to those who do not believe in the *Vedas*. The Sâṅkhyas and Mīmâṃsakas do not believe in God, but they believe in the *Vedas* and hence they are not Nâstikas. The Buddhists, Jains, and Cârvâkas do not believe in the *Vedas*; hence they are Nâstikas.[12]

In non-technical usage, the term *astika* is sometimes loosely translated as "theist" while *nastika* is translated as "atheist".[13] However, this interpretation is distinct from the use of the term in Hindu philosophy. Notably even among the *astika* schools, *samkhya* and the early *mimamsa* school do not accept a God while accepting the authority of the *Vedas*; they thus are "atheistic *astika* schools".

The different usages of these terms are explained by Chatterjee and Datta as follows:

> "In modern Indian languages, 'âstika' and 'nâstika' generally mean 'theist' and 'atheist', respectively. But in Sanskrit philosophical literature, 'âstika' means 'one who believes in the authority of the *Vedas*' or 'one who believes in life after death'. (*Nâstika*' means the opposite of these). The word is used here in the first sense. In the second sense, even the Jaina and Buddha schools are 'âstika', as they believe in life after death. The six orthodox schools are '*âstika*', and the Cârvâka is '*nâstika*' in both the senses."[14]

The three main heterodox schools of Indian philosophy do not base their beliefs on Vedic authority:

- Buddhism
- Jainism
- Cârvâka

The use of the term nâstika to describe Buddhism and Jainism in India is explained by Gavin Flood as follows:

At an early period, during the formation of the *Upanishads* and the rise of Buddhism and Jainism, we must envisage a common heritage of meditation and mental discipline practiced by renounces with varying affiliations to non-orthodox (*Veda*-rejecting) and orthodox (*Veda*-accepting) traditions. These schools [such as Buddhism and Jainism] are understandably regarded as heterodox (*nâstika*) by orthodox (*âstika*) Brahmanism.[15] So far if we want to discuss all divisions, we may miss the main subject (the relationship between religion and modern science), we will discuss the viewpoints of the subject of some great modern thinkers of the *Vedanta* school:

1. Swami Vivekananda
2. Mahatma Gandhi
3. Sarvepalli Radhakrishnan

Vivekananda was a renowned thinker in his own right. One of his key contributions was to demonstrate how *Advaitin* thinking is not merely philosophically far-reaching, but also has social, and even political consequences. Everyone of the twentieth century Indian leaders of note have acknowledged his influence, from Gandhi to Subhas Bose. Mahatma Gandhi is universally acknowledged as the greatest man of his age. His greatness came from the realm of spirit, his influence and unparallel leadership from his universal love and faith in mankind. Radhakrishnan, like Gandhi, occupied a unique position of distinction and eminence in the national life of India. He was an exceptionally brilliant writer, spell-binding orator and above all a Master of Wisdom.

The earliest poetry of India already contains many traces of the essential character of the philosophy of India. In nothing indeed does the continuity of Indian life show itself more strikingly than this: the gods of India change, but the alteration of the higher thought is far less marked.

Philosophy in India shows that its beginnings are often in the expression of skepticism: the normal belief in the gods here and there seems to have been questioned and it is not unnatural that the questioning should have arisen in the case of the most human of the gods, him whom the seers most closely fashioned in their own likeness, the vehement Indra. Hindus are distinctly told that there were men who asked, 'Who is Indra, whoever saw him?' or asserted that he did not exist at all. There were, they learn, faithless men, who did not believe in the gods of the *Brahmans* and did not—perhaps a worse thing—give the priests their fees for sacrifice, men who did not believe in Indra.

Hindu Theories of Creation

In Hindu philosophy, the existence of the universe is governed by the *Trimurti* of *Brahma* (the Creator), *Vishnu* (the Sustainer) and *Shiva* (the Destroyer).

The sequence of *Avatars* of *Vishnu* the *Dasavatara* (Sanskrit: *Dasa* = ten, Avatara = incarnation) is generally accepted by most Hindus today as correlating well with Darwin's theory of evolution, the first *Avatar* generating from the environment of water.

Hindus thus do not see much conflict between creation and evolution. An additional reason for this could also be the Hindu concept of cyclic time, such as *yugas*, or days of *Brahma* in approximately 4.3 billion year cycles (unlike the concept of linear time in many other religions). In fact, time is represented as *Kaala Chakra*—the Wheel of Time.

In Hinduism, nature and all of God's creations are manifestations of Him. He is within and without his creations, pervading the entire universe and also observing it externally. Hence, all animals and humans have a divine element in them that is covered by the ignorance and illusions of material or profane existence.

What makes this creation? *Brahman*. There is no suitable word for this in English. He is eternal, eternally pure, eternally awake, the almighty, the all-knowing, the all-merciful, the omnipresent, the formless, and the partless. If this is so, then why is there partiality in the world? Why is one person happy and another unhappy? Who makes it? *Vedanta* says: We ourselves. There is a cloud shedding its rain on all fields alike. But it is the field that is well cultivated is the one that takes the best advantage of it. The fault is not in the cloud. The mercy of God is eternal and unchangeable. It is we who make the difference. We reap what we have sown in several previous births.

According to the *Rig Veda* the One Supreme God did not create the Universe by fashioning it from preexisting material, but transformed himself into the Universe.

In earlier *Vedic* thinking, the universe was created by

Hiranyagarbha (here interpreted as 'the golden embryo') or by *Prajapati* who was born from the *Hiranyagarbha* (here interpreted as 'the golden womb'). *Prajapati* was later identified with the *puranic Brahma*. Other gods are credited with acts of creation, primarily the act of propping apart the sky and the Earth-gods who are said to have done this include *Indra*, *Varuna* and *Vishnu*.

Another myth which began in late *Rig-Vedic* times with the *Purusha Sukta* hymn was the story of the creation of the universe from the remains of the primaeval cosmic male *Purusha*, who had sacrificed himself or been sacrificed by other primaeval beings (not the most popular *Vedic* gods because they were said to have been born from *Purusha* after the sacrifice) at the *Purushamedha yajna*.

According to the *Upanishads*, the universe is a manifestation of God. All matter contains innate divinity and evolution is the process of realizing that divinity. The *Upanishads* discuss creation at a philosophical level, quite different from some of the hymns of the *Rig Veda* and also different from the narratives of creation in the later *Puranas*. The fundamental point is that life or consciousness cannot evolve from matter unless matter has the innate potential to provide life and consciousness. Similarly Divine Bliss cannot be the end of evolution unless it is present in the beginning, even if not in a manifest form. Evolution proceeds by the removal of obstruction to move to a higher plane. Hence life, consciousness and divinity are innate in all matter. When the obstruction to life is removed, matter takes the form of living beings. When the obstruction to consciousness is removed, matter takes the forms of animals. When the obstruction to reasoning is removed, matter takes the forms of humans. When the obstruction to divinity is removed humans realize their divine aspect.[16]

According to Hindu Mythology, creation happened gradually. The universe in primitive form was made up of *Ishwar Tattva*, primarily spread homogeneously throughout the universe.

The Hindu tradition perceives the existence of the cyclical nature of the universe and everything within it. The cosmos follows one cycle within a framework of cycles. It may have been created and reached an end, but it represents only one turn in the perpetual "wheel of time", which revolves infinitely through successive cycles of creation and destruction. Within this cycle of creation and destruction of the universe, the soul (*atman*) also undergoes its own version of cycle called *samsara*, the cycle of rebirth in which individual souls are repeatedly reincarnated.

"In the beginning there was neither existence nor non-existence; there was no atmosphere, no sky, and no realm beyond the sky. What power was there? Where was that power? Who was that power? Was it finite or infinite?

There was neither death nor immortality. There was nothing to distinguish night from day. There was no wind or breath. God alone breathed by his own energy. Other than God there was nothing.

In the beginning darkness was swathed in darkness. All was liquid and formless. God was clothed in emptiness.

Then fire arose within God; and in the fire arose love. This was the seed of the soul. Sages have found this seed within their hearts; they have discovered that it is the bond between existence and non-existence.

Who really knows what happened? Who can describe it? How were things produced? Where was creation born? When the universe was created, the one became many. Who knows how this occurred?

Did creation happen at God's command, or did it happen without his command? He looks down upon creation from the highest heaven. Only he knows the answer—or perhaps he does not know."[17]

On the other hand, the authors of *Upanishads* struggled with this question of origins. Ultimately, they contended that the source of creation is profoundly unknowable.

The universe is often said to be born from the sacred syllable *Om*, or from an inert void in which "there was neither being nor non-being death nor non-death", a single principle from which emerged the diversity of life. From this void desire was born, and from desire came humans, gods and demons.

"Those who deny God, deny themselves. Those who affirm God, affirm themselves.

"God said: 'Let me multiply! Let me have offspring!' So he heated himself up; and when he was hot, he emitted the entire world, and all that it contains.

"And after emitting the world, he entered it. He who has no body, assumed many bodies. He, who is infinite, became finite. He, who is everywhere, went to particular places. He, who is totally wise, caused ignorance. He who sees all truth, caused delusion. God becomes every being, and gives reality to every being.

"Before the world was created, God existed, but was invisible. By means of the soul all living beings can know God; and this knowledge fills them with joy. The soul is the source of abiding joy. When we discover the soul in the depths of our consciousness, we

are overwhelmed with delight. If the soul did not live within us, then we should not breathe—we should not live.

"The soul is one. The soul is changeless, nameless, and formless. Until we understand the soul, we live in fear. Scholars may study the soul through words; but unless they know the soul within themselves, their scholarship merely emphasizes their ignorance, and increases their fear."[18]

But sometimes it was said that often there is a bad mix-up of science and religion. For example, astrology is included in Hindu scriptures, and some leading astrologers regard astrology as scientific.

Swami Vivekananda[19]

In the *Bhagavad Gita* Krishna says, "Whenever virtue declines and evil increases, I incarnate myself to rescue the holy, to destroy evil and to establish righteousness".[20]

1. Vivekananda, Religion and Science

History shows that from time to time world teachers have arisen who have done just this. Swami Vivekananda was such a world teacher. He believed that there existed no conflict between Hinduism and science; because he knew that the conflict in the West between religion and science was one of the main issues of the day. Such a conflict should have been resolved, but could not be except on the basis of an all inclusiveness such as that exhibited by Hinduism.

He then said that Hinduism is based on the revelations of the *Vedas*, an idea that sounds like the Christian belief in the *Bible* as divine revelation, but he went on to say that the *Vedas* are not books but are immutable spiritual laws like the laws discovered by Western science. Here described the meaning of divine laws revealed to the spiritual seers in terms of the Western belief in the universal and timeless laws discovered by science. Note that he is not repudiating or belittling science, but rather is using it to show that science and religion are harmonious, in that both are engaged in the discovery of immutable laws that exist beyond limited time and space. This was an appeal to the scientific West to accept Oriental religion on the same basis as it accepted science: experimental proof. Thus, in one deft stroke he destroyed the Western idea that science and religion are necessarily at war with one another.[21]

According to Vivekananda, the union of science and religion will bring harmony and peace to the humanity. He accepts unselfish moral goodness to be the test of religion. According to him the various religions that exist in the world, although they differ in the form of worship they take, are really one.

2. Vivekananda and Creation and Science

According to the ancient Vedantic philosophy *atman* or the life force moves from one *yoni* or level of organization to another. In stories of *Panchtantra* and Aesop's Fables human qualities were attributed to animals.

In the Middle Ages, when religion dominated Man's thinking, he regarded himself as a superior being, far superior to other living forms. Gods were humanized. In the Christian scripture it was said that God had created Man out of his own image.

In about the middle of the last century an important event took place in the scientific world; Charles Darwin, in his book *Origin of Species* (1859) offered us the concept of organic evolution as a scientific theory. According to this theory living forms are not static; they change with the passage of time in order to become better adapted to the existing conditions. When this happens in populations of the same species, living in different areas with somewhat different conditions, this may lead to the populations becoming, in due course, different and new species. Similar views had been expressed by some biologists and thinkers before Darwin, but Darwin was the first to put forth these views adequately supported by a large mass of evidence.

The publication of Darwin's "Origin of Species" has been described as the most important event and a turning point in the history of Biology. The concept of evolution became generally accepted among people of science, following the publication of the book, and in the next few years the entire science of biology underwent a rapid remoulding on the basic theme of organic evolution.

Swamiji opened up this insoluble paradox of how God, who is eternal, could have created the world at a particular time, by saying that according to Hinduism, creation is that which is cyclic and never begins or ends, but, from the point of view of time, continues like a revolving wheel for ever, with its *Kalpas* or aeons for ever succeeding one another. Time is thus shown as one with eternity, as eternity perceived in bits, as it were, not something separate from it. In all this Swamiji is not really refuting Western beliefs but enlarging them to infinity.[22]

He then said that the human being is not the body but the spirit, a statement that agrees with the Christian teaching, a teaching which was all but forgotten under the avalanche of materialism that was burying the West. He went on to say that the soul is immortal, which means, according to Hinduism, that the soul is not only deathless but birthless as well. This destroys the barriers erected by Western orthodoxy against the prenatal eternity of the soul, thus giving the soul an all-dimensional immortality instead of a one-way immortality—as does the traditional Western view which says that the soul is created by God at the conception of the body.

It seems that, Vivekananda used the West's intensive involvement in the development of science to show how the Infinite alone is the true individuality and the true reality. He said that science reveals that matter is one unbroken ocean, and that the so-called individual body is a delusion. What I call "my body is simply a wave or a bubble in that ocean; through it flows the whole material universe. It has no real boundaries either. Then he made the point he later expanded upon many times. Science, he said, is the search for unity by sorting out particulars into classes, and smaller classes into larger classes. So science consists in the search for and the finding of unity. But why stop before ultimate unity is reached?, he asks. Religion is the search for ultimate unity or God. He did not say that one should stop being scientific. Instead, he said one should carry science to its logical conclusion and reach the final unity of all, the Absolute One, which is the goal of all sciences and all religions.

Since Swamiji spoke these words in 1893, modern scientists in their search for unity have produced results that bear out the mystical view of the final unity of all beings. Einstein's Relativity Theory and his Unified Field Theory[23] broke down many barriers of belief that had previously appeared to separate various phenomena that are not really separate.

Fritjof Capra, professor of physics at the University of California at Berkeley, has shown the harmony he believes exists between Eastern religions and modern physics in his book *The Tao of Physics*. In an article of the same title published in the *Prabuddha Bharata* magazine of March 1979, Dr. Capra summarizes his views. Thus, we can see that science, using scientific methods, is getting closer and closer to the universal unity behind phenomena as it was urged to do by Swamiji in 1893.[24]

Mahatma Gandhi[25]

1. Gandhi and Religion

Mahatma Gandhi, as a great leader, recognized the major religions of the world as historical and cultural phenomena.

Though the meaning of religion in the Hindu concept of *dharma* is not without complexities, Gandhi tried to make it broad enough to lend it a universal character. His idea of religion was not totally esoteric. He knew that every religion was connected with some belief system supported by rituals. He tried to get rid of the rituals as far as possible. To Gandhi, religion was a human institution made by human ingenuity to solve practical affairs as well as spiritual matters.[26]

He said: "By religion, I do not mean formal religion, or customary religion, but that religion which underlies all religions, which brings us face to face with our Maker. It is the permanent element in human nature which counts no cost too great in order to find full expression and which leaves the soul utterly restless until it has found itself. Again, he observed: Religion which takes no account of practical affairs and does not help to solve them, is no religion. He did not define religion in exact and definitive language. One of his attempts was to bring religion closer to common man. In this regard his approach was functional. But most of the times Gandhi felt that religion could not be understood without knowing its relation with God.

Mahatma also believed that real religion that transcends all these religions should pervade everyone of our actions. Here religion does not mean sectarianism. It means a belief in ordered moral government of the universe. It is not less real because it is unseen. This religion transcends Hinduism, Islam, Christianity, etc. It does not supersede them. It harmonises them and gives them reality.

Gandhi's perspective of religion was entirely different from that of others. In the past, *dharma* was considered as one of the societal values. He insisted on the praxis of religion to the extent of saying: "I have come to this fundamental conclusion that if you want something really important to be done, you must not merely satisfy reason, you must move the heart also. The appeal of reason is more to the head but the penetration of the heart comes from suffering. It opens up the inner understanding in man". For him, religion and morality are inseparable. Politics bereft of religion is absolute dirt, even to be shunned.

Although Gandhi is a firm believer of God, he is not a speculative metaphysician. For him spiritual life is the same as unselfish ethical life and to realize God, to realize Truth, i.e., the true ultimate goal of life, is the same as to realize ethical perfection. For him, Truth is the ultimate goal and non-violence is means. Gandhi accepts the supremacy of reason: Scriptures cannot transcend reason and truth. They are intended to purify reason and illuminate truth. He would not accept any interpretation of scriptures which conflicts with reason. He would consider such a view to be a false interpretation or an interpolation in the scripture. Since scientific beliefs are empirically well justified, Gandhi would not accept any interpretation of a scripture when conflicts with science. Contrary to popular belief, he is not against science and technology, but he would not accept any use of science and technology which conflicts with morality. He also said, "I would reject all authority if it is in conflict with sober reason or the dictates of the heart. Authority sustains and ennobles the weak when it is the handiwork of reason, but it degrades them when it supplants reason sanctified by the still small voice within. He says further: "Scriptures cannot transcend reason and truth. They are intended to purify reason and illuminate truth. Error can claim no exemption even if it can be supported by the scriptures of the world. An error does not become truth by reason of multiplied propagation, nor does truth become error because nobody sees it."[27]

According to Gandhi, the whole gamut of man's activities constitutes an indivisible whole; it must be inspired by one's religious faith, a faith in God, and living in the presence of God, it means faith in a future life in Truth and *Ahimsa*. After long study and experience he concluded that all religions are true. All religions have some error in them. All religions are almost as dear to him as his own close relatives. He also believed that all religions are God-given and, therefore, stressed the necessity of religion. He compares the atheist and agnostic to 'a man saying that he breathes but that he has no nose.' Vows and observances taken in his religion not only facilitate the spiritual progress of the individual but also harmonious community living on the basis of spirituality, mutual help, and collective salvation. Hence, removal of evils, inequalities, and injustices becomes part of one's own religious duties. Thus, his entire view of religion is an integrated one. Beyond these particular forms there is the religion of humanity, which is reflected as faith in the moral order. This religious belief, Gandhi held, is common to all particular religions. He said: "The soul of religions is one, but it is encased in a multitude of forms." For him, the moral order which governs the universe is *satya* and the process by which life is continued is *ahimsa*. All religions are nothing but appropriations of *satya* under the condition of cultural limitation and human finitude. Thus, religions as cultural and historical phenomena are more or less true. They are equal in the sense that no single religion has the absolute or exclusive truth. He said: "Religions are different roads converging on the same point. What does it matter that we take different roads as long as we reach the same goal? In reality, there are as many religions as there are individuals."

According to Gandhi, true religion is not narrow dogma. It is not external observance. It is faith in God and living in the presence of God, it means faith in a future life, in truth and *ahimsa*. He understood the fact that religion is a binding force which ultimately calls "to accelerate the process of realization of fundamental unity. He gives a simile of a faithful husband who would love no other woman. Even her faithlessness would not wean him from his faith. The bond is more than blood relationship, so is the religious bond if it is worth anything. It is a matter of the heart.[28]

Gandhian philosophy is not only at the same time political, moral and religious; it is also traditional and modern, simple and complex. It embodies numerous Western influences to which Gandhi was exposed, but being rooted in ancient Indian culture and harnessing eternal and universal moral and religious principles, there is much in it that is not at all new. This is why Gandhi could say: "I have nothing new to teach the world. Truth and non-violence are as old as the hills". Gandhi is concerned even more with the spirit than with the form. If the spirit is consistent with truth and non-violence, the truthful and non-violent form will automatically result. In Gandhi's thought the emphasis is not on idealism, but on practical idealism. It is rooted in the highest religious idealism, but is thoroughly practical.[29]

2. *Gandhi and Marx and Religion*

Sometimes, in Hindustan, people say that Karl Marx was a great admirer of India. He wrote a number of books (*The British Rule in*

India, The First War of Independence, and *Notes on Indian History*) and a large number of articles on India and the British rule. He is the first person to call the so-called Sepoy Mutiny of 1857 the First War of Independence of India. Marx's admiration and sympathy for India are reflected in his writing when he compared India to Italy, one of the two (Greece being the other) foundations of European civilization. He wrote:

"Hindustan is an Italy of Asiatic dimensions, the Himalayas for the Alps, the Plains of Bengal for the Plains of Lombardy, the Deccan for the Apennines, and the Isle of Ceylon for the Island of Sicily. The same rich variety in the products of the soil and the same dismemberment in the political configuration."[30]

Dr. Dipak Basu wrote also: "It is unknown in India, but Karl Marx and Swami Vivekananda had similar views on the historical cycle of the world. According to Marx the world history has four cycles starting with primitive communism of tribal societies, then feudalism, capitalism and ultimately socialism followed by advanced communism. For Marx, history is deterministic; these cycles are bound to happen due to the contradictions or dialectics in the existing system? In Karl Marx, changes occur in society because of contradictions in the prevailing ideology, in its social, economic and political order. These contradictions arise from hostilities between the social classes."[31]

Swami Vivekananda similarly divided world history into four cycles, starting with the Age of the Priests, Age of the Warriors, and Age of the Merchants as we are now in and ultimately the Age of the Worker, which is coming. With each cycle, society rises to higher and still higher stages and is perfected.[32]

Religion has historically played important roles in most civilizations; hence it is worthwhile to consider it in some depth, although it has several functions. In Gandhi's view all religions are practical ways towards truth (*satya*). The twin cardinal principles of Gandhi's thought are truth and non-violence. It should be remembered that the English word "truth" is an imperfect translation of the Sanskrit, "*satya*", and "non-violence", an even more imperfect translation of "*ahimsa*". Derived from "*sat*"—that which exists—"*satya*" contains a dimension of meaning not usually associated by English speakers with the word "truth". The absolute truth is the Ultimate Reality and this ultimate truth is God (as God is also Truth) and morality—the moral laws and code—its basis. *Ahimsa*, far from meaning mere peacefulness or the absence of overt violence, is understood by Gandhi to denote active love—the polar opposite of violence, or "*himsa*", in every sense.[33] Gandhi's philosophy has much in common with several Western philosophies which uphold the ideal of a more just and equitable society. For example, the Gandhian social order has been described as "communism minus violence". However, Marxists have traditionally rejected Gandhi because of what they regard as his "bourgeois" outlook. Gandhi rejected violent class conflict and the centralization of political and economic power in the hands of the State as counterproductive to the development of a non-violent society. Nevertheless, Gandhian philosophy, particularly in the Sarvodaya ideal, does contain many socialist sentiments. In fact, such an entity as Gandhian Socialism emerged in theoretical literature during the 1970s and 1980s. Gandhi's thought has also been likened to Utopian Socialism and Philosophical Anarchism, and can be compared with strands of Maoist thought (though not a Western philosophy), and even Western liberal thought. However, Gandhism is incompatible with many aspects of Liberalism and is virtually entirely incompatible with the modern, intensely competitive, ecologically destructive and materialistic capitalism of the West.

The ultimate station Gandhi assigns non-violence stems from two main points. First, if according to the Divine Reality all life is one, then all violence committed towards another is violence towards oneself, towards the collective, whole self, and thus "self"-destructive and counter to the universal law of life, which is love.

Second, Gandhi believed that *ahimsa* is the most powerful force in existence. Had *himsa* been superior to *ahimsa*, humankind would long ago have succeeded in destroying itself. The human race certainly could not have progressed as far as it has, even if universal justice remains far off on the horizon. From both viewpoints, non-violence or love is regarded as the highest law of humankind.

Religion's ugly role as a tool of oppression has led to much apathy, even prompting some people to conclude that religion is intrinsically bad. Religion is the opiate of the masses, declared Karl Marx.

It is necessary to say that we consider in this part of our search, about Gandhi and Marx as social subjects who have some points about religions themselves and not as political subject, but in the researcher's opinion Gandhi does not respect politics without religion as he said: "For me there is no politics without religion—not the religion of the superstitious and the blind, religion that hates and fights, but the universal religion of toleration. Politics without morality is a thing to be avoided.[34]

Gandhi as a philosopher may have viewpoint about the creation of man, as we know according to Hindus' scriptures creation of man cannot follow randomly. Hindus believe that there is no end or beginning to God and His Creation. God creates and destroys this Universe in a cyclical pattern. The creation and destruction repeated in a cycle of four *yugas* (eras).[35]

Dr. Sarvepalli Radhakrishnan[36]

In private conversation Dr. Radhakrishnan used to say that three great men made a deep impression on his life and thinking – Rabindranath Tagore, Vivekananda and Gandhi. And among these three, he was profoundly influenced by Mahatma Gandhi. Within a few years Radhakrishnan felt that Gandhi was undoubtedly the greatest and the noblest man in the contemporary world. Once Radhakrishnan asked Gandhi three questions:

1. What is your religion?
2. How are you led to it?
3. What is its bearing on life?

Gandhi replied "I believe in God", now I say, "I believe in Truth". "God is truth", that is what I was saying and today I say, "Truth is God". There are people who deny God. There are no people who deny Truth.

In the concluding portion of Radhakrishnan 'Introduction' he made the following tribute:

> "Gandhiji is the immortal symbol of love and understanding in a world wild with hatred and torn by misunderstanding. He belongs to the ages, to history."

This issue that is sacred in the minds of some and evil in others must be discussed openly. Not questioning religion has brought certain secrecy about them. That is the root of our problems. According to thinkers like Robert Ingersoll, Dr. Radhakrishnan, Karl Marx and many others, religion requires more discussion and research. To reveal the truth we should ask questions; the question is why do we have no permission (sometimes) to ask about religion? We have no platform to stand on. Question is that the first platform of freedom and the first cry by a new born baby is the real Freedom that is born with the baby and that should not be silenced.

1. Radhakrishnan and Religion

Radhakrishnan's hierarchy of religions is well-known. "Hinduism," he affirms, "accepts all religious notions as facts and arranges them in the order of their more or less intrinsic significance": "The worshippers of the Absolute are the highest in rank; second to them are the worshippers of the personal God; then come the worshippers of the incarnations like Rama, Krishna, Buddha; below them are those who worship ancestors, deities and sages, and the lowest of all are the worshippers of the petty forces and spirits."

It seems that Dr. Radhakrishnan in contrast to Marx, believes in religion as a whole, and as a system that can help men and societies to solve their problems. Several diverse religions and cultures have been the tributaries of the mighty river of Indian civilization. All religions of the world find a place under the Indian sun. India is home to all faiths and beliefs. Diverse religions and cultures lend man unique richness, so he must nurture these traditions and values and endeavour to build a healthy understanding and harmony among people of different religious denominations.

It seems that we ought to educate our children about the richness of our diverse religions and cultures so that they imbibe the values of tolerance of diversity and respect for all religions. The seeds of such a value system planted in young minds, will in due course grow into mighty trees with deep and strong roots to sustain for ever our way of life in peace and harmony. All the religions practiced in our country have one core essence: that of universal tolerance and that all religions are true.

The philosopher-President, Dr. Radhakrishnan said:

> I quote, "secularism does not mean irreligion. It means we respect all faiths and religions. Our State does not identify itself with any particular religion."

It means that all religions aim to elevate the spiritual and moral foundations of people, make a person a better human being, and enlighten him to pursue the path of virtue and thus attain sublime goals of life. Indeed, religion has always had great influence on people. This power of religions needs to be harnessed and canalized and directed towards achieving the goals of national development. Religion should be an effective instrument to guide human behaviour and conduct to achieve social reforms, social integration and social harmony.

Religion should inspire us to serve the poor and the deprived so as to improve their lot. To be religious should also mean being motivated and committed to the objective of uplift of the needy and the downtrodden. The goal of promoting welfare of the common man needs to be at the centre-stage of all religion-guided actions.

Radhakrishnan's distinction between "religion" and "religions" will be helpful here. At its most basic, religions, for Radhakrishnan, represent the various interpretations of experience, while integral experience is the essence of all religions. "If experience is the soul of religion, expression is the body through which it fulfils its destiny. We have the spiritual facts and their interpretations by which they are communicated to others."

"It is the distinction between immediacy and thought. Intuitions abide, while interpretations change." But the interpretations should not be confused with the experiences themselves.

For Dr. Radhakrishnan, the creeds and theological formulations of religion are but intellectual representations and symbols of experience. "The idea of God," Dr. Radhakrishnan affirms, "is an interpretation of experience."

For Dr. Radhakrishnan, the context of religious experiences is relative and, therefore, imperfect. They are informed by and experienced through specific cultural, historical, linguistic and religious lenses. Because of their contextuality and subsequent intellectualization, experiences in the religious sphere are limited. It is in this sense that we may refer to experiences which occur under the auspices of one or other of the religions as "religious experiences". Dr. Radhakrishnan spends little time dealing with "religious experiences" as they occur in specific religious traditions. And what little he does say is used to demonstrate the theological preconditioning and "religious" relativity of such experiences. However, "religious experiences" have value for Dr. Radhakrishnan in so far as they offer the possibility of heightening one's religious consciousness and bringing one into ever closer proximity to "religious intuition".

Dr. Radhakrishnan is explicit and emphatic in his view that religious intuition is a unique form of experience. Religious intuition is more than simply the confluence of the cognitive, aesthetic, and ethical sides of life. However, vital and significant these sides of life may be, they are but partial and fragmented constituents of a greater whole, a whole which is experienced in its fullness and immediacy in religious intuition.

For instance on Buddhism, Dr. Radhakrishnan says: "When we pass from the *Upanishads* to early Buddhism we pass from a work of many minds to the considered creed of a single individual. In the *Upanishads*, we have an amazing study of an atmosphere, in Buddhism the concrete embodiment of thought in the life of a man. This unity of thought and life worked wonderfully on the world of the time. The singular personality and life of Buddha had much to do with the success of early Buddhism."[37]

To Dr. Radhakrishnan's mind, religious intuition is not only an autonomous form of experience, but a form of experience which informs and validates all spheres of life and experience. Philosophical, artistic, and ethical values of truth, beauty, and goodness are not known through the senses or by reason. Rather, "they are apprehended by intuition or faith." (IVL 199-200). For Dr. Radhakrishnan, religious intuition informs, conjoins, and transcends an otherwise fragmentary consciousness.

Informing Dr. Radhakrishnan's interpretation of religious intuition is his affirmation of the identity of the self and ultimate reality. Throughout his life, Dr. Radhakrishnan interpreted the *Upanisadic* mahavakya, *tat tvam asi*, as a declaration of the non-duality (*advaita*) of *Atman* and *Brahman*. His *advaitic* interpretation allows him to affirm the ineffability of the truth behind the formula. Dr. Radhakrishnan readily appropriates his acceptance of the non-dual experience to his interpretation of religious intuition. Dr. Radhakrishnan not only claimed to find support for his views in the *Upanishads*, but believed that, correctly understood, the ancient sages expounded his interpretation of religious intuition. Any attempt at interpretation of the intuition could only approximate the truth of the experience itself. As the ultimate realization, religious intuition must not only account for and bring together all other forms of experience, but must overcome the distinctions between them. Dr. Radhakrishnan goes so far as to claim that intuition of this sort is the essence of religion. All religions are informed by it, though all fail in varying degrees to interpret it. "Here we find the essence of religion, which is a synthetic realization of life. The religious man has the knowledge that everything is significant, the feeling that there is harmony underneath the conflicts and the power to realize the significance and the harmony."

With this, the present discussion of intuition and the varieties of experience has come full circle. Dr. Radhakrishnan identifies intuition—in all its contextual varieties—with integral experience. The two expressions are, for Dr. Radhakrishnan, synonymous. Integral experience coordinates and synthesizes the range of life's experiences. It furnishes the individual with an ever-deepening awareness of and appreciation for the unity of Reality. As an intuition, integral experience is not only the basis of all experience but the source of all creative ingenuity, whether such innovation is philosophical, scientific, moral, artistic, or religious. Moreover, not only does integral experience find expression in these various spheres of life, but such expression, Dr. Radhakrishnan believes, quickens the intuitive and creative impulse among those it touches.

2. Dr. Radhakrishnan and the Darwinian Theory

Based on these ideas, we may conclude that Dr. Radhakrishnan, like Gandhi, could not accept Marx's view about religions because they strongly believe that religions can be used for solving social problems and for development.

Nature and all of God's creations are manifestations of Him. He is within and without his creations, pervading the entire universe and also observing it externally. Hence, all animals and humans have a divine element in them that is covered by the ignorance and illusions of material or profane existence.

Dr. Radhakrishnan in his books[38] (Indian philosophy) has examined the views of many schools of Indian thought on various issues. He concluded that throughout the history of Indian thought, the idea of a world behind the ordinary world of human strivings as more real and more intangible, which is the true home of the spirit, has been haunting the Indian race.[39]

Summary of Chapter Four

- The word "Hindu" originally meant those who lived on the other side of the river Indus (in Sanskrit, '*Sindhu*'). Alternate names for the people following the religion can be '*Vaidikas*', followers of the *Vedas*, or '*Vedantists*', followers of the *Vedanta*. So, let us have a brief overview of the *Vedas*.

- According to Hinduism, nature and all of God's creations are manifestations of Him. He is within and without his creations, pervading the entire universe and also observing it externally. Hence, all animals and humans have a divine element in them that is covered by the ignorance and illusions of material or profane existence.
- According to the *Upanishads,* the universe is a manifestation of God. All matter contains innate divinity and evolution is the process of realizing that divinity. The *Upanishads* discuss creation at a philosophical level, quite different from some of the hymns of the *Riga Veda* and also different from the narratives of creation in the later *Puranas*.
- It discussed the viewpoints of three of the greatest thinkers of the *Vedanta* school on the subject: Vivekananda, Mahatma Gandhi, Dr. Sarvepalli Radhakrishnan and their viewpoint about religion and Marx's view and creation and evolution.
- Swami Vivekananda, believed that there is no conflict between Hinduism and Science. He held that the conflict in the West between religion and science was one of the main issues of the day, a conflict which must be resolved, but could not be except on the basis of an all inclusiveness such as that exhibited by Hinduism.
- Vivekananda believed that the union of science and religion will bring harmony and peace to humanity.
- Though the meaning of religion in the Hindu concept of *Dharma* is not without complexities, Gandhi tried to make it broad enough to lend it a universal character. His idea of religion was not totally esoteric, therefore, Gandhi's perspective of religion was entirely different from that of others. Although Gandhi is a firm believer of God, he is not a speculative metaphysician. For him spiritual life is the same as unselfish ethical life and to realize God, to realize Truth, i.e., the true ultimate goal of life, is the same as to realize ethical perfection. For him, Truth is the ultimate goal and non-violence is the means.
- Marxists have traditionally rejected Gandhi because of what they regard as his "bourgeois" outlook. Gandhi rejected violent class conflict and the centralization of political and

economic power in the hands of the State as counterproductive to the development of a non-violent society.

- Gandhi as a philosopher may have some viewpoints about man's creation, as we know according to Hindus' scriptures creation of man cannot follow random or something like that. The Hindus believe that there is no end or beginning to God and His Creation.
- Dr. Radhakrishnan's hierarchy of religions is well-known. "Hinduism," he affirms, "accepts all religious notions as facts and arranges them in the order of their more or less intrinsic significance".
- It would seem that Dr. Radhakrishnan, in contrast to Marx, believes in religions as a whole, and as a system that can help men and societies solve their problems.
- We may say that Dr. Radhakrishnan as a Hindu and grand philosopher, affirms what the Hindu scriptures revealed. Hindu tradition perceives the existence of cyclical nature of the universe and everything within it. The cosmos follows one cycle within a framework of cycles. He believed that nature and all of God's creations are manifestations of God. He is within and without his creations, pervading the entire universe and also observing it externally. Hence, all animals and humans have a divine element in them that is covered by the ignorance and illusions of material or profane existence, so he could not accept the theory of evolution or any others that contradict the scriptures.
- Hindu thought has no concept of the creation of the universe, assuming that everything—the universe, God, scripture and humanity—has existed without beginning. Within this view is the idea of cycles of creation with relative beginnings. Each cycle begins from a pre-existent seed state, grows, flowers, withers and dies. But, just as a dying flower leaves seeds for its own propagation, each cycle drops a seed which begins the next state.[40]

FOOTNOTES

1. Such as Hindi, Bengali and other contemporary Indo-Aryan languages, as well as in several Dravidian tongues like Tamil and Kannada. The

word "Hindu" comes from the name of the river Indus, which flows 1800 miles from Tibet through Kashmir and Pakistan to the sea.

2. Ed. John Bowker, *The Concise Oxford Dictionary of World Religions*. Oxford University Press, 2000; The term can be traced to late nineteenth century Hindu reform movements (J. Zavos, *Defending Hindu Tradition: Sanatana Dharma as a Symbol of Orthodoxy in Colonial India*, Religion (Academic Press), Volume 31, Number 2, April 2001, pp. 109-123; see also R.D. Baird, "Swami Bhaktivedanta and the Encounter with Religions," *Modern Indian Responses to Religious Pluralism*, edited by Harold Coward, State University of New York Press, 1987).
3. Word Religions Index, See: wri.leaderu.com/wri-table2/hinduism.html.
4. See: www.vishnumandir.com/htm/meaning.htm.
5. *Aum* is the main symbol of Hinduism. It is the sound heard in deepest meditation and is said to be the name most suited for God.
6. Osborne, E., "Accessing R.E. *Founders and Leaders, Buddhism, Hinduism and Sikhism Teacher's Book Mainstream.*", p. 9. Folens Limited, 2005. Klostermaier, K. *A Survey of Hinduism*, page 1. SUNY Press, 1994.
7. e.g. in "Hinduism and the Clash of Civilizations" by David Frawley, *Voice of India*, 2001. ISBN 81-85990-72-7, also see the National Geographic site.
8. Major Religions of the World Ranked by Number of Adherents, see: WWW.Adherents.com (2005 figure)
9. Flood, Gavin (1996). *An Introduction to Hinduism.* Cambridge: Cambridge University Press, pp. 82, 224-49. For an overview of this method of classification, with details on the grouping of schools, see: Radhakrishnan, Sarvepalli; and Moore, Charles A. *A Source Book in Indian Philosophy.*
10. Chatterjee, Satisschandra and Datta, Dhirendramohan, *An Introduction to Indian Philosophy*, ISBN: 964-8090-106.
11. See: Monier-Williams, Monier, "*Monier-Williams Sanskrit Dictionary*", Nataraj Books, 2006, ISBN 18-81338-58-4, And: V.S. Apte, *A Practical Sanskrit Dictionary*, p. 240.
12. Bhattacharyya, N.N. *History of the Tantric Religion*, Second Revised Edition. (Manohar: New Delhi, 1999), p. 174. ISBN 81-7304-025-7.
13. For instance, the "*Atheist Society of India*" produces a monthly publication *Nasthika Yugam* which it translates as "The Age of Atheism". See also: *Encyclopædia Britannica*, 2007.
14. Chatterjee, Satisschandra and Datta, Dhirendramohan, *An Introduction to Indian Philosophy*, ISBN: 964-8090-10-6, p. 5, footnote 1.

15. Flood, Gavin (1996). *An Introduction to Hinduism,* Cambridge: Cambridge University Press, p. 82.
16. Harsh Nevatia, See: WWW.hinduism.suite101.com/article.cfm/creation_in_the_upanishads.
17. *Rig Veda* 10:129.1-7.
18. *Taittiriya Upanishad* 2:6; 7. Source: *World Mythology* by Donna, See: WWW.1stholistic.com/Prayer/Hindu/hol_Hindu-creation-of-the-universe.htm
19. Swami Vivekananda (स्वामी विवेकानन्द) (January 12, 1863-July 4, 1902), whose pre-monastic name was Narendranath Dutta, was one of the most famous and influential spiritual leaders of the philosophies of *Vedanta* and *Yoga* and a major figure in the history of Hinduism and India. He was the chief disciple of Ramakrishna Paramahamsa and the founder of Ramakrishna Math and Ramakrishna Mission. While he is widely credited with having uplifted his own nation, simultaneously he introduced *Yoga* and *Vedanta* to America and England with his popular lectures and private discourses on *Vedanta* philosophy. Vivekananda was the first known Hindu Swami to come to the West, where he introduced Eastern thought at the World's Parliament of Religions, in connection with the World's Fair in Chicago, in 1893. It was there that he was catapulted to fame by wide audiences in Chicago and then later elsewhere in America.
20. *Bhagvad Gita*, 4.7-8.
21. See: Swami Atmaramananda Dr. M. Sivaramkrishna, *Art, Culture and Spirituality*, Advaita Ashrama, Publication Department, Calcutta, 1997. pp. 507-528.
22. *Ibid.*, p. 508.
23. See: Lincoln Barnett, *The Universe and Dr. Enistein* (New York: Mentor, 1950).
24. Advaita Ashrama, *The Life of Swami Vivekanand*, Calcatta, 1960, p. 145 and see: Dr. M. Sivaramkrishna, *Art, Culture and Sprituality*, Advaita Ashrama, Publication Department, Calcutta 1997, pp. 512-513.
25. Mohandas Karamchand Gandhi (Gujarati: मोहनदास करमचंद गांधी, Hindi: मोहनदास करमचंद गांधी, IAST: mohands karamcand gâdhī, IP A., (October 2, 1869-January 30, 1948) was a major political and spiritual leader of India and the Indian independence movement. In India, he is recognized as the Father of the Nation. October 2nd, his birthday, is commemorated each year as Gandhi Jayanti, and is a national holiday. He was the pioneer of *satyagraha*—the resistance of tyranny through mass civil disobedience, firmly founded upon *ahimsa* or total non-violence—which led India to independence and inspired movements

for civil rights and freedom across the world. Gandhi is commonly known in India and across the world as Mahatma Gandhi (Hindi: महात्मा, mahâtmâ; from Sanskrit, mahâtmâ; Great Soul) and as Bapu (in Gujarati, Father).

26. Ranjit Chaudhari, www.mkgandhi.org.
27. N.K. Bose, *Selections from Gandhi,* Navajivan Publishing House, Ahmedabad, India, 1972, p. 260.
28. A. Jayabalan, CMF/www.mkgandhi.org
29. Stephen Murphy, Adapted from: *Why Gandhi is Relevant in Modern India: A Western Gandhian's Personal Discovery,* Gandhi Peace Foundation, New Delhi; Academy of Gandhian Studies, Hyderabad, 1991. www.mkgandhi.org
30. In New York *Daily Tribune*, June 25, 1853 and London, Friday, June 10, 1853. Dr. Dipak Basu, CPI (M) and Karl Marx, www.ivarta.com (articles).
31. *Ibid*., Dr. Dipak Basu, CPI (M) and Karl Marx, www.ivarta.com
32. *Ibid*., Dr. Dipak Basu, CPI (M) and Karl Marx, www.ivarta.com
33. *Ibid*., Dr. Dipak Basu, CPI (M) and Karl Marx, www.ivarta.com
34. M.K. Gandhi, *In search of the supreme*, Navajivan Publishing House, Ahmedabad, India, 2002, VII, p. 308.
35. These are: 1. *Krita Yuga* (1,728,000 years), 2. *Treta Yuga* (1,296,000 years), 3. *Dwapara Yuga* (864,000 years) and 4. *Kali Yuga* (432,000 years) Our universe is now in Kali Yuga. It has been approximately 5,042 years since the beginning of *Kali Yuga* (according to Swami Dayananda). At the end of each of these four-yuga periods, there is a transition period which is characterized by rains and flooding.

    If we count the combined total of the four *yugas* as one unit (one four-yuga period), then 71 of such units comprise the rule of one Manu (ruler of the men). Since the creation, it has been six different Manus who ruled our part of the Universe. The current time period is the 28th four-*yuga* cycle of the seventh Manu. He will rule for 43 more four-*yuga* periods. Then there will be seven more such Manus who will rule in the future before the entire Universe will come to an end and recreated again.

    A thousand four-*yuga* periods comprise one day of the creator Brahma and another thousand four-*yuga* periods make one night for him. The Universe lasts for the duration of one creator's-day (=4.320 billion years). The Universe stays unmanifested for the duration of his night. When he wakes up, the Universe is set in motion again. The Principal *Upanishads* by Sarvepalli Radhakrishnan see: www.dfwhindutemple.org.
36. Sarvepalli Radhakrishnan (Telugu: సర్వేపల్లి రాధాకృష్ణ, Tamil: சர்வபள்ளி ராதாகிருஷ்ணன), (September 5, 1888 – April 17,

1975), was a philosopher and statesman. One of the foremost scholars of comparative religion and philosophy in his day, he built a bridge between Eastern and Western thought showing each to be comprehensible within the terms of the other. He introduced Western idealism into Indian philosophy and was the first scholar of importance to provide a comprehensive exegesis of India's religious and philosophical literature to English speaking peoples. His academic appointments included the King George V Chair of Mental and Moral Science at the University of Calcutta (1921-?) and Spalding Professor of Eastern Religions and Ethics at Oxford University (1936-1939). Dr. Sarvepalli Radhakrishnan was a most distinguished diplomat, scholar and teacher, apart from being the President of India. As a tribute to this great teacher, his birthday is observed as Teacher's Day. President of India Late Dr. S. Radhakrishnan was born on September 5, 1888, at Tiruttani, forty miles to the Northeast of Madras, in South India. His early years were spent in Tiruttani and Tirupati, both famous as pilgrim centres. He graduated with a Master's Degree in Arts from Madras University. In April 1909, he was appointed to the Department of Philosophy at the Madras Presidency College. From then onwards, he was engaged in the serious study of Indian philosophy and religion, and was a teacher of Philosophy. In 1918, Doctor Radhakrishnan was appointed Professor of Philosophy in the University of Mysore. Three years later, he was appointed to the most important philosophy chair in India, King George V Chair of Mental and Moral Science in the University of Calcutta. Dr. Radhakrishnan represented the University of Calcutta at the Congress of the Universities of the British Empire in June 1926 and the International Congress of Philosophy at the Harvard University in September 1926. In 1929, Dr. Radhakrishnan was invited to take the post vacated by Principal J. Estin Carpenter in Manchester College, Oxford. From 1936-39, Dr. Radhakrishnan was the Spalding Professor of Eastern Religions and Ethics at Oxford University. In 1939, he was elected Fellow of the British Academy. From 1939-48, he was the Vice Chancellor of the Banaras Hindu University. He later held offices that dealt with India's national and international affairs. He was the leader of the Indian delegation to UNESCO during 1946-52. He was the Ambassador of India to U.S.S.R. during 1949-1952. He was the Vice President of India from 1952-1962 and the President, General Conference of UNESCO from 1952-54. He held the office of the Chancellor, University of Delhi, from 1953-62. He became the second President of India in 1962, an office he held until 1967. When he became the President of India in 1962, some of his students and friends requested him to allow them to celebrate his birthday, September 5. He replied, "Instead of celebrating my birthday, it would be my proud privilege if 5 September is observed as Teachers' Day." Since then, Teachers' Day has been celebrated in India on this day.

See: www.iep.utm.edu/r/radhakri.htm and www.en.wikipedia.org/wiki/Sarvepalli_Radhakrishnan, Ashok Vohra, K. Satchidananda Murty, *Radhakrishnan: His Life and Ideas*, State University of New York Pr, ISBN-10: 0791403440, 1990, p. 98, Kotta Satchidananda Murty, Ashok Vohra, *Radhakrishnan: His Life and Ideas*, Published 1990 SUNY Press, ISBN 0791403432, B.K. Ahluwalia, *Facets of Radhakrishnan*, Published 1978, Newman Group of Publishers, Original from the University of Michigan, Digitized July 12, 2006. *Radhakrishnan: An Anthology,* Sir Sarvepalli Radhakrishnan, Published 1952, G. Allen Unwin, Original from the University of California, Digitized December 19, 2006.

37. Sir SarvepallI Radhakrishnan, *Radhakrishnan: An Anthology*, Published 1952, G. Allen Unwin, Original from the University of California, Digitized Dec. 19, 2006. p. 188.
38. Radhakrishnan, *Indian Philosophy*, Oxford University Press. ISBN 0195623495, 1993, London, Volume two, p. 767.
39. *Ibid.*, p. 766.
40. www.thecanadian encyclopedia.com

5

Ethics and Science: According to Islam and Hinduism

What is Ethics?

Ethics,[1] a major branch of philosophy, is the study of the values and customs of a person or group. It covers the analysis and employment of concepts such as right and wrong, good and evil, and responsibility. In other words, Ethics has been defined as:

> "The normative science of the conduct of human beings living in societies—a science which judges this conduct to be right or wrong, to be good or bad or in some similar way."[2]

Some key terms used in this definition are briefly explained for a better understanding of the concept.

Ethics in Philosophy

Philosophy is concerned with questions of a very different kind: What should we do? How should we organize society? What is right? How should we understand the idea of justice? On what basis can we choose between different courses of action? These lead to a study of ethics, and of political philosophy and the philosophy of law.

Although the pre-Socratic philosophers of ancient Greece had probed many questions about the nature of reality, questions to which their answers are still interesting in terms of both epistemology and the natural sciences, with Socrates, Plato and Aristotle, the emphasis shifted towards issues of morality. For example, Plato's Republic is not based on the question "what is society?, but "what is justice?" and it is through that question that many other issues about society and how it should be ruled are explored. Aristotle (in *Nicomachean Ethics)* asked about the 'good' which was the aim of every action, and about what could constitute a 'final good'—something that was to be sought for its own sake, rather than for the sake of something higher. He came to the view that the highest good for man was eudemonia, which literally means 'having a good spirit', but perhaps can be translated as 'happiness'. He saw it as the state in which a person was fulfilling his or her potential and natural function. It expressed a form of human excellence or virtue *(arête).* This tied in with his general view that everything had a 'final cause' 'a goal and a purpose' to which it moves. If you understand the final cause of something, you also understand its fundamental essence, which finds its expression in that goal. If a knife had a soul, Aristotle argued, that soul would be 'cutting'; that is what makes it a knife. That is what it is there to do. What then is the essence of humankind? What is it there to do? What is its goal? The study and evaluation of human conduct in the light of moral principles includes many dimensions today. Moral principles may be viewed either as the standard of conduct that individuals have constructed for themselves or as the body of obligations and duties that a particular society requires of its members.

'**Normative Science**' (as opposed to 'descriptive' or 'positive' sciences) in simple words, is a discipline, which describes or sets standards or rules for the field under consideration. For example, a 'normative grammar' of a language describes how its authors think that the language should be spoken or written. In other words, a normative science deals with 'how things ought to be' rather than 'how things really are'. 'Normative Sciences', primarily comprise three fields:

- 'Aesthetics' deals systematically with the standards by which we judge the beauty or the ugliness of objects of sense, perception, commonly sights and sounds. Thus, setting the standards of beauty or ugliness is related to the field of 'aesthetics'.

- 'Logic' deals systematically with the standards by which we judge the validity or invalidity of arguments. Thus, setting any standards for validity and invalidity is related to the field of 'logic'.
- 'Ethics' deals systematically with the standards by which we judge the right or wrong in human action. Thus, setting any standards of 'right' or 'wrong' behaviour in a society is related to the field of 'ethics'.

'Conduct' is a collective name for voluntary actions. A voluntary action is an action that a man could have done differently if he had so chosen.

Our definition has limited the conduct with which we deal in ethics in two ways:

We deal with human actions and not with the actions of the lower animals; we confine ourselves to the study of the conduct of human beings living in societies. Moralists sometimes go further and hold that the standards of ethics only apply to the relations of men with one another; the conduct studied in ethics is not only conduct done in a society, but conduct that affects some other member or members of that society. Although, it may be considered convenient to include, in a single normative science, all human activities, including those that appear to have no effects on other people or relations with them, yet common usage would certainly make a social activity like speaking the truth more directly the concern of ethics that a purely private activity with no marked effects like playing a guitar in one's private room or a religious activity like fasting. Of course, even such activities may have indirect social effects; however, as soon as such activities start having a social effect, they shall be included in the study of ethics. For instance, a man playing his guitar may start disturbing his neighbours. At this juncture, his apparently private activity would now be included in the scope of 'ethics'.

The subject of ethics essentially comprises issues fundamental to practical decision-making in case of all such actions, which bring one in an active or a passive interaction with other human beings. For this reason, the discipline, though long considered a branch of philosophy, is closely linked with many other fields of inquiry, including anthropology, economics, politics, and sociology. Ethics, however, remains distinct from such areas of study, as it deals with human conduct as it ought to be, rather than as it actually is.

Division of Ethics

According to one division, it is divided into three primary areas: meta-ethics (the study of the concept of ethics), normative ethics (the study of how to determine ethical values), and applied ethics (the study of the use of ethical values):

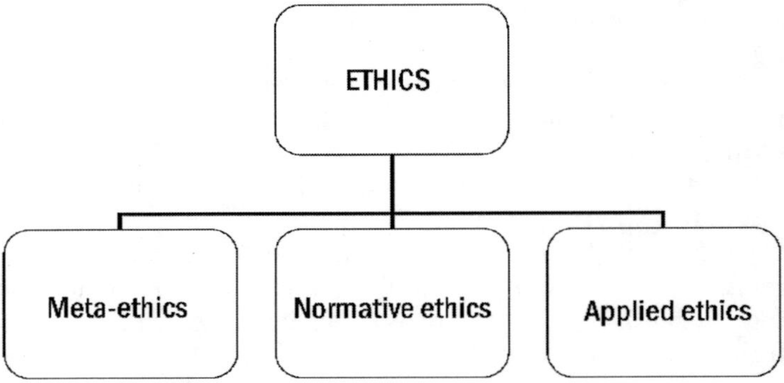

Fig. 5.1: Division of Ethics

Meta-Ethics centres on questions relating to the nature and origin of moral concepts and judgments. Philosophers in meta-ethics have taken markedly different positions on this matter. There also has been much disagreement over whether moral judgments are objective or subjective, absolute or relative.

Normative Ethics is primarily concerned with establishing standards or norms for conduct and is commonly associated with general theories about how one ought to live. One of the central questions of modern normative ethics has to do with whether human actions are to be judged right or wrong solely according to their consequences. Traditionally, theories that judge actions by their consequences have been known as 'teleological', though the term 'consequentiality' has in large part supplanted it. Another class of theories in normative ethics, designated as 'deontological', judges action by their conformance to some formal rule or principle (for example, the ethical system of the philosopher Immanuel Kant).

Applied Ethics is the application of moral theories to practical moral problems. Such moral issues as racial and sexual equality, human rights, and justice have become prominent, as have questions about the value of human life raised by controversies over abortion and euthanasia[3]. Related to the latter, are the ethical implications of various developments in regard to reproduction, as for example, in *vitro* fertilization[4], sperm banks, gene manipulation, and cloning[5]. Perhaps the most striking development in the study of ethics during the second half of the twentieth century has been the growing interest in applied ethics among philosophers.

In other words, ethics is a branch of philosophy concerned with the nature of ultimate value and the standards by which human actions can be judged right or wrong.

Many people think ethics has to do with a set of social conventions or a religious decree. In professional philosophy we do not typically consider this to be the definition of ethics. Philosophical ethics could be called the study of what is good and bad. Generally, philosophical ethics concerns itself with discovering a system one may use to determine who or what is good, or with evaluating systems that others have proposed. The pursuit of moral knowledge dates back to ancient Greek philosophers, but it is mostly the influence of the Enlightenment on moral thought that continues to shape ethics today. There are many well-known figures in the history of ethics, including the Greek philosophers Plato and Aristotle, but some of the most important modern influences include such people as Immanuel Kant, Jeremy Bentham, John Stuart Mill, D.W. Ross, C.L. Stevenson, Alasdair Macintyre, and John Rawls. In ethics, a premium is placed upon defining "the good". Different approaches to defining the good, the nature of moral properties, the source of moral knowledge, and the status of moral facts have played an important role in shaping various branches of moral theory. The three major divisions of ethical philosophy may be called Virtue Ethics, Deontology, and consequentiality.

Ethical mandates from society and church do not qualify as genuine philosophical ethics. This last statement causes concern in that it reeks of negative presuppositions. First of all, ethical mandates always have ethical undertones. It is inescapable. An ethical mandate may not fit certain schools of thought, but then certain schools of thought can be erroneous. All ethics are religious by nature, if one defines religion as an attempt to discover the good.

Ethics are rules for behaviour, based on beliefs about how things should be. Ethical statements involve: (1) assumptions about humans and their capacities; (2) notions of what is good and desirable.

Ethical systems (sets of rules for acceptable behaviour) concern the "shoulds" and "should nots" of life, the principles and values on which human relations are based.

The assessment of whether a behaviour is ethical is divided into four categories, or domains: consequences, actions, character, and motive. In the domain of consequences, a behaviour is determined to be "right" or "wrong" based on the results of the action, whereas the domain of actions looks only at the act itself. The domain of character looks at whether a person's overall character is ethical; a person who is deemed as "virtuous" has consistently ethical behaviour. The motive domain evaluates a person's intentions, regardless of the consequences. It considers whether the person intended to do well, even if the result was bad. A behaviour may be deemed "ethical" according to one domain of assessment, but appear "unethical" according to another. For example, a poor person steals a small amount of food to feed her starving child from a wealthy, well-fed person who does not even notice that the food is missing. This act would be considered ethical in the domain of consequences, since the child can be fed, and motive, since the person is caring for her child, but unethical in the domain of actions, because stealing in itself is wrong. The poor person's general behaviour would have to be evaluated to determine whether she is ethical in the domain of character.

Ethics can also be divided into two main schools:

Absolutism and ***Relativism***: Absolutists believe that ethical rules are fixed standards (for example, stealing is always wrong, no matter what the circumstances). Relativists, on the other hand, believe that all ethics are subject to context (for example, stealing may be wrong in certain circumstances but not in others). Few people are actually pure absolutists or pure relativists, but rather fall somewhere along the spectrum between the two extremes, tending towards one or the other. Most who tend towards absolutism will allow for special circumstances and bend the rules on occasion, while those who tend towards relativism will admit to some universal standards that form a "bottom line" of behaviour.

In order to develop ethical maturity, people must have moral awareness and moral agency (or autonomy). Moral awareness is the ability to recognize the ethical element of a given situation. For some, eating beef is simply an act of appetite and habit, with no thought given to its ethical implications. For others, whether to eat beef is a complicated moral question involving the ethics of land use (grazing cattle *vs*. growing food crops), conservation (the destruction of rain forests to increase grazing grounds), and the global economy (the transformation of underdeveloped countries into cattle farms for Western industrialized nations).

Moral agency or autonomy; means the freedom to choose between alternative behaviours. A person cannot develop ethical maturity without being able to choose from alternatives. Without moral awareness and moral agency, ethics becomes meaningless because behaviours are simply automatic, or forced.

The question of moral agency becomes complicated by the tendency to equate ethical behaviour with obedience. Because humans first learn ethics as small children from adult authority figures, our initial understanding of ethics is "obeying". When we do what adults want us to, we are told we are "good". If we disobey, we are "bad". Some people never outgrow this, continuing throughout life to believe that being "good" means obeying external authorities. These people have never developed a sense of moral agency, even though they are capable of making choices. A prime example of this dilemma is the numerous soldiers and citizens who carried out or assisted in the torture and murder of millions of peoples, soldiers, gays, and others in Second World War. Do their claims that they were "just following orders" exempt them from ethical responsibility? Likewise, in situations of oppression where people have been traumatized into blind obedience to their oppressors, are the oppressed ethically responsible for their actions, or do they lack moral agency? These questions illuminate the essential character of freedom to choose in the development of ethical maturity.

Ethical maturity involves accepting full responsibility for one's ethical choices and their consequences. An ethically mature person obeys her or his own, inner authority (or conscience), rather than an outside authority figure. Moving from the infantile state of externally determined obedience to the mature state of self-determination is a long and difficult process.

Bioethics

Bioethics is the philosophical study of the ethical controversies brought about by advances in biology and medicine. We can say that this is a new branch of ethical issues related to a new scientific subject. Bioethics are concerned with the ethical questions that arise in the relationships among life sciences, biotechnology, medicine, politics, law, philosophy, and theology. Bioethics is concerned with questions about basic human values such as the rights to life and health, and the rightness or wrongness of certain developments in healthcare institutions, life technology, medicine, and the health professions and about society's responsibility for the life and health of its members.

Bioethics ask these questions in the context of modern medicine and draw on a plurality of traditions, both secular and religious, to help society understand and keep pace with how advances in science and medical technology can change the way we experience the meaning of health and illness and, ultimately, the way we live.

Bioethics is related to different subjects. It blends law, philosophy, insights from the humanities and medicine to bear on complex interaction of human life, science and technology. Although its questions are as old as humankind, the origins of bioethics as a field are more recent and difficult to capture in a single view. Bioethics has been used in the last twenty years to describe the investigation and a study of ways in which decisions in medicine and science touch upon our health and lives and upon our society and environment.

The Nature of Good

One of the differences in the approach to ethical problems revolves around the question of absolute good as opposed to relative good. Throughout the history of philosophy thinkers have sought an absolute criterion of ethics. Frequently moral codes have been based on religious absolutes. Immanuel Kant, in his categorical imperative, attempted to establish an ethical criterion independent of theological considerations. Rationalists (Plato, Baruch Spinoza, and Josiah Royce) founded their ethics on metaphysics. All the various methods of building an ethical system pose the question of the degree to which morality is authoritative (i.e., imposed by a power outside the individual). If the authority is a religion, then that religion is the ethical teacher. Hedonism, which equates the good with pleasure in its various forms, finds its ethical criterion either in the good of the individual or the good of the group. An egoistic hedonism (Aristippus, Epicurus, Julien de La Mettrie, and Thomas Hobbes) views the good of the individual as the ultimate consideration. A universalistic hedonism, such as utilitarianism (Jeremy Bentham, James Mill), finds the ethical criterion in the greatest good for the greatest number[6].

On the other hand, in Virtue ethics, when looking at actions and asking if they are right and wrong, one could start by asking the basic question: what does it mean to be a 'good' person?, and then develop this to explore the qualities and virtues that make up the 'good' life. This approach had been first taken by Aristotle who linked the displaying of certain qualities with the final end or purpose of life. Virtue ethics, for example, was seen as naturalistic, in that it moved away from the idea of simply obeying rules, to an appreciation of how one might express one's own fundamental nature, and thus fulfil one's potential as a human being. Virtue ethics raises some basic questions:

- Do we have a fixed essence? Are there, particular masculine or feminine qualities that give rise to virtues appropriate to each sex? Or is our nature the product of our surroundings and upbringing?
- If our nature has been shaped by factors over which we have no control (e.g., the culture into which we have been born; traumatic experiences in childhood) are we responsible for our actions?
- How should we relate the expression of an individual's virtues to the actual needs of society?
- How are we able to decide between different ways of expressing the same virtue? For example, a sense of love and compassion might lead one person to help a seriously ill person to die, yet another might find that love and compassion lead them to struggle to keep that same person alive. In some way, we need to fall back on other ethical theories if we want to assess the actions that spring from particular virtues.

It seems that beneath some of these 'virtue ethics' approaches lay the basic questions raised by Aristotle about the end or purpose of human life. Virtue ethics examines human qualities in terms of their overall place within human life, and the appropriate ways in which they may be expressed.

Twentieth Century Ethical Thought

Among ethical theories debated in the first half of the twentieth century were instrumentalism (John Dewey), for which morality lies within the individual and is relative to the individual's experience; emotivism (Sir Alfred J. Ayer), wherein ethical considerations are merely expressions of the subjective desires of the individual; and intuitionism (G.E. Moore), which postulates an immediate awareness of the morally good. Agreeing with Moore that the morally good is directly apprehended through intuition, deontological intuitionists, (H.A. Prichard, W.D. Ross) went on to distinguish between good and right and to argue that moral obligations are intrinsically compelling whether or not their fulfilment results in some greater good. Important ethical theories since the mid-twentieth century have included the prescriptivism of R.M. Hare, who has compared moral precepts to commands, a crucial difference between them being that moral precepts can be universally applied. In his arguments for virtue ethics, Alasdair C. Macintyre has cautioned against unbridled individualism and advocated correctives drawn from Aristotle's discussion of moral virtue as the mean between extremes. Thomas Nagel has held that, in moral decision-making, reason supersedes desire, so that it becomes rational to choose altruism over a narrowly defined self-interest.

The Role of Ethics in Science

Although whether one is a good or bad person depends essentially one's motive whether an action is good or bad cannot be independent of its harmful or beneficial efforts. But the knowledge of what are the harmful or beneficial efforts of an ethics is a scientific knowledge. Hence, such ethical knowledge is some kind of empirical scientific knowledge. Similarly the knowledge about how to transform one's life into a life of ethical perfection is also some kind of special scientific knowledge. Vivekananda, Gandhi and Radakrishnan explicitly accept that one could programme towards ethical perfection by the conscious effort of exercising one's freewill and reason, and thus discover directly, various deeper immortal spiritual truths about life.

The question arises as to why students should study ethical issues in science and technology. One reason is that several recent scientific developments, such as cloning and genetic engineering of plants and animals, have raised pressing ethical issues. Many universities and research funding agencies have determined that science and technology majors should increase their awareness of the ethical issues they are likely to face in their careers and have made courses such as this one mandatory. Also, many members of the public wish to increase their understanding of current debates about ethical issues in biotechnology and other areas of science that will affect their lives and well-being. The reasons for studying ethical issues in science and technology extend beyond current controversies to the pervasive influence of science and technology in our lives leading to long standing debates and deeper questions about why ethical issues continue to arise in science and technology. For example, some people argue that our attitude towards the natural environment as a resource to be dominated and exploited is at the root of these issues.

Gandhi, Marx and Ethics

The nature of Marx's views on morality and ethics has long been a matter of considerable dispute. One widespread view is that Marx had no ethics; he rejected morality, and envisioned a communism beyond both[7].

Marx is supposed to have founded a science which sought in an objective, morally neutral manner to understand the origin, growth, and collapse of capitalism as well as the ultimate succession of communism. One has only to read the history of Marxism to appreciate how generally this view has been defended. Comments such as the following are wholly common:

Marxism is distinguished from all other socialist systems by its anti-ethical tendency. In all of Marxism from beginning to end, there is not a grain of ethics, and consequently no more of an ethical judgment than an ethical postulate.[8]

The nature of Marx's views on morality and ethics has long been a matter of considerable dispute. But we know that morality, ethics and religion are convertible terms, a moral life without reference to religions is like a house built upon sand as Gandhi said. He sees clearly that unselfish ethical struggle against exploitation injustice oppression, etc., is essentially a religious struggle. Thus, Marx's view that "religion is an opiate of the people" is essentially false. Unlike Gandhi he fails to see that ethical life based on internal sanction, constitutes the essence of religious life and one could lead a religious life even if one does not believe in external religious sanction.

Although all religions accept the external religious sanction for morality based on some metaphysical beliefs, they do have fundamental differences in the field of metaphysics. Since metaphysics is beyond the scope of *a priori* reason, if science has no answer on the problem, then there is no way for us to know the view of which religion on same metaphysical problem is true. At present science has no answer to the problem of the existence of God, the soul and life after death. Marx's belief in the non-existence of God, soul, life after death and so on is a metaphysical belief, not a scientific belief.

The Gandhian view which states that there is fundamental unity and truth in all great religions, is essentially true with reference to their ethics. Since ethics constitutes the core of religion and fundamental ethical questions are within the scope of reason, the Gandhian view that critical ethical and religious dialogue is conducive to inter-religious harmony and growth of religions is essentially correct.

Mahatma Gandhi, one of India's prominent spiritual leaders, though largely known for his *Satyagraha* (non-violent resistance as truth-force) means of freedom struggle in the Indian Independence Movement, has also contributed to the field of Ethics to a great extent. Gandhi was influenced by the Indian Scriptures like *Gita* and *Upanishads*. Also the teachings of Tolstoy (conscientious objection and non-violent non-cooperation) and Thoreau (civil disobedience against unjust laws, e.g., slavery and war) influenced him greatly. In the simplest terms, Gandhi's philosophy can be summarized into two important principles of *Satya* (Truth) and *Ahimsa* (Non-violence).

'*Satya* (Truth)' stands for the Indian philosophical thought that God alone has absolute existence and God is absolute truth/being (*Sat*), consciousness (*Chit*), bliss (*Ananda*). Hence, Gandhi equated Truth with God and said that Truth is there in the hearts of all and sustains all creation. When doing so, by Truth Gandhi meant absolute truth and not mere truthfulness and honesty, which are means to truth. Truth is the end and not a means to something beyond itself. Gandhi said that to find Truthfully means to realize oneself and one's destiny and to become perfect.

'*Ahimsa* (Non-violence)' for Gandhi is to patiently adhere to the Truth in spite of whatsoever sufferings come in our way, even at the cost of one's life. While Truth is the goal, *Ahimsa* is the means without which the realization of Truth is not possible. Like Buddha, Gandhi also explained *Ahimsa* as not injuring any living being, neither by body nor by mind. In a broader sense, *Ahimsa* includes love, charity, and compassion. Gandhi asserted Christ's saying 'love your enemy'.

Non-violence should not be taken for weakness, Gandhi said that his doctrine of Non-violence is a highly active force and has no room for cowardice or weakness. According to him, Non-violence is the law of the human species, as violence is the law of brutes.

According to Gandhi, the principle of *Ahimsa* involves different noble practices like non-stealing, non-covetousness, no untouchability, religious tolerance and equanimity, conservation of ecology and nature, celibacy (gentleness and compassion instead of addiction and sexual violence), control of the palate, physical labour, and *swadeshi* (serving one's immediate neighbour first).

According to Gandhian morals, ethics and religion are convertible terms: "A moral life without reference to religion is like a house built upon sand. And religion divorced from morality is like 'sounding brass', good only for making a noise and breaking heads. Morality includes truth, *Ahimsa* and continence. He also held that every virtue that mankind has ever practiced is referable to and derived from these three fundamental virtues. Non-violence and continence are again derivable from Truth, which for me is God."[9]

Gandhi believed that morality is the basis of religion as he said: "As soon as we lose the moral basis, we cease to be religious. There is no such thing as religion overriding morality. Man for instance cannot be untruthful, cruel or incontinent and claim to have God on his side."[10]

Clarification of the Ethical Theory of Islam[11]

A significant matter to be noticed here and to be reasonably and philosophically clarified and justified is how human manner and permanent qualities become possessed of value through 'worship to Allah and perfect obedience and humbling oneself before Allah'. In this regard, from the outlook of Islam and verses of *Holy Quran* and *Hadith*, we have no doubt, for the Almighty Allah says:

و ما خلقت الجن و الانس الّا ليعبدون

> *"And I have not created the jinn and the man except that they should worship* Me (51:56)."

The only aim of the creation of man and of *jinn*, who from the viewpoint of the *Holy Quran* are two kinds of responsible (entrusted with duties) beings is just (their) worshipping the One God (Allah—The One and only). Of course, taking into consideration other verses (of *the Holy Quran)* we come to realize that this is not the final goal, for this very *ibadah* (worship) to Allah has in another *ayah* of the *Holy Quran* has been propounded as the right way.

و ان اعبدوني هذا صراط مستقيم

"And that you should serve Me; this is the right way (36:61)"

Worship Allah, this is the right way. The same thing which in the former *ayah* (51:56) had been mentioned as the aim of creation, has been introduced as the right way in the latter (36:61), meaning that *ibadah* (worship) is a medium goal and above it there is another goal. That very act of *ibadah* (worship) itself has been considered for a higher goal and that is attaining nearness to the Almighty Allah (attaining Allah's pleasure) in which all human virtues and perfections are summed up.

But for this theory to be presentable and defendable in the face of the other ethical and value theories of the world, and particularly so that our educated youth will be able to defend the righteous position of Islam before other schools of thought, it is necessary to clarify this theory on the basis of the following reasons and philosophical discussions.

According to Islam the criterion for the goodness and value of the action is the effect which a free conduct has on man's spiritual and intellectual perfection. For the clarification of this basic principle we express an analysis of the concept of value and anti-value and their equivalent in the Islamic culture, namely, 'good' and 'evil'.

What makes man superior to and more perfect than the animals and other beings is that unlike them human beings can reach spiritual perfection. *The Holy Quran* says:

و نفخت فيه من روحي .

"*...And I breathed into him of My spirit...* (15:29 and 38:72)."

And,

فتبارك الله احسن الخالقين ...

"*...so blessed be Allah, the best of the creators* (23:14)."

The question which is raised here is whether value is only in the superiority of man's spiritual perfections or whether plant and animal perfections are also of value?

Let us consider an apple tree. In an apple tree, taking root, turning green, bearing branches, leaves and even blossoms, are considered perfection in so far as they cause fruit bearing; if not, they would not be of value. These kinds of perfections are preliminary perfections which are not of value in themselves, rather they are preliminaries for eventual and genuine perfection, and value is acquired through them.

In man this is also the case. If a growth emerges in the body alone and does not cause that main, basic and eventual growth, it is an animal growth and will not be of any value for man from the viewpoint that he is man. A healthy body is valuable for man if he uses it for his spiritual and intellectual progress, and not if he misuses his health for hurting others. The same is true of other qualities as well. For example, bravery is desirable from the Islamic viewpoint when it is used in the way of man's spiritual and intellectual perfection and in the way of getting near to the Almighty Allah (winning Allah's pleasure and favour); otherwise the great (notorious) enemy of Islam and others were also brave and had this animal value. The superiority of a brave man, apart from his spiritual goal and perfection to another man is like the superiority of a rhinoceros to a horse and the superiority of an elephant to a gazelle. This preliminary perfection will be of value when it is used for attaining that eventual human perfection, when it has been achieved for that and used in the way of attaining it (eventual human perfection). Justice, too, which in today's world culture has absolute value, in the view of the *Holy Quran* is valuable since it is a preliminary stage for getting near to *taqwa*:

..اعدلوا هو اقرب للتقوى ...

"*...Act equitably, that is nearer to piety...* (5:8)."

In the value system of Islam, justice is of value when it is in the way of Allah and for attaining a loftier goal and moves man towards that highest point of perfection.

The point which is necessary to be paid attention to here is the relationship between the philosophical good and the ethical good, but before clarifying this relationship, we will discuss about good and evil and their criteria.

The Aim of Ethics in Islam: The Purification of the Soul[12]

Moral virtues in man gain him eternal happiness, while moral corruption leads him to everlasting wretchedness. It is, therefore, necessary for man to purge and purify himself of all evil traits of character and adorn his soul with all forms of ethical and moral virtues. Moreover, without having cleansed oneself of all evil habits, it would be impossible to nourish and develop moral virtues in oneself. The human soul can be compared to a mirror in this regard. If we wish to see something beautiful reflected in a mirror, we must first cleanse the mirror, so that dust and dirt do not disfigure the reflection. Any attempt to obey God's commands would be fruitful and successful only when one has purified himself of evil habits and tendencies; otherwise, it would be like putting on jewels on a dirty and unwashed body. When self-purification has been completed and one is completely rid of all evil habits of thought, speech and action, then the soul is ready to receive the unlimited grace of God. Such reception is the ultimate reason for which man was created.

In truth, God's grace and the Divine mysteries are always accessible to man, it is man that must purify his soul and develop within himself the necessary receptivity to benefit from the infinite grace of his Creator. In order to attain the ultimate and final perfection, it is necessary to traverse the path of struggle against selfish lusts and immoral tendencies which may exist within the soul, and thus to prepare the soul to receive the grace of God. If man sets foot on the path of self-purification, God shall come to his aid and guide him along the path:

"و الذين جاهدوا فينا لنهدينهم سبلنا"

> *And [as for] those who struggle in our cause, surely we guide them in our ways.* (29:69)

Theory of *Jihad* or the Spiritual Significance of *Jihad* (*Tazkieh*)

> "*And those who perform* jihad *for Us, We shall certainly guide them in our ways, and God is surely with the doers of good.*" (*Quran* 39: 69)

> *You have returned from the lesser* jihad *to the greater* jihad. (Hadith)

The Arabic term *jihad* usually translated into European languages as holy war or holy defense, more on the basis of its juridical usage in Islam rather than on its much more universal meaning in the *Quran* and *Hadith*, is derived from the root j-h-d whose primary meaning is to strive or to exert oneself. Its translation into holy war combined with the erroneous notion of Islam prevalent in the West as the 'religion of the sword' has helped to eclipse its inner and spiritual significance and to distort its connotation. Nor has the appearance upon the stage of history during the past century and especially during the past few years, of an array of movements within the Islamic world, often contending with or even opposing each other, and using the word *jihad* or one of its derivative forms, helped to make known the full import of its traditional meaning which alone is of concern to us here. Instead, recent distortions and even the total reversal of the meaning of *jihad* as understood over the ages by Muslims, has made it more difficult than ever before to gain insight into this key religious and spiritual concept.

To understand the spiritual significance of *jihad* and its wide application to nearly every aspect of human life as understood by Islam, it is necessary to remember that Islam bases itself upon the idea of establishing equilibrium within the being of man as well as in human society where he functions and fulfils the goals of his earthly life. This equilibrium, which is the terrestrial reflection of Divine Justice and the necessary condition for peace in the human domain, is the basis upon which the soul takes its flight towards that peace which, to use Christian terms, 'passeth understanding'. If Christian morality sees the aim of the spiritual life and its own morality as based on the vertical flight towards that perfection and ideal which is embodied in Christ, Islam sees it in the establishment of equilibrium both outward and inward as the necessary basis for the vertical ascent. The very stability of Islamic society over the centuries, the immutability of Islamic norms embodied in the Shari'ah, and the timeless character of traditional Islamic civilization which is the consequence of its permanent and immutable prototype are all reflections of both the ideal of equilibrium and its realization, as is so evident in the teachings of the Shari'ah (or Divine Law) as well as works of Islamic art, that equilibrium which is inseparable from the very name of Islam as being related to *salam* or peace.

The preservation of equilibrium in this world, however, does not mean simply a static or inactive passivity since life by nature implies movement. In the face of the contingencies of the world of change, of the withering effects of time, of the vicissitudes of terrestrial existence, to remain in equilibrium requires continuous exertion. It means carrying out *jihad* at every stage of life. Human nature being what it is, given to forgetfulness and the conquest of our immortal soul by the carnal soul or passions, the very process of life of both the individual and the human collectivity implies the ever-present danger of the loss of equilibrium and the fact of falling into the state of disequilibrium which if allowed to continue cannot but lead to disintegration on the individual level and chaos on the scale of community life. To avoid this tragic end and to fulfil the entelechy of the human state which is the realization of unity (*al-tawhid*) or total integration, Muslims as both individuals and members of Islamic society must carry out *jihad*, that is they must exert themselves at all moments of life to fight a battle both inward and outward against those forces that if not combated will destroy that equilibrium which is the necessary condition for the spiritual life of the person and the functioning of human society. This fact is especially true if society is seen as a collectivity which bears the imprint of the Divine Norm rather than an antheap of contending and opposing units and forces.

Man is at once a spiritual and corporeal being, a microcosm complete unto himself; yet he is a member of a society within which alone are certain aspects of his being developed and certain of his needs fulfilled. He possesses at once an intelligence whose substance is ultimately of a divine character and sentiments which can either veil his intelligence or abet his quest for his own Origin. In him are found love and hatred, generosity and covetousness, compassion and aggression. Moreover, until the present time, there have been not just one, but several 'humanities' with their own religious and moral norms, and national, ethnic and racial groups with their own bonds of affiliation. As a result the practice of *jihad* as applied to the world of multiplicity and the vicissitudes of human existence in the external world has come to develop numerous ramifications in the fields of political and economic activity and in social life, and come to partake on the external level of the complexity which characterizes the human world.

In its most outward sense, *jihad* came to mean the defense of dar-al-islam, that is, the Islamic world, from invasion and intrusion by non-Islamic forces. The earliest wars of Islamic history which threatened the very existence of the young community came to be known as *jihad* par excellence in this outward sense of 'holy war'. But it was upon returning from one of these early wars, which was of paramount importance in the survival of the newly established religious community and, therefore, of cosmic significance, that the Prophet nevertheless said to his companions that they had returned from the lesser holy war to the greater holy war, the greater *jihad* being the inner battle against all the forces which would prevent man from living according to the theomorphic norm which is his primordial and God given nature. Throughout Islamic history, the lesser holy war has echoed in the Islamic world when parts or the whole of that world have been threatened by forces from without or within. This call has been especially persistent since the nineteenth century with the advent of colonialism and the threat to the very existence of the Islamic world. It must be remembered, however, that even in such cases when the idea of *jihad* has been evoked in certain parts of the Islamic world, it has not usually been a question of religion simply sanctioning war but of the attempt of a society in which religion remains of central concern, to protect itself from being conquered either by military and economic forces or by ideas of an alien nature. This does not mean, however, that in some cases especially in recent times, religious sentiments have not been used or misused to intensify or legitimize a conflict. But to say the least, the Islamic world does not have a monopoly on this abuse as the history of other civilizations including even the secularized West demonstrates so amply. Moreover, human nature being what it is, once religion ceases to be of central significance to a particular human collectivity, then men fight and kill each other for much less exalted issues than their heavenly faith. By including the question of war in its sacred legislation, Islam did not condone but limited war and its consequences as the history of the traditional Islamic world bears out. In any case, the idea of total war and the actual practice of the extermination of whole civilian populations did not grow out of a civilization whose dominant religion saw *jihad* in a positive light. On the more external level, the lesser *jihad* also includes the socio-economic domain. It means the reassertion of justice in the external environment of human existence starting with man himself. To defend one's rights and reputation, to defend the honour of oneself and one's family is itself a *jihad* and a religious duty. So is the strengthening of all those social bonds from the family to the whole of the Muslim people (*alummah*) which the *Shari'ah* emphasizes. To seek social justice in accordance with the tenets of the *Quran* is a way of re-establishing equilibrium in human society, that is, of performing *jihad*, as are constructive economic enterprises, provided the well-being of the whole person is kept in mind and material welfare does not become an end in itself; provided one does not lose sight of the Quranic verse, 'The other world is better for you than this one'. To forget the proper relation between the two worlds would itself be instrumental in bringing about disequilibrium and would be a kind of *jihad* in reverse.

All of those external forms of *jihad* would remain incomplete and in fact contribute to an excessive externalization of human being, if they were not complemented by the greater or inner *jihad* which man must carry out continuously within himself, for the nobility of the human state resides in the constant tension between what we appear to be and what we really are and the need to transcend ourselves throughout this journey of earthly life in order to become what we 'are'.

From the spiritual point of view all the 'pillars' of Islam can be seen as being related to *jihad*. The fundamental witnesses, 'There is no divinity but Allah and Muhammad is the Messenger of Allah, through the utterance of which a person becomes a Muslim are not only statements about the Truth as seen in the Islamic perspective but also weapons for the practice of inner *jihad*. The very form of the first witness (*La ilaha illa' Lah* in Arabic) when written in Arabic calligraphy is like a bent sword with which all otherness is removed from the Supreme Reality while all that is positive in manifestation is returned to that Reality. The second witness is the blinding assertion of the powerful and majestic descent of all that constitutes in a positive manner the cosmos, man and revelation, from that Supreme Reality. To invoke the two witnesses in the form of the sacred language in which they were revealed is to practice the inner *jihad* and to bring about awareness of who we are, from whence we come and where our ultimate abode is.

The daily prayers (*salat*) which constitute the heart of the Islamic rites are again a never ending *jihad* which punctuates human existence in a continuous rhythm in conformity with the rhythm of the cosmos. To perform the prayers with regularity and concentration requires the constant exertion of our will and an unending battle and striving against forgetfulness, dissipation, and laziness. It is itself a form of spiritual warfare.

Likewise, the fast of *Ramadan* in which one wears the armour of inner purity and detachment against the passions and temptations of the outside world requires an asceticism and inner discipline which cannot come about except through an inner holy war. Nor is the *hajj* to the centre of the Islamic world in Mecca possible without long preparation, effort, often suffering and endurance of hardship. It requires great effort and exertion so that the Prophet could say, "The *hajj* is the most excellent of all *jihads*". Like the knight in quest of the Holy Grail, the pilgrim to the house of the Beloved must engage in a spiritual warfare whose end makes all sacrifice and all hardship pale into significance, for the *hajj* to the House of God implies, for the person who practices the inner *jihad*, an encounter with the Master of the House who also resides at the centre of that other *Ka'ba* which is the heart.

Finally, the giving of *Zakat* or religious tax (*khums*) is again a form of *jihad* not only in that in departing from one's wealth man must fight against the covetousness and greed of his carnal soul, but also in that through the payment of *zakat* and *khums* in its many forms, man contributes to the establishment of economic justice in human society. Although *jihad* is not one of the 'pillars of Islam', it in a sense resides within all the other 'pillars'. From the spiritual point of view in fact all of the 'pillars' can be seen in the light of an inner *jihad* which is essential to the life of man from the Islamic point of view and which does not oppose but complements contemplatively the peace which results from the contemplation of the One.

The great stations of perfection in the spiritual life can also be seen in the light of the inner *jihad*. To become separate from the impurities of the world in order to repose in the purity of the Divine Presence requires an intense *jihad*, for our soul has its roots sunk deeply into the transient world which the soul of fallen man mistakes for reality. To overcome the lethargy, passivity and indifference of the soul, qualities which have become second nature to man as a result of his forgetting who he is constitutes likewise a constant *jihad*. To pull the reins of the soul, to prevent it from dissipating itself outwardly as a result of its centrifugal tendencies and to bring it back to the centre wherein reside Divine Peace and all the beauty which the soul seeks in vain in the domain of multiplicity, is again an inner *jihad*. To melt the hardened heart into a flowing stream of love which would embrace the whole of creation in virtue of the love for God, is to perform the alchemical process of solve "Internal conflict" through a 'work' which is none other than an inner struggle and battle against what the soul has become, in order to transform it into that which it 'is' and has never ceased to be, if only it were to become aware of its own nature. Finally, to realize that only the Absolute is absolute and that only the Self can ultimately utter 'I', is to perform the supreme *jihad* of awakening the soul from the dream of forgetfulness and enabling it to gain the supreme principal knowledge for the sake of which it was created. The inner *jihad* or warfare seen spiritually and esoterically, can be considered, therefore, as the key for the understanding of the whole spiritual process, and the path for the realization of the One which lies at the heart of the Islamic message seen in its totality. The Islamic path towards perfection can be conceived in the light of the symbolism of the greater *jihad* to which the Prophet of Islam, who founded this path on earth, himself referred.

In the same way that with every breath the principle of life which functions in us, irrespective of our will and as long as it is willed by Him who created us, exerts itself through *jihad* to instil life within our whole body, at every moment in our conscious life we should seek to perform *jihad* in not only establishing equilibrium in the world around us but also in awakening to that Divine Reality which is the very source of our consciousness. For the spiritual man, every breath is a reminder that he should continue the inner *jihad* until he awakens from all dreaming and until the very rhythm of his heart echoes that primordial sacred Name by which all things were made and through which all things return to their Origin. The Prophet said, 'Man is asleep and when he dies he awakens'. Through inner *jihad* the spiritual man dies in this life in order to cease all dreaming, in order to awaken to that Reality which is the origin of all realities, in order to behold that Beauty of which all earthly beauty is but a pale reflection, in order to attain that Peace which all men seek but which can in fact be found only through the inner *jihad*[13].

Clarification of the Criterion for the Good and the Bad

One of the most disputed human matters in the course of the history of man's life has been the issue of the criterion for good and bad action and good and evil. Today, many of the world's philosophical schools which have the great universities of the Western World under their domination, including the Positivists, maintain that good and bad are subjects to the persons' taste and inclination and that there is no reality beyond this like and dislike. But Islam says: "Basically, action is a means not an end. A free action is performed for an end and receives its value from that end. In the philosophy of the morality of Islam, good is an action which drives man towards his eventual perfection, namely getting near Allah and bad is an action which drives man away from that end (i.e., from attaining nearness to Allah) and from this it becomes clear why in Islam so much emphasis is laid on *niyyah* (intention); in fact it is man's *niyyah* (intention) which gives direction to his action.

As for the relationship between philosophical good and ethical good, ethical good is propounded in relation to man's free conduct and actions which is the means for philosophical good, the ultimate meaning of life.

So, the ethical good is in one sense other than philosophical good, but is, however, not separate from it either and there is a cause and effect relationship between these two. In other words, ethical good is the preamble to philosophical good. Therefore, when we say that good action causes perfection for man's soul, the goodness of the action is an ethical concept, but the perfection of the soul is a philosophical concept.

In the clarification of the criterion for the evaluation of actions is the fact that perfection of the soul which man should attain through (good) free actions is nearness to Allah (winning Allah's pleasure and favour). About the meaning and concept of this *qurb* (to seek Allah's pleasure-nearness) to Allah, various statements and views have been expressed, about each of which we will give some explanation to the extent necessary.

Various Meanings and Cases of the Application of *Qurb* (to seek Allah's pleasure-nearness)

The first concept which in common conversations is applied to the term '*qurb*' is in terms of place. For example, as when two persons are seated near or in proximity to each other, 'this person is near that person and/or this person is away from that person'. Is man's being near to Allah understood in this sense? Where (in the *Holy Quran)* Asiyah—the wife of *Fir'awn* (pharaoh) says:

..ربِّ ابن لي عندك بيتا في الجنة ...

"*My Lord! Build for me a house with Thee in the garden.* (66:11)."

Did she (by saying so) mean that a faithful person attains nearness of place with Allah in the Paradise? Those who know even the fundamentals of the Islamic beliefs will know that nearness to Allah is definitely not in this sense, because nearness of place is imagined among objects and Allah is not an object to have a place, to whom another object becomes near or from whom another object gets away. So, getting near to Allah does not mean nearness of place.

One of the other cases (of the application) of *qurb* in our conversations is the nearness in terms of time. About two persons living in a time close to each other it is said that they are *qaribul-'asr* (near in terms of time), *vis-à-vis* two beings, two individuals and/or two societies which have a great time gap, one living thousands years ago and the other living today, about them it is said that they are away from each other. It is obvious that man's getting near Allah is not in terms of time either, because, firstly, Allah does not have a time, rather He encompasses all times, just as He has no place and is available at all places. Besides, being near and/or being away in terms of time and place in them do not create any perfection. Anyhow, nearness in terms of place and time is impossible with regard to the Almighty Allah and getting near Him in these two definitions is false. So, how is man to get near Allah?

One other kind of *qurb* which we have in common conversations is that two things are compared with each other in respect of resemblance in specifications, perfections and characteristics apart from time and place. Can it be said in this sense that man gets near Allah? Does *qurb* (to seek Allah's pleasure-nearness) to Allah mean that a greater resemblance to Allah is achieved? Some have attempted to interpret *qurb* to Allah in this way, but in reality this sense is incorrect too. Because firstly, Allah does not resemble anything, (as says the *Holy Quran):*

..ليس كمثله شيء ...

"*...Nothing is like a likeness of Him...* (42:11)"

And that sometimes the interpretation of "being likes God" is applied is a neglectful interpretation. Allah's perfection is infinite and each being, at least in the stage of existence has a phase of finiteness and limitation, and the finite is never comparable with the infinite. If you consider a line with a length of one metre and ask what proportion this one metre line has with an infinite line, those who are even a little conversant with mathematics know that the answer to this question is that there is no proportion between the finite and the infinite. Now, if instead of a one metre line, a two-metre line is considered, again the answer is nothing and even if we draw a line as long as the distance between the earth and the sun, and it is asked that what proportion does this line have to an infinite line, the answer will still be "nothing". No matter how much man attains perfection, he is after all limited and is not a party in proportion to Allah's infinite perfections, for it to be said about him that he has now got somewhat nearer to Allah. Therefore, that some imagine that when man's perfection becomes more, his difference with Allah becomes less and in this sense he gets nearer to Allah, is due to short-sightedness in knowing Allah.

Also some have imagined that by *qurb* is meant just what the following verse of the *Holy Quran* refers to:

و نحن اقرب اليه من حبل الوريد ...

"...*And we are nearer Him than his life-vein*... (50:16)."

Namely, Allah is nearer to man than his life-vein.

Though this matter is true and no firmer and closer relationship between this (relation) can be assumed between Allah and His creatures, but it is clear that this *qurb* and nearness is not particular to the believers and that it exists not only for all men, whether believers, or disbelievers, the pious or the lewd, but it also exists for all creatures and all creatures have this relationship with Allah.

Sometimes *qurb* is also applied in the sense of honour and formality. For example, we say that such and such a person is near to such and such a minister and is favoured by him. By this we mean that they have friendly relations with each other and if the former has a request, the latter will not reject it and will listen to him. About man's *qurb* (to seek Allah's pleasure-nearness) to Allah, the interpretation is sometimes made in this sense, that a man gets so near to Allah that Allah heeds his words, pays attention to his requests and hears his prayers.

Among these five meanings, only the last-mentioned meaning conforms to *qurb* of Allah, a *qurb* which is attained through worship and obedience to the Almighty Allah, as is said in a *hadithun-qudsiyy*.

..لا يزال العبد يتقرب الي بالنافلة حتي اكون سمعه الذي يسمع به و بصره الذي يبصر به و يده التي يبطش بها

> "A servant (of Allah) owing to servitude (to Allah) attains such a position where the Almighty Allah becomes his hearing ears, his seeing eyes and his mighty hands[14]."

A servant (of Allah) owing servitude (to Allah) attains such a position, that in accordance with the interpretation of the above *hadith*, the Almighty Allah becomes his hearing ear, his seeing eye and his capable hand and it is clear that the prayer of such a servant (of Allah) will be heard (by Allah) and that the Almighty Allah will secure his needs and wants. But the question (which may be raised here) is whether such a position is just a honorary and formal position or whether it is an existential and true perfection? And our reply is that this position of *qurb* to Allah is a true perfection for the human soul and that to become *mustajabud-da'wah* (one whose prayer is heard by Allah) and even the acceptance of one's intercession for the others with Allah, are the effects of this spiritual perfection, and not merely a credit and an agreement. In other words, the true meaning of *qurb* to Allah is the sixth meaning which we will now explain to the extent the situation demands.

The Principles for More Clarification

For the clarification of this meaning, we should point out two noble philosophical matters, the details of which should be sought in their own place and in the related books.

The First Principle

The existence of each creature is the relation itself between the Creator and the creature and no creature has any independence of the existence-giving Creator.

The clarification of this principle is rated among the great achievements of the great Islamic expert Sadrul-Muta'allihin Ash-

Shirazi. The philosophical expression of the fourth meaning of the above-mentioned meanings is also based on this very matter, that is, the reason why the Almighty Allah is nearer to each being than any other thing is the very fact that the existence of each creature is the relation itself to and dependence on Him (the Creator) and if this relation is cut off, it will no longer have any existence.

The Second Principle

The existence of the soul is of the category of the existence of knowledge.

In other words; just as the requisite for each physical existence is extension, the requisite for each abstract existence is also "knowledge" which requisite is of course not anything outside the existence of the soul.

Taking into consideration these two matters, we conclude that whenever the existence of man's soul becomes more perfect, his knowledge will become more perfect. The first stage of the perfection of the soul is attaining self-awareness and when one's self-awareness becomes perfect, he will find the reality of his existence which is the same as relation, belonging to and dependence on the Almighty Allah. In other words, he will attain self-awareness and it is for this reason that in the Islamic culture "self-awareness" and "God-awareness" are coupled together. On the one hand, it has been said that:

من عرف نفسه عرف ربه

"*Anybody who knew himself knew his Lord.*"

And on the other hand, the *Holy Quran* says:

...نسوا الله فانساهم انفسهم ...

"*...Those who forsook Allah, so He made them forsake their own souls...* (59:19)"

Those who forsook themselves became afflicted with Allah's forsaking.

So, an inseparable relation exists between knowing one's self and knowing Allah and also between forsaking one's self and Allah's forsaking. The reality of forsaking oneself and self-alienation in the

Islamic culture is precisely that a person forgets his human identity and his attention is so diverted to this world's luxuries and pleasures that he forsakes his reality and his human perfection and felicity, namely, he forgets about his relation to and dependence on the Almighty Allah.

The conclusion is this that true perfection of man's soul is God-awareness (awareness of Allah) which has innumerable stages and more the man's celestial soul becomes perfect, the more his awareness of Allah will increase and this awareness of one's self and of one's God is the same as the existence of the soul. Therefore, man's eventual perfection is his attaining perfect awareness and his innate and intuitive knowledge (knowledge acquired not through the five senses, but through illumination of one's heart) about the Almighty Allah and this awareness about Allah is the very true *qurb* to Allah which should be attained through efforts and endeavours. Therefore, the true meaning of *qurb* to Allah as an acquired perfection for man's soul consists of intuitive and inner *qurb* and the realization of this fact that man's existence is nothing but relation and attachment to the Almighty Allah and that it is not merely knowledge and acquired learning which are attained through concepts and by way of intellectual reasoning.

The Third Principle

The clarification of the moral and value theory of Islam says that this perfection and *qurb* to Allah is attained just in the light of the conducts the general title of which is *ibadah*, worshipping Allah, and virtuousness. To prove this principle from the philosophical point of view, too, requires a technical and complicated expression.

Here, we restrict ourselves to a simple explanation of the principle. We came to know that the Almighty Allah is not a physical and place-occupying being whom we could get near to with the movement of the body or traversing material distance, and that no kind of physical action and reaction and body change and development can in itself have any role in changing man's relation to the Almighty Allah and that the truth of man's *qurb* to Allah is inner and intuitive nearness and attaining man's existential relationship with Him. Taking these points into consideration it can easily be accepted that what plays the main role in man's getting near to the Almighty Allah is that very man's power of perceiving and witnessing, namely, the truth of his soul which in many cases is called 'heart'. The free (voluntary) relationship which is established between man's heart and the Almighty Allah is by means of attention (to Allah), and this very attention itself is termed "*dhikr* (remembrance of Allah) of the heart. When this attention and remembrance become the source of performance of an action and a conduct, it is rated as the *niyyah* (intention) and motive for the action. Since the perfection of man's soul and spirit is attained by means of free actions, and each kind of conduct can have a role in the promotion or regression of the soul in one of its dimensions, therefore, we conclude that man's all-sided perfection is attained when all distinct conducts are fulfilled with divine motive and the main stimulant and the giver of direction to these conducts is attention to Allah. In other words, just as physical forces determine the direction of the movement of objects, so also psychic motives, which stem from attention to and remembrance of Allah, are spiritual forces which determine the spiritual direction of man's actions and conducts and which give value to them. As already explained, such conducts have two general terms in Islamic culture: one is *taqwa* in its general sense and the other *ibadah* in its general sense.

The conclusion is that each free action, to the extent it enjoys divine intention and motive, will have positive value; and to the extent it stems from ungodly, egoistic and polytheistic intention, it will have negative value. Thus, the role of *At-Tawhid* in the value system of Islam becomes clear.

Quranic Expressions about the Philosophy of Morality

So far, we have explained the theory of Islam in the philosophy of morality and values with the simplest rational expressions which were available to us. Now we refer to some examples of Quranic expressions concerning the principles of this theory:

In *Suratush-Shams* (chapter 91 of the *Holy Quran*) in the wake of a number of verses in which the Almighty Allah swears by the sun, by the moon, by the night, by the day and the like, He says:

و نفس و ما سواها * فالهمها فجورها و تقواها * قد افلح من زكاها * و قد خاب من دساها

> *"And the soul and Him Who made it perfect, then He inspired it to understand what is right and wrong for it; He will indeed*

> *be successful who purifies it. And he will indeed fail who corrupts it* (91:7-10)."

Of the many points inferred from these verses, we content ourselves with citing three points:

The first point is that Allah swears by the human soul, the soul which Allah has made and delivered well, and among all creatures man has a particular privilege to determine his destiny with his own freewill: to choose either the way of felicity and salvation or the way of adversity and corruption. Certainly, Allah's goal of the creation of man, is that he attains felicity and salvation, but since human felicity is a matter to be attained by the way of man's own will-power and free choice, so there should necessarily exist another point in the face of it too towards which would retrogress of his own ill-choice anybody who chooses to. It is important to note that all religions explicitly or implicitly accept that a life of spiritual perfection is an intrinsically happy life and such a life brings hereafter eternal happiness and intrinsic and extrinsic goodness.

The second point is that selection of either of the two points' exaltation and perfection or fall and retrogression demands recognition. Because it is obvious that without awareness and recognition proper selection and choice does not take place. Hence, the Almighty Allah has made two general ways known to man: one the way of *taqwa* and the other the way of *fujur* (wrong behaviour), and from this very interpretation it is inferred that the criterion for the positive conduct values is *taqwa* and the criterion for the negative moral values is *fujur*, as was already explained in the foregoing expressions.

The third point is that to traverse the way of *taqwa* is the very "purification of the soul" and its result is the growth and perfection of the soul, just as to traverse the way of *fujur* is the very pollution of the soul, the result of which is the fall and destruction of the soul itself. So man, by selecting the way of *taqwa*, gives growth and perfection to his soul and by selecting the way of *fujur* and licence pollutes and destroys his own soul. Therefore, the result of man's free conducts, be they in the direction of growth and perfection or in the direction of fall and retrogression, will accrue to man himself. From here it can well be inferred that the value conducts have a true effect on the perfection and imperfection of the soul and that the positive or negative value criterion is this very perfection and imperfection of man's soul. This is that same first principle in the expression of the logical reason we referred to previously.

From another set of the verses of the *Holy Quran* it is inferred that man's eternal felicity and adversity is the result of his own faith and infidelity and praiseworthy and indecent actions:

> و ان ليس للانسان الّا ما سعى
>
> *"And that man shall have nothing but what he strives for* (53:39)."
>
> لها ما كسبت و عليها ما اكتسبت ...
>
> *"...For it, is what it has earned, and against it what it has incurred.* (3:286)."
>
> ..و وفيت كل نفس ما كسبت ...
>
> *"...And every soul is paid off whatever it has earned.* (3:25)."
>
> ... يوم تجد كل نفس ما عملت من خير محضرا
>
> "**The** *day when every soul shall find present what it has done of good.* (3:30)."

There are many other verses in the *Holy Quran* indicating that the blessings and torments in the Hereafter are the result of the actions which man has himself fulfilled in this world, rather they are those very actions of his, which in the Hereafter world appear in the form of blessing or torment. Of course, the language of most of the verses of the *Holy Quran* is that the blessings or torments in the Hereafter are the reward or punishment for the conducts in this world. With our mind having got acquainted with the concepts of reward and punishment, it might at first be imagined that the relation of good and bad actions with their results in the Hereafter is a nominal and conventional relation, but taking into view the cited verses of the *Holy Quran* it becomes clear that beyond these nominal concepts a series of creational facts and true and real relations are hidden, though our knowledge is not sufficient for the discovery of these true relations, because we have no experience of such relations.

Included among the verses to be considered in this discussion are the verses which have just been mentioned about spiritual light and darkness. These terms have been largely applied with regard to truth and falsehood, moral and value, good and evil and with regard to the affairs related to them in the *Holy Quran* and also in the sayings of the Holy Prophet of Islam and the Infallible Imams and which have a particular position in Islamic culture.

On the one hand, the *Holy Quran* introduces the Almighty Allah as "*nur* (the light) of the heavens and the earth" and it is obvious that by this light the generally known physical light is not meant and on the other hand, the Holy Prophet of Islam has been introduced (by *the Holy Quran)* as

سراجا منيرا ...

"...*A light-giving torch* (33:46)."

And on the other hand, the *Holy Quran* has itself been named "*nur*" (light).

قد جاء كم من الله نور و كتاب مبين ...

"...*There has come to you a light and a clear Book from Allah* (5:15)."

And also the aim of the revelation of The *Holy Quran* to the Holy Prophet of Islam has been considered (by *The Holy Quran)* to be taking the people out of darkness and bringing them into the "light":

..لتخرج الناس من الظلمات الي النور ...

"...*That you may bring forth men, by their Lord's permission from darkness into light*...(14:1)."

Also, the believers have been introduced (by the *Holy Quran*) as those who in this world are possessed of light (*nur*), *versus* the infidel and those who are disobedient to Allah's commands that have sunk into darkness:

او من كان ميتا فاحييناه و جعلنا له نورا يمشي به في الناس كمن مثله في الظلمات ليس بخارج منها ...

"*Is he who was dead then We raised him to life and made for him a light by which he walks among the people, like hint whose likeness is that of one in utter darkness whence he cannot come forth?* (6:123)."

Finally, among the descriptions of the Resurrection Day, the *Holy Quran* says:

يوم ترى المؤمنين و المؤمنات يسعى نورهم بين ايديهم و بأيمانهم...

> *"On that day you will see the faithful men and the faithful women—their light shining before them and on their right hand-.* (57:12)."

يوم يقول المنافقون و المنافقات للذين امنوا انظرونا نقتبس من نوركم قيل ارجعوا وراء كم فالتمسوا نورا ...

> *"On the day when the hypocritical men and the hypocritical women will say to those who believe: Wait for us, that we may have light from your light; it shall be said: Turn back and seek a light (hinting that for seeking light you should return to the world, which is impossible).* (57:13)."

And the most comprehensive *ayat* in this connection are the verses 35 to 40 of *Suratun-Nur* (Chapter 24) of the *Holy Quran* which start with this sentence:

الله نور السموات و الارض ...

> "*Allah is the light of thee heavens and the earth.* (24:35)."

And end with this sentence:

و من لم يجعل الله له نورا فما له من نور ...

> "*And to whomsoever Allah does not give light, he has no light* (24:40)."

In these verses, after the Almighty Allah has been introduced as the light of the heavens and of the earth (the light of the worlds); a parable has been given for His light in *ayah* 35 of chapter 24.

> "*A likeness of His light is as a niche in which is a lamp, the lamp is in a glass, (and) the glass is as it were a brightly shining star; lit front a blessed olive-tree, neither eastern nor western.* (24:35)."

(Hinting that the sun shines from all its sides perfectly and no unripe fruit remains in it). Such oil is so susceptible for being inflamed that it is as if it automatically lights without any fire touching it.

In fact, it is the remembrance of Allah which makes their (holy men's) lives lit and luminous and which gives value to all their conducts and deeds.

On the opposite side of these, there are the disbelievers, who due to forgetting Allah have sunk into darkness and whose actions have become null and valueless. And in the two last-mentioned verses, two parables have been cited for the actions of the disbelievers: The first parable is

> "*The mirage in a desert, which the thirsty, man deems to be water; until when he comes to it he finds it to be naught, and there he finds Allah, so He pays back to him his reckoning in full. (24:39).*"

That is, the disbelievers engage in efforts and endeavours in hope of felicity and attach their hearts to their own deeds, but when they should derive benefit from these efforts (in the Hereafter), they see no useful thing and the Almighty Allah will make it clear to them that they have done no useful work for their felicity.

The second parable for the disbeliever and the value of their deeds is:

> "*Utter darkness in the deep sea: there covers it a wave above which is another wave, above which is a cloud (layers of) utter darkness one above another; when he holds out his hand he is almost unable to see it.* (24:40)."

The above *ayah* ends with the following sentence:

> و من لم يجعل الله له نورا فما له من نور ...
>
> "...*And to whomsoever Allah does not give light, he has no light* (24:40)."

Whatever ambiguity, if any, might exist about the reality (the true meaning) of "*misbah*" (lamp), "*zujajah*" (glass) and *mishkat* (niche) (The expressions applied in *surah* 24 of the *Holy Quran*, in *ayah* 35 referred to) and whatever discussion, if any, might be made regarding the sea, the waves and the clouds surrounding it, there is no room for any doubt and ambiguity about the fact that these *ayats* regard the men of Allah (the believers) to be those who are blessed with light and felicity, who through remembrance of Allah and heart-felt attention to the Creator make their lives valuable and that the disbelievers, through forgetting Allah, destroy the value of their deeds and will finally be afflicted with darkness and adversity. So, the criterion for good, felicity, light and true value is relation with the original source of light which is attained by means of faith in Allah and the attention of one's heart to Him and the criterion for evil, adversity, darkness, valuelessness and futility is lack of relationship and connection with the original source of light which develop as a result of disbelief (in Allah), forgetting Allah and turning away from His remembrance, like an electric light which on connection with the electricity-generating system is lit and on disconnection is extinguished. And these are the purports of those very principles to which in the last expression of logical reason we referred and thus the conformity of the expression of logical reason with the Quranic expressions becomes manifest.

The Ethical Philosophy of Islam

Islam, like other great religions, lays great emphasis on ethics for all situations of the man's life; it contains a variety of instructions such as worship of God (*Salaat* "prayer", *Sowm* "Fasting", *Hajj* "pilgrimage", etc.) and some physical actions.

Morals can be classified either as secular or religious. Secular morality tries to establish a moral system that is independent of God and religious faiths. With regard to motives for morality, various explanations have been given. One explanation is that people are ethical in pursuit of happiness or perfection. Another suggests that pressure by political power or social means forces people to follow a certain code of conduct. Yet another explanation is that a feeling of duty makes people moral.

Another problem in this classification for morals is that it lacks clarity in defining ethical knowledge. For example, is happiness mental, physical, or spiritual?

As for religious morality, it is fundamentally based on two things; first, the belief in God as the Creator of the universe, and second, the belief in the Hereafter.

"Religious morality" is not a uniformly used term because the fundamentals of religious morality are not the same for all religions.

Al-Kindi, the first genuine philosopher of Islam, appears from his extensive ethical writings to have been particularly influenced by Socrates and Diogenes the Cynic. Other classical influences can be seen in the work of Platonists such as Abu Bakr al-Razi, who followed Plato's division of the parts of the souls, and Neoplatonists such as al-Farabi, while Aristotelian influences can be seen in al-Farabi, (who also discussed the problem of evil) Ibn Sina and Ibn Rushd. Ibn Sina developed a theory of the conjunction of the soul with the active intellect; with this conjunction is bound up the ultimate perfection of the soul which has attained the highest degree of wisdom and virtue. Islam is the loving, conscious, and voluntary submission to the will of God.

Neoplatonism again surfaces in the work of Ibn Miskawayh and his followers, to whom we owe the groundwork of a whole ethical tradition which flourished in Persia well into the twelfth century A.D. and beyond. (Eighteenth century A.D.) Onto Plato's three-fold division of the soul, Ibn Miskawayh grafts a three-fold division of virtue into wisdom, courage and temperance. His views were elaborated upon by al-Tusi and al-Dawwani, among others. A blend of philosophical and religious ethics is characteristic of the work of some later writers such as al-Ghazali and Fakhr al-Din al-Razi, in which the road to moral and spiritual perfection has mystical overtones[15].

Finally, it can be said that Islamic Ethical philosophy differs from other philosophies on two basic counts:

1. The origin or the motivating factor in adherence to ethical principles under the Islamic ethical philosophy is primarily the articles of faith of Islam. In other words, ethical behaviour, under the Islamic ethical philosophy, is a requisite of the articles of Islamic faith. An attitude of deviation from ethical principles is a practical negation of ascription to the very elements of Islamic faith.
2. The practical application of ethical principles of the *Shari'ah*, with the basic universal ethical principles themselves, are a part of the code of basic ethical conduct in Islam.

Thus, to summarize, the ethical teachings of Islam may be classified into two categories:

1. Where the *Holy Quran* has reminded man of the basic ethical values with the implication that if man consciously deviates from such values, he shall then have no excuse to defend himself from facing the consequences of such deviation.
2. Where the *Holy Quran* has applied the basic ethical principles on practical life situations and has prescribed or prohibited a particular code of conduct.

Summary of Chapter Five

- Ethics, a major branch of philosophy, is the study of values and customs of a person or group. It covers the analysis and employment of concepts such as right and wrong, good and evil, and responsibility. It is divided into three primary areas: meta-ethics (the study of the concept of ethics), normative ethics (the study of how to determine ethical values), and applied ethics (the study of the use of ethical values).
- Ethics means a set of rules for behaviour, based on beliefs about how things should be.
- Ethical systems (sets of rules for acceptable behaviour) concern the "shoulds" and "should nots" of life, the principles and values on which human relations are based.
- Ethics can also be divided into two main schools: Absolutism and Relativism. Absolutists believe that ethical rules are fixed standards (for example, stealing is always wrong, no matter what the circumstances). Relativists, on the other hand, believe that all ethics are subject to context (for example, stealing may be wrong in certain circumstances but not in others).
- Bioethics is the philosophical study of the ethical controversies brought about by advances in biology and medicine. We can say that this is a new branch of ethical issues which are related to the new scientific subject.
- One reason for studying ethical issues in science is that several recent scientific developments such as cloning and genetic engineering of plants and animals have raised pressing ethical issues, and also the reasons for studying ethical issues in science and technology extend beyond current controversies to the pervasive influence of science and technology in our lives.

- The nature of Marx's views on morality and ethics has long been a matter of considerable dispute. But we know that moral, ethics and religion are convertible terms. A moral life without reference to religion is like a house built upon sand, as Gandhi said. The chapter argues that the Gandhian view that unselfish ethical struggle against injustice, exploitation, etc., is a religious struggle.
- Islam, like other great religions, lays great emphasis on ethics for all situations of the man's life. According to Islam, man has not come into existence on his own and neither is he a product of natural forces that had somehow, by pure chance, combined to produce life. Moral virtues in man gain him eternal happiness, while moral corruption leads him to everlasting wretchedness. It is, therefore, necessary for man to purge and purify himself of all evil traits of character and adorn his soul with all forms of ethical and moral virtues. Moreover, without having cleansed oneself of all evil habits, it would be impossible to nourish and develop moral virtues in oneself. One of the most important ethical issues of Islamic thought that is called *Taqwa,* which we call an internal *Jihad* or internal purification that Prophet Mohammad had put great emphasis on.
- *Taqwa* as a word means; fear of God. It is the fear of earning His displeasure and being deprived of His all abounding mercy. Keeping the foregoing in mind, a person can attain *taqwa* if he submits wholeheartedly to every order of His Lord. The great stations of perfection in the spiritual life can also be seen in the light of the inner *jihad*. To become separate from the impurities of the world in order to repose in the purity of the Divine Presence requires an intense *jihad*, for our soul has its roots sunk deeply into the transient world which the soul of fallen man mistakes for reality. The Islamic path towards perfection can be conceived in the light of the symbolism of the greater *Jihad* to which the Prophet of Islam, who founded this path on earth, himself referred.

FOOTNOTES

1. via Latin ethica from the Ancient Greek →θική [φιλοσοφία] "moral philosophy", from the adjective of →θος ēthos "custom, habit"

2. (William Lillie, *An Introduction to Ethics,* 3rd edition, Methuen & Co. Ltd., 1971, pp. 1-2)
3. Mercy killing.
4. Like producing test tube babies.
5. All these concepts are related to the field of bio ethics.
6. See: Mel Thompson, *Philosophy, Teach Yourseif,* London 2000, p. 98.
7. There can be a distinction between ethics and 'morality. Morality' refers to an actual or an ideal (i.e. reflective) set of moral principles, virtues, standards, etc., according to which people should live and/or act. 'Ethics' or 'moral philosophy' refers either to the process in which one engages while reflecting on morality, its nature and bases, or to the result of that reflection. In the latter instance, ethics and (ideal) morality overlap—at least in part. They might be said to be not identical because one's ethics may include various logical and methodological views which would not, as such, be part of one's (ideal) morality.
8. Werner Sombart, Barun's Archiv fur Socia e Gesetzgebung und Statistik, vol. 5, 1892, p. 489, cited in Robert C. Tucker, *Philosophy and Myth in Karl Marx,* Cambridge University Press, 1971, p. 12. Other commentators who have held, in one place or another, that Marxism is essentially a science would include B. Croce, R. Hilferding, and K. Kautsky.
9. M.K. Gandhi, *In Search of the Supreme*, Navajivan Publishing House, Ahmedabad, India 2002, Vol. I, p. 131.
10. *Ibid*, p. 131.
11. See: *At-Tawhid or Monotheism* by Muhammad Taqi Misbah Yazdi, p. 146.
12. See: Jami' al-Sa'adat, *The Collector of Felicities,* pp. 9-11, by Muhammad Mahdi ibn Abi Dhar al-Naraqi.
13. S. Mohammad. Nasr.
14. Al-Usulul Kafi, Mohammad Koleini, Iran 1990, Vol. 2, p. 352.
15. For more study see: al-Tusi (1201-74) *Akhlaq-i Nasiri (The Nasirean Ethics),* trans. G.M. Wickens, London: Allen & Unwin, 1964. (Translation of al-Tusi's *Akhlaq-i Nasiri* from Persian, Reliable on the whole) and related books.-www.usc.edu/dept/MSA?quran/The Noble Quran
www.shiaweb.org/quran.net/tafseer/Meeza/index.html-6k
-تفسير الميزان
www.holyquran.net/tafseer/majma/index/html/10k
.تفسير مجمع البيان
www.qurancomplex.org/Quran/tafseer/Tafseer.asp?t =TABARY&TabID=3&Subltemld=1&1=arb تفسير طبرى

www.qurancomplex.org/Quran/tafseer/Tafseer.asp?1=arb&1= katheer & nSora=1&nAya= 1 • 1_1 تفسير ابن كثير
www.alhikmeh.com/Arabic/akhlaq/quran/index.htm. اخلاق قرآن
www.alhikmeh.com/Arabic/akhlaq/nama/index.htm.
اخلاق در حديث شيعه
www.al-eman.com/Islamlib/viewtoc.asp?BID=383
متن احياء العلوم غزالى
www.wri.leaderu.com/wri-table2/hinduism.html.

6

Conclusion

In this chapter, the analysis of the relationship between religion and science, and the Islamic and Hindu viewpoints about the ethical approach to modern science and its issues has been discussed. We have seen that according to both (Islam and Hinduism), there is no clash between religious scriptures and science. Marx's view and Evolution theory as examples have been examined. The internal aspect of religion is the body of ideas, convictions and emotions concerning man's relations with God, while its external aspect is the system of prayers, ceremonies and rites through which the religious feeling is manifested, as well as one's ethical relations with others and nature.

Many scientists believe that science is made and applied to solve modern problems which consist of technological and humanist issues. The quarrel between science and religion was a very fateful quarrel in the history of Europe. And it was not a product of a conspiracy, ill will, malice or ir-religiosity. In fact, it was a very natural quarrel: there was growth in the natural sciences, in geology, biology, astronomy. And new information came to light that was in conflict with the contents of Scripture and the conflict intensified to the point where it became impossible to hide or deny these differences. There were the cases of Copernicus, Kepler, Galileo and Newton and, later, Buffon and Darwin. Some of these people were religious themselves. As it happens, Galileo was a religious man. Copernicus was once a priest. Kepler was someone who had gone several steps beyond the common religion of the masses to the point of being superstitious. But the product of these people's work was something that was not in anyway in keeping with the contents of Scripture, especially on the subject of the motion of the earth and the sun and the planets. The Church tolerated these ideas for a while but, in time the quarrel flared up anew. The status that the Church and Scripture acquired thereafter never went back to what it had been before the quarrel. In all fairness, despite all its hostility towards science, the Church did not go down the path of fanaticism. The Church allowed the publication of Copernicus's book. In *The Revolutions of the Heavenly Spheres*, Copernicus explicitly stated that the earth was in motion and that the sun was still, whereas, according to Scripture, it was the sun that moved and the earth that was still. From the 400 copies of the book that were published in the sixteenth century, 200 still exist today. The tales about Galileo having been put to death are all untrue. Of course, they did put Galileo under house arrest. The Church allowed the publication of Copernicus's book but insisted on an introduction being added which made an important point: "what is stated in this book is a theory and not the absolute truth". This was a laudable and sensible solution.

The big and small discoveries that were being made here and there gradually robbed Scripture of the status that it had had heretofore. Religion lost its former power and status and, from then on, it was no longer the actor on the social and political stage that it had been before. As long as religion was strong, it was in the political arena. When faith diminished and religion's status declined, this actor ended up playing a smaller role. It was not as if anyone evicted religion from the political stage; it just grew weaker and moved to the sidelines. The political stage is for powerful players. When religion was strong, there was no need for anyone to invite religion onto the political stage. And, when it grew weak, it inevitably left the stage; there was no need for anyone to evict it.

Science alone, and without the cooperation of religion, is incomplete. Sciences do not deal with values but religions do. Science cannot make man happy, hopeful and serious in looking for the goal of the life. So science itself is not enough for his happiness. The experience of the Second World War made it clear that science by itself and without religion could not bring happiness and goodness. Because at that time science was used only for waging war more efficiently, destroying and killing more. The world is not free from war even for a single day. Science without religion cannot lead man towards happiness. Science is a powerful instrument under man when he wants to remove or increase his suffering. It is not possible to separate man's way of thinking from his way of living and his dealing with life. Theistic religions base their interpretation and viewpoint on believing that this universe, life, and man have a Creator, a Lord, a God; and that man's existence on this earth is neither a meaningless nor aimless one nor it is a random happening. Life and man have their goals and values exceeding the time span of man's existence on the earth's surface. Although some theistic religions like Buddhism do not believe in God, every religion has an ethical system to guide one's action, and a metaphysical worldview with the belief that good will be necessarily properly rewarded and evil will be punished in this life or in the life after death.

The question of whether religion is compatible with science occupied a prominent place in the discussions of the nineteenth century and some thinkers held that science and religion are incompatible. Those who believe that religion and science cannot be opposed to each other argue that they are two aspects of the same facts of life. One aspect touches the soul while the other indicates material advancement. Religion gives peace to a scientifically advanced and worried society. It is also said that both try to pierce into the realm of unknown. They also argue that in every society there are eminent scientists who believe in God. They, therefore, feel that it is not correct to say that both are absolutely opposed to each other. It cannot be denied that there is a conflict between the two. Religion fears that the free enquiry of science may damage or shatter its image, if not wholly at least partially.

It seems that there are four approaches by which science and religion can be related to each other:

Conflict: The conviction that science and religion are fundamentally irreconcilable.

Contrast: The claim that there can be no genuine conflict since religion and science are each responding to radically different questions.

Contact: An approach that looks for dialogue, interaction, and possible "consonance" between science and religion, and especially for ways in which science shapes religious and theological understanding.

Confirmation: A somewhat quieter, but extremely important perspective that highlights the ways in which, at a very deep level, religion supports and nourishes the entire scientific enterprise.

The main goal of this book was to analyze the solution offered by the different religions to resolve the conflict between religion and science. But some of these approaches are themselves not free from major mistakes.

The relationship between ethics and religion and modern science is stricter when we consider the main purpose of religions. In other words, religions have to improve the moral activities in human's life, and they have to be leading him to goodness and happiness. The ethics of religion could solve many problems of mankind, for example faith and purification to complete goodness can open new horizons of human perfection.

It should be noted that a competent and successful scientist today can be found in all four categories. We should avoid giving simplistic answers to questions about science and religion. It is suggested that other researchers work on these issues:

- Religious laws and modern sciences.
- Ethics and religious scriptures.
- Secularism and the relationship between religion and science.
- Abortion and religious scriptures.
- Religion and science and globalization.
- Religions and Bioethics issues.
- And many other issues.

In the second chapter, various viewpoints such as those of Marx, Galileo, Darwin and other religions or scientists, and their relationship have been discussed. It is not possible to separate man's way of thinking from his way of living and his dealing with life. Man thinks for himself, wants to comprehend his surroundings and tries to know the beginning and the end of everything, in order to be able to understand the mysteries of the world and life. He tries to discover: How did this world begin? Where is it going to? Why is he here in this life? What is the goal of his existence? What does ethics means? Where will he end? What does life itself mean? How should he conduct his life?

Man has always been looking for convincing answers to these questions. The answer to them either leads him to happiness and welfare, or wretchedness and misfortune.

The answers, though short in their form and brief in their expression, are yet great in their meanings, important in their reality and deep in their effects.

These answers define how man should live, behave, and understand life and estimate the importance of his own existence. By providing correct answers one may resolve an important crisis of thought—the crisis from which man has long been suffering, unable to find correct answers. He has been tormented by anxiety and uncertainty and forced to walk through as chasm of suffering. The correct answers to these questions have always been confined to two contradictory theories, and in the resulting constructions that are based upon them. The two answers are: The first given through religion, lighting the path of righteousness and faith with rational proof; the second given by error and denial, aiming at invoking a mist to obliterate clear visibility, to envelope man's conscience and prevent it from directing itself towards Allah, the Beginning and the end of existence.

Evolution (Darwinian Theory) is a purely scientific theory that need not be cast in either materialist, or religious terms. Islam tells us that the same God who creates the universe also promises to save it from all its travail, suffering, and death. This would mean then that the whole story of cosmic evolution, in all its detail and incredible breadth, is permanently taken into God's loving memory. A model or combination of models that a person adopts for relating science and religion is likely to depend strongly on his or her up bringing, as well as on the fundamental presuppositions he or she brings to the issue. We should note that today, competent and successful scientists can be found in all four categories. We should avoid giving simplistic answers to questions about science and religion.

It should be stressed, as we know Darwin's theory is opposed to Christianity scriptures in some interpretation. Islamic scriptures also describe the story of creation. But in the *Bible*, the creation by God is direct. For instance, we have in the *Holy Quran* the verses that illustrates that God created all animals, the earth and sky indirectly while this concept is not mentioned in the scriptures of *Bible*. Therefore, the evolution theory of Darwin does not clash with Quranic verses. Therefore, the question whether the theory of evolution is opposed to the creation of Adam and Eve or not, depends on the interpretations. Thus, Darwin's theory of evolution is not necessarily a contrast to religion.

Under the headings of conflict, contrast, contact and conformation, we can present the positions of each approach as it responds to the attractive questions that science is raising for religion today. But in our understanding, religions, especially Islam and Hinduism do not oppose scientific and technological progress, on the contrary, they encourage it. Islam, like other great religions, has laid great emphasis on ethics for all situations of the man's life. According to Islam, man has not come into existence on his own and neither is he a product of natural forces that had somehow, by pure chance, combined to produce life. Moral virtues in man gain him eternal happiness, while moral corruption leads him to everlasting wretchedness. It is, therefore, necessary for man to purge and purify himself of all evil traits of character and adorn his soul with all forms of ethical and moral virtues. Moreover, without having cleansed oneself of all evil habits, it would be impossible to nourish and develop moral virtues in oneself. One of the most important ethical issues of Islamic thought is called *taqwa,* which we can call it as an internal *jihad* or internal purification on which Prophet Mohammad had put great emphasis. The meaning of *taqwa* is fear of God; it is the fear of earning His displeasure and being deprived of His all abounding mercy.

Regarding the theory of *jihad* it seems that (to my understanding) the great stations of perfection in the spiritual life can also be seen in the light of the inner *jihad.* To become separate from the impurities of the world in order to repose in the purity of the Divine Presence requires an intense *jihad* for our soul whose roots are sunk deeply into the transient world, which the soul of fallen man mistakes for reality. The Islamic path towards perfection can be conceived in the light of the symbolism of the greater *jihad* to which the Prophet of Islam, who founded this path on earth, himself referred.

Religion's answer offers, through its call and message, and its interpretation of the universe and life, an explanation of man's existence, and of his links with them. Religion bases its interpretation and viewpoint on believing that this universe, life and man have a Creator, a Lord; and that man's existence on this earth is neither a meaningless or aimless one, nor is it random happening. Life and man have their goals and values exceeding the time span of man's existence on the earth's surface. He has a supreme objective to pursue, embodying it through his attitudes, his deeds and his general activities in a world that goes beyond perception.

According to both religions, scripture and traditions do not have any clash with reference to their fundamental ethics although they have fundamental differences in the domain of metaphysics.

On the contrary, it encourages different scientific researches, the goal of which is exalted and manlike, because they divulge secrets of creation and of the divine particulars in the world. However, some researches, such as "human cloning", are meddling in creation and their prejudicial results cannot be anticipated.

Marx's view and the evolution theory as examples have been examined in this study. Although the *Quran* and Hindu scriptures do not have a scientific purpose to illustrate scientific facts, we could not say that, religions are against scientific facts. As a final conclusion about the accuracy or validity of Marx's ideas on religion, we should recognize that he provided an invaluable service by forcing people to take a hard look at the social states in which religion always performs. Because of his work, it has become impossible to study religion without exploring its ties to various social and economic forces. People's spiritual lives can no longer be assumed to be totally independent of their material lives. In addition to this point we can find many social reforms which are based on religions such as the Gandhian movement, Islamic revolution of Iran and Tobacco Concession (1891). There are many interpretations on evolution. Some of them are acceptable according to Islam, while others are not acceptable. If by evolution, it means the development and growth that Allah Almighty has placed in the nature of His creation, then this is acceptable and the *Quran* itself talks about it. According to the Islamic view, human beings are the special creation of Allah. Allah created the Body of Adam and his wife Eve from the soil; it does not mean that scientific rules have not been accepted.

Gandhi's views, such as that modern civilization is essentially irreligious, i.e. unspiritual, is essentially correct, although one may not agree with him that it is immoral. According to him, unselfish ethical life of love constitutes the essence of religion and modern civilization is essentially a civilization of selfishness. He rightly considered modern Western civilization to be a false civilization in the sense that what it considers to be the ultimate goal of life is false. He would not accept the form of development of modern Western civilization which causes the destruction of thousand and thousand species and continues to cause great harm to our life sustaining natural systems.

It does not mean that religion is against development. Both Islam and Hinduism would accept development within the limits of ethics.

Considering the main purpose of religions, the relationship

between ethics and religion and modern science is stricter. In other words, religions have come to improve the moral activities in human's life, and they have to lead him to goodness and happiness, because science cannot create value for man, but religion can. The ethics of religion can solve many problems of mankind, for example purification to complete goodness and bring new horizons of human's perfection. The result of this study shows that the majority of man's problems have arisen because of his disbelieving in religions and missing its role. As a last comment it can be concluded that it is possible that religion and science converge in the future world and their convergence would bring lasting peace and happiness to humanity. Therefore, man's need for religion has not terminated.

As The *Quran* says:

> *"And be not ye as those who forgot Allah, therefore He caused them to forget their souls. Such are the evil-doers"*[1].

And also *The Upanishad says:*

> *"Those who deny God, deny themselves. Those who affirm God, affirm themselves"*.[2]

FOOTNOTES

1. *Holy Quran*; chapter 59/19. The Gathering "Al-Hashr".
2. *Taittiriya Upanishad* 2:6; 7. Source: *World Mythology* by Donna.

Bibliography

Asimov Isaac, *Toward Freedman,* University Press of Mississippi, 2005.

Anscombe, Elizabeth, *Modern Moral Philosophy, Philosophy,* 1958, Vol. 33, reprinted in her Ethics, Religion and Politics (Oxford: Blackwell, 1981).

Bose, N.K., *Selections from Gandhi,* Navajivan Publishing House, Ahmedabad, India, 1972.

Burtt, A. Edwin, *The Metaphysical Foundation of Modern Science,* Humanities Press, 1951.

Bagvad-Gita, 4.7-8.

Bishop, C.L., *Does Science deny God?* William Earl & Company Ltd., London, 1970.

Baird, R.D., 'Swami Bhaktivedanta and the Encounter with Religions', in *Modern Indian Responses to Religious Pluralism,* edited by Harold Coward, State University of New York Press, 1987.

Barbour, Ian Graeme, *Issues In Science and Religion,* Harper Torch Books, New York, 1971.

Benz Ernst, *Evolution and Christian Hope,* Garden City, N.Y: Doubleday, 1996.

Bhattacharyya, N.N., *History of the Tantric Religion.* (Second Revised Edition), Manohar: New Delhi, 1999.

Bohm, David, *Causality and Chance in Modern Physics,* Princeton. N. J. D. van Nostrand Co., 1957.

Burckhardt, Titus, *Science of the Cosmos, Science of the Soul,* 1997, Vitae www.cis-ca.org.

Catholic University of America, *New Catholic Encyclopaedia,* the Catholic University of America-Washington, D. C. volume 11, 2003.

Campanini, M.: Al-Ghazzali, in S.H. Nasr and O. Leaman, *History of Islamic Philosophy,* 1996. www.mullasadra.org

Chattrjee, Satisschandra & Datta, Dhirendramohan, *An Introduction to Indian Philosophy.*

Copleston, Frederick, *A History of Philosophy*, Image Book, A Division of Doubleday & Company, Inc., Garden City, New York, 1985.

Corbin, H. The Encyclopaedia Britannica, *History of Islamic Philosophy* London, Keagan Paul International, 1993.

Craig, Edward, *Routledge Encyclopedia of Philosophy* London and New York, volume 8, 1998.

Darwin, Charles, "*Science and Civilization in Islam*", Cambridge: Harvard University Press, 1968, The Origin of Species: A Facsimile of the First Edition, Harvard University Press, 1964, and Stefan Bengston, Nature, Vol. 345, 1990.

Darwin, Charles, *The Origin of Species,* A Facsimile of the First Edition, Harvard University Press, 1964.

Derek V. Ager, *The Nature of the Fossil Record,* Proceedings of the British Geological Association, Vol. 87, 1976

Edeard H. Cotton, *Has science discovered God?,* Yhomas Y. Crowell Company Publishers, New York, Second Printing, 1931.

Edelglass, William, *Between Two Worlds: East and West: An Autobiography* (review), Philosophy East and West, Volume 55, Number 1, January 2005.

Edwards, A. *Episodes in the Mathematics of Medieval Islam.* New York: Springer-Verlag.

Edwards, Paul, *The Encyclopedia of Philosophy,* Macmillan Company, New York, volume 7, 1967.

Eliade, Mircea, *The Encyclopedia of Religion,* Volume 15, Macmillan Publishing Company, New York, 1986.

Frank R.M., *Al-Ghazali and the Ash'arite School,* Duke University Press, London, 1994.

Fieser, James, *The Internet Encyclopaedia of Philosophy,* Immanuel Kant's Metaphysics (Free online encyclopedia. Hosted by the University of Tennessee at Martin.www.iep.utm.edu).

Flood, Gavin, *An Introduction to Hinduism*, Cambridge: Cambridge University Press, 1996.

Frawley, David, *Hinduism and the Clash of Civilizations* by Voice of India, 2001. Website of National Geographic.

Galileo, Galilei, *Dialogues Concerning Two New Sciences,* trans. T. Salusbury, Chicago, University of Chicago, 1953.

Gandhi, M.K., *Hind Swaraj or Indian Home Rule,* Navajivan Publishing House, Ahmedabad, 1995.

Gandhi, M.K., *In Search of the Supreme,* Volume III, Navajivan Publishing House, Ahmedabad, reprint 2002.

Gandhi, Mohandas Karamchand, *The Collected Works of Mahatma Gandhi,* Vol. 35. New Delhi: Publications Division, Government of India. 1995.

George Sarton Published 1927, Published for the Carnegie Institution of Washington by the Williams & Wilkins, Co. Original from the University of Michigan Digitized June 9, 2006.

Gharavian, M., *Interpretation of Sahife Sajjadyyeh*, Maaref Publishing, Qom, 2002.

Golshani, Mehdi, *Can Science Dispense with Religion?* Hardcover ed. I.H.C.S., 1998.

Golshani, Mehdi, *Holy Quran and the Sciences of Nature,* Global Scholarly Publications, 1997.

Good, P. K.; Hatt, William J., *Methods in Social Research,Mc*Graw Hill Book Company, Singapore, 1952.

Guenon, Rene, *The Free Encyclopaedia,* http://en.Wikipedia,org.

Holmyard, E.J., *Encyclopaedia Britannica* (ed.) ,*The Arabic Works of Jabir ibn Hayyan,* translated by Richard Russel in 1678. New York, E.P. Dutton, 1928.

Haught, John F., *Religion and Science,* Paulist Press, Mahwah, New Jersey, 1995.

Hogendijk, J.P., *Bibliography of Mathematics in Medieval Islamic Civilization,* January 1999.

Imam Ali ibn Abu Talib, *Nahjul Balagha (Peak of Eloquence),* Islamic Foundation Press, Kerala, India, 1990.

Imam Muslim, *Sahih Muslim,* Abdul Hamid Siddiqi (translator).

In New York Daily Tribune, June 25, 1853 and London, Friday, June 10, 1853. Dr. Dipak Basu, *CPI (M) and Karl Marx*, 1853.

Jay Gould Stephen, *Ever Since Darwin,* New York : Washington Square Press, 1982.

King Winston, *Encyclopedia of Religion,* The University of Chicago Press, 1990.

Khosro Panah, *A New Theology,* Imam Sadegh (A.S.) Publisher Qom, 2000.

Kung Hans, *Does God Exist?* Trans by Edward Quinn, New York: Doubleday, 1980.

Klostermaier, K., *A Survey of Hinduism,* Suny Press, 1994.

Lennart, J., *The Encyclopedia Britannica* & Berggren, 1986.

Lincoln, Barnett, *The Universe and Dr. Enistein*, New York: Mentor, 1950.

Masterson, P., *Atheism and Alienation,* Gil & Macmillan, 1971.

Majlisi, M.B., *Bihar al-Anwar*, Islamiyeh Publisher, Beyrout, 1995.

Majid, Fakhry Al-Farabi, *Founder of Islamic Neoplatonism: His Life, Works, and Influence,* Oxford: Oneworld Publications, 2002.

Mesbah Yazdi, Taghi, *Philosophy of Ethics,* Ettelaat Institute, Tehran, 1990.

Malekiyan, Mostafa, & others, *kherade javidan,* University of Teheran, Tehran, 2002.

Monier-Williams, Monier, *Monier-Williams Sanskrit Dictionary,* Nataraj Books, 2006.

Nasr, Seyyed Hossein, *Man and Nature, The Spiritual Crisis in Modern Man,* Published ABC International Group, Inc, Chicago, 1997.

Nasr, Seyyed Hossein, *The Need for a Sacred Science,* U.K., Curzon Press, 1993.

Nasr, Seyyed Hossein, *Knowledge and The Sacred,* Pakistan, Suhail Academy Lahore, 1988.

North, J., *Marx's Religion of Revolution, Regeneration Through Chaos*, 1984.

Nietzsche, Friedrich, *The Gay Science,* The Nietzsche Channel, www.geocities.com.

Newton, Roger G., *Galileo's,* Vinod Vasishtha, New Delhi, 2005.

Naini, Majid *M., The Mysteries of the Universe and Rumi's Discoveries on the Majestic Path of Love,* Universal Vision & Research, 2002.

Osborne, E., *Accessing R.E. Founders & Leaders, Buddhism, Hinduism and Sikhism* Teacher's Book Mainstream Folens Limited, 2005.

Popper, Karl R., *Conjectures And Refutations: the Growth of Scientific Knowledge,* New York and Evanston, Harper Torch Nooks, 1968.

Peterson, M. and others, *Reason and Religious Belief,* trans. by E. Soltani, Oxford University Press, 1991.

Phil Dowl, *Galileo, Darwin, and Hawking*, William B. Eerdmans Publishing Company, Grand Rapids, Michigan/Cambridge, U.K.

Popper, Karl R., *Conjectures And Refutations; the Growth of Scientific Knowledge,* New York and Evanston, Harper Torch Books, 1968.

Randall, John. H. *The making of the modern mind: a survey of the intellectual background of the present age*, translate by A. Payandeh, Elmi Pub. Tehran, 1997.

Rauta, K.C., *An Integrated Study in Philosophy,* Vol. I, I.I.A.S. Shimla.

Radhakrishnan, *Indian Philosophy,* Oxford University Press, London, Volume two 1993.

Radhakrishnan, Sarvepalli, *Anthology*, Published 1952, G. Allen and Unwin, Original from the University of California, Digitized Dec. 19, 2006.

Radhakrishnan, Sarvepalli; and Moore, Charles A. *A Source Book in Indian Philosophy.* Published by Princeton University, 1967.

Rahner, Karl, *Hominization,* Trans. by W.J. O'Hara (New York: Harder & Herder, 1965.

Ranganathananda, Swami, *Universal Message of The Bhagavad Gita,* Volume 1, Calcutta, 2000.

Raup, David, 'Conflicts Between Darwin and Paleontology', Bulletin, Field Museum of Natural History, Vol. 50, January 1979.

Richard Monastersky, 'Mysteries of the Orient', *Discover,* April 1993.

Rig Veda, English translation by Ralph T.H. Griffith 10:129.1-7,1896.

Routledge *Encyclopedia of Philosophy,* Version 1.0, London: Routledge 2001.

Russell, Robert; Stoeger, William R.; Coyne, G.V., *Physics, Philosophy, and Theology: A Common Quest for Understanding,* translated by H. Hemmati, Tehran, 2004.

Safavi, Seyed Gholam, *Rumi's Thoughts,* edited by London Academy of Iranian Studies, 2003.

Scott, Andrew, Ananda Coomaraswamy, www.Virtual Library. Sri Lanka.

Sidgwick, H., *Outlines of the History of Ethics* (1902); A.C. MacIntyre, A Short History of Ethics 1965.

Sivaramkrishna, M., *Art, Culture and Spirituality,* Advaita Ashrama Publication Department, Calcutta, 1997.

Sophia, *Journal of Traditional Studies*, vol. 4, no. 2, Winter 1998 & http: //www.salaam.co.uk.

Sobhani, Jafar. *Some Issues in New Theology*, Tawhid Publication, Qom, 1995.

Stephen, Murphy, Adapted From: *Why Gandhi is Relevant in Modern India: A Western Gandhian's Personal Discovery,* Gandhi Peace Foundation, New Delhi; Academy of Gandhian Studies, Hyderabad, 1991.

Swami Atmaramananda, Dr. M. Sivaramkrishna, *Art, Culture and Spirituality*, Advaita Ashrama, Publication Department, Calcutta, 1997.

Taittiriya Upanishad 2:6; 7. Source: World Mythology by Donna The Catholic Encyclopedia, Volume XV, Copyright 1912 by Robert Appleton Company, Online Edition Copyright 2003 by K. Knight.

The Atheist Society of India, produces a monthly publication Nasthika Yugam which it translates as *"The Age of Atheism"*. Pithani Dibba, Visakhapatnam-300002, Andhra Pradesh, India

The Columbia Encyclopaedia, New York, Columbia University Press, Sixth Edition, 2001-5.

The Concise Oxford Dictionary of World Religions. Ed. John Bowker. Oxford University Press, 2000; Symbol of Orthodoxy in Colonial India, Religion (Academic Press), Volume 31, Number 2, April 2001.

The Encyclopaedia Britannica,*The Life of Swami Vivekanand,* Calcutta: Advaita Ashrama, 1960.

The Glorious Qur'an.

The Internet Encyclopedia of Philosophy, Continental Rationalism, www.iep.utm.edu

The New Testament, scriptures.lds.org/

The Oxford English Dictionary, second edition 1998, Volume xiv.

The Political Aspects of Islamic Philosophy, Cambridge, MA: Harvard University Press. 1992.

Tucker, *Philosophy and Myth in Karl Marx,* Cambridge University Press, 1971.

Ward & Trent, *et al. The Cambridge History of English and American Literature,* New York: G.P. Putnam's Sons, 1907-21; New York: Bartleby.com, 2000.

Williams, B., *Ethics and the Limits of Philosophy,* (1985) P. Singer, ed., Applied Ethics, 1986.

Warnock, M., *Ethics since 1900,* (1979); W. D. Hudson, A Century of Moral Philosophy, 1980.

White A.D., *A history of the warfare of science with theology in Christendom,* Prometheus Books, 1896 (Reprinted 1993).

Webster's *New World Dictionary* (Third College Edition).

Walker, P., 'The Political Implications of al-Razi's Philosophy', in C. Butterworth (ed.) *The Political Aspects of Islamic Philosophy*, Cambridge, MA: Harvard University Press, 1992.

Whitehead, Alfred N., *Science and the Modern World,* New York, The Macmillan Company, 1925.

William R., Shea, *Galileo's Intellectual Revolution,* second Edition, Neal Watson Academic Publications, Inc., New York, 1977.

Wittgenstein, Ludwig, *Philosophical Investigations,* translated by G. E. M. Anscombe, Oxford, Basil Blackwell, 1972.

Zalta, N., Edward, *Stanford Encyclopedia of Philosophy,* David Hume, U.S.A. (Stanford University, www. Plato. Stanford. Edu)

Websites

www.shiaweb.org/quran.net/tafseer/Meeza/index.html-6k تفسیر المیزان
www.holyquran.net/tafseer/majma/index/html/10k تفسیر مجمع البیان
www.qurancomplex.org/Quran/tafseer/Tafseer.asp?t=TABARY&TabID=3&SubltemId=1&1=arb تفسیر طبری
www.qurancomplex.org/Quran/tafseer/Tafseer.asp? 1=arb&1=katheer&nSora=1&nAya=1≠1—1 تفسیر ابن کثیر
www.alhikmeh.com/Arabic/akhlaq/quran/index.htm. اخلاق قرآن
www.alhikmeh.com/Arabic/akhlaq/nama/index.htm. اخلاق در حدیث شیعه
www.al-eman.com/Islamlib/viewtoc.asp?BID=383 متن احیاء العلوم غزالی
www.Drsoroush.com دکتر عبدالکریم سروش
www.manaviat.blogfa.com مصطفی ملکیان
wri.leaderu.com/wri-table2/hinduism.html.
ww.websters-online-dictionary.org
www.1stholistic.com/Prayer/Hindu/hol_Hindu-creation-of-the-universe.htm
www.about (atheism).com
www.Adherents.com
www.iep.utm.edu
www.bartleby.com
www.ivarta.com
www.iep.utm.edu
www.crystalinks.com/vedic.html
www.dfwhindutemple.org.
www.en.wikipedia.org/wiki/Sarvepalli_Radhakrishnan
www.hinduism.suite101.com/article.cfm/creation_in_the_upanishads.
www.iep.utm.edu/r/radhakri.htm
www.imanway.com.
www.irfi.org
www.islaam.net.
www.mkgandhi.org.
www.revision-notes.co.uk.
www.tebyan.net
www.vishnumandir.com/htm/meaning.htm.

Index